HELPING PERSONS WITH
SEVERE MENTAL RETARDATION
GET AND KEEP EMPLOYMENT

HELPING PERSONS WITH SEVERE MENTAL RETARDATION GET AND KEEP EMPLOYMENT
SUPPORTED EMPLOYMENT STRATEGIES AND OUTCOMES

M. SHERRIL MOON, Ed.D.
Training and Research Institute
for People with Disabilities
The Children's Hospital
Boston, and
Rehabilitation Research and Training Center
on Supported Employment
Virginia Commonwealth University
Richmond

KATHERINE J. INGE, O.T.R., M.Ed.
PAUL WEHMAN, Ph.D.
VALERIE BROOKE, M.Ed.
and
J. MICHAEL BARCUS, M.Ed.
Rehabilitation Research and Training Center
on Supported Employment
Virginia Commonwealth University
Richmond

·P A U L·H·
BROOKES
PUBLISHING C?

Baltimore • London • Toronto • Sydney

Paul H. Brookes Publishing Co.
P.O. Box 10624
Baltimore, Maryland 21285-0624

Typeset by Brushwood Graphics, Inc., Baltimore, Maryland.
Manufactured in the United States of America by
The Maple Press Company, York, Pennsylvania.

Library of Congress Cataloging-in-Publication Data

Helping persons with severe mental retardation get and keep
    employment: supported employment strategies and outcomes/
    M. Sherril Moon . . . [et al.].

        p.   cm.
    Includes bibliographical references.
    ISBN 1-55766-042-5
    1. Mentally handicapped—Employment.   I. Moon, M. Sherril,
1952–   .
HV3005.H44   1990
362.3′84–dc20   89-25371
                                                                CIP

CONTENTS

About the Authors

M. Sherril Moon, Ed.D. currently serves as School-Community Development Coordinator at the Training and Research Institute for People with Disabilities at The Children's Hospital, Boston. She is also Associate Professor at Virginia Commonwealth University and Associate Director of the Rehabilitation Research and Training Center on Supported Employment. She is interested in all aspects of community integration for persons with disabilities and in the acquisition and preservation of civil rights for all citizens of this country.

Katherine J. Inge, O.T.R., M.Ed. is a Training Associate at the Rehabilitation Research and Training Center on Supported Employment at Virginia Commonwealth University. She has been the coordinator of several demonstration projects that served individuals with severe disabilities, including the Supported Employment Project for Youth with Severe Disabilities. She is most interested in the development and implementation of systematic training procedures for persons with severe disabilities.

Paul Wehman, Ph.D. is a Professor in the Department of Rehabilitation Medicine in the Medical College of Virginia and Director of the Rehabilitation Research and Training Center on Supported Employment at Virginia Commonwealth University. He is nationally recognized for his work in creating employment opportunities for persons with mental retardation. He is especially interested in enhancing parental involvement in advocacy planning and employment.

Valerie Brooke, M.Ed. is the Acting Assistant Director of Training at the Rehabilitation Research and Training Center on Supported Employment at Virginia Commonwealth University. She has extensive national experience working with persons with severe disabilities in competitive employment situations as well as providing consultation and technical assistance to supported employment programs.

J. Michael Barcus, M.Ed. is the Acting Director of Training at the Rehabilitation Research and Training Center on Supported Employment at Virginia Commonwealth University. He has been a frequent presenter, consultant, and publisher of articles on the subject of supported employment for persons with severe disabilities.

PREFACE

During the 1980s supported employment was one of the major initiatives of the rehabilitation and developmental disabilities networks. Many citizens with significant disabilities are now working in real jobs because of this movement. However, despite the nationwide progress in providing integrated, community-based employment to all citizens, there is overwhelming evidence that persons with severe mental retardation and other more significant handicapping conditions are still being excluded from job training programs. In other words, the people for whom supported employment was intended often are not the consumers who are receiving supported employment services!

This book provides information specifically related to helping citizens with severe mental retardation or multiple severe handicapping conditions get and keep real jobs. Chapters 1–5 address a variety of issues, including strategies for assessment prior to job placement (Chapter 5) and methods for helping young persons who may still be in school to get jobs (Chapter 3). A discussion of present employment outcomes (Chapter 2) for persons with severe mental retardation is also provided. The first half of the book should challenge the reader to consider all the work that remains to be done in supported employment implementation. The last five chapters of the book are more technical in nature and address job placement, training, and maintenance activities that have been implemented successfully in community work settings with persons who have severe mental retardation or other severe or profound handicapping conditions. These chapters are intended to serve as a day-to-day guide for persons directly involved in supported employment training.

The authors of this text understand that there are a *multitude* of ways to approach job training for persons with severe handicapping conditions, and the strategies described here are by no means the only ones, perhaps not even the best. They simply describe methods that are tried and true and that we feel are worthy of replication.

Finally, we wish to acknowledge all the topics related to successful supported employment outcomes that are not addressed in this book. We recognize that working is only one aspect of a good quality of life and that employment must be approached in conjunction with improving residential, educational, and social options for citizens with severe disabilities. This resource can be effective only when teamed with many others addressing an array of political and programmatic issues.

ACKNOWLEDGMENTS

We would like to thank the young people and their families who participated in the Supported Employment Project for Youth with Severe Disabilities. Without family support and the enthusiasm of the individuals who were placed through this project, we would not have been able to develop the materials within this book. In addition, we would like to recognize the contributions of the employment specialists for their expertise and commitment to serving persons with severe mental retardation. These individuals include Amy Armstrong, Marguerite Faina, Valorie MacInnis, Perry Mathews, Wendy Parent, and Kelly Tait. We would also like to acknowledge the teachers and staff of Amelia Street School and Virginia Randolph School. This team of individuals continued to believe in the employability of individuals with severe disabilities under sometimes difficult and trying circumstances. Finally, the deadline for completion of this book would have been impossible to meet without the persistance of our secretarial staff. Jan Smith, Jeanne Dalton, and Brenda Robinson once again kept our heads above water!

HELPING PERSONS WITH SEVERE MENTAL RETARDATION GET AND KEEP EMPLOYMENT

EMPLOYMENT FOR PERSONS WITH SEVERE MENTAL RETARDATION

ISSUES AND STRATEGIES

1

Supported employment offers paid work in integrated community settings with permanent follow-along or supervision to citizens with severe disabilities. It is a job placement and training approach intended for persons who have been traditionally ineligible for state vocational rehabilitation services because of their need for continuing support to maintain a job (*Federal Register*, August 14, 1987). Current supported employment guidelines for programs operating with federal and state vocational rehabilitation dollars are outlined in Public Law 99-506, the Rehabilitation Act Amendments of 1986. The major points delineated in the law are presented in Table 1.1

Great strides have been made in the 1980s toward the national implementation of supported employment, and there is now an abundance of literature describing research, demonstration, and training programs in the area. One book reviewer compared the supported employment movement with the civil rights movement. However, persons with truly severe handicaps may not be receiving the benefits of a movement designed particularly for them (Sailor, Gee, Goetz, & Graham, 1988; Wehman, 1988).

Failure to understand who should receive supported employment could be the major pitfall of this great vocational rehabilitation movement. As Wehman (1988) has written, federal definitions and guidelines can be interpreted loosely or vaguely. He suggests that persons receiving supported employment must exhibit levels of mental retardation in the moderate, severe, or profound range (IQ <55) or have severe or multiple physical or sensory handicaps, autism, severe traumatic brain injury, or a history of chronic mental illness. He presents case studies of persons who should be considered for supported employment. All of these individuals have truly severe disabilities and were employed, except one, Kelly, who had profound physical handicaps, spent a large portion of the day strapped to a posture board, had profound mental retardation (IQ <10), and was not employed in the community. As several authors have pointed out (Sailor et al., 1988; Wehman, Hill, Wood, & Parent, 1987; Wehman, Parent, Wood, Kregel, & Inge, 1989), the literature does not yet include accounts of persons such as Kelly working for pay in integrated community job settings.

1

Table 1.1.   Supported employment criteria according to Public Law 99-506

Funds will be made available for persons not traditionally eligible for rehabilitation services who must have ongoing support for the duration of employment.

Persons receiving supported employment must have an individualized work rehabilitation plan (IWRP) reflecting ongoing support from other state, federal, or private programs.

A person must average 20 hours per week over the course of his or her normal pay period.

No more than eight persons with handicapping conditions will be at a supported employment work site.

A worker with handicapping conditions must be able to have regular contact with people who do not have disabilities, other than personnel providing support services, while at the job site.

A competitive wage must be paid in accordance with fair labor standards.

The state vocational rehabilitation agency can provide funding for supported employment for up to 18 months beginning at the time of placement.

Individuals, except those with chronic mental illness, need as part of their ongoing services, job skills training at least twice monthly.

Off-site, ongoing support services are not limited.

Although we may not be capable of finding the right job for Kelly at this time, there are many people with severe or profound mental retardation, autism, or other multiple, severe disabilities who should be working. The fact that professionals do not believe these people can work, do not know how to implement training for them, or do know that programs for them can be as costly as existing sheltered employment, is no longer justification for the "status quo." The purpose of this book is to provide a framework for employment of citizens with severe mental retardation and other very severe handicapping conditions.

DEFINING THE POPULATION

This book addresses issues and methods of supported employment for persons with functional severe or profound mental retardation. Generally, such individuals have a measured IQ below 40 and exhibit poor social skills. Many display behaviors such as self-stimulation, self-abuse, inappropriate verbalizations, and lack of some daily living or personal care skills, such as independent eating and appropriate grooming skills. These citizens do *not* possess functional language, reading, or math skills and cannot, without direct instruction, move about independently in the community. Many have other handicapping conditions such as autism, deafness, blindness, and cerebral palsy. The following case descriptions provide a clearer picture of the barriers that persons with severe mental retardation face in finding employment.

Case Study #1

John is 20 years old, with a primary diagnosis of mental retardation and a secondary diagnosis of autism. His IQ is 30, which falls within the severe range of mental retardation. John is nonverbal and does not possess any functional communication skills. He does, however, make loud humming noises that can be heard 40–50 feet away. John is able to see to all of his self-care needs, but he does not display any academic skills, that is, reading, math, or simple money identification. There have been reports of aggressive behavior, including hitting a classmate, when he becomes upset or agitated. His school does not consider him a candidate for community placement due to his limited interactions with people.

Case Study #2

Angela is 21 years old and has an IQ of 33, within the severe range of mental retardation. She has a secondary diagnosis of cerebral palsy, hemiplegia type, which is manifested in a slow, awkward gait and functional use of only one hand. In addition, Angela has seizures that are only partially controlled with medication. She frequently falls backwards due to her physical limitations as well as the seizure disorder. Her medical condition has been a concern for placement into a supported employment position.

Case Study #3

Sam is 22 years old, with an IQ of 27. He has limited communication skills and speaks in two- to three-word phrases. At times, Sam has had problems with self-abusive behavior, that is, biting his hands and fingers until raw. He has poor social skills and he usually avoids interacting with people, even familiar individuals. His teacher reports that he displays autistic-like behaviors and does not feel that he is an appropriate candidate for employment.

Supported Employment Work History

1. John has been successfully employed as a maintenance assistant washing windows for 25 months.
2. Angela has been successfully employed as a restroom attendant for 12 months.
3. Sam has been successfully employed as a maintenance assistant emptying trash for 10 months.

We are not claiming to know how to find and help maintain jobs for persons with the most profound handicapping conditions, such as those defined by the TASH Subcommittee on Services for Students with Multiple and Profound Handicaps (1987):

> These unresponsive students do not demonstrate understanding of daily routines, gestures, or other bases for communication, although they may grimace or groan with discomfort. They show no recognition of even significant persons in their lives. They may sit or grasp objects, but they engage in no purposeful movement. They demonstrate little if any observable response to noise, movement, touch, odors, or other stimuli. When compared to normal children, these students frequently lack the abilities even newborn infants possess. They rarely function higher than the six-month level in many developmental areas. While some likes and dislikes may be suggested, true reinforcers that increase the occurrence of a behavior are elusive. Unresponsive, profoundly retarded students may be of any age and may live in any setting. They may have received attention ranging from virtual neglect to intensive programming. (p. 33)

As Sailor et al. (1988) so aptly pointed out, we are all still looking for the best methods to improve the quality-of-life of these persons. We believe that the only way to make this improvement is to try to include them in supported employment training whenever possible.

There are few data-based reports in the literature on the successful implementation of supported employment for persons with severe or profound mental retardation or other severe or multiple disabilities, such as autism, deafness or blindness. We do know, however, that only a small number of these citizens are being served. A recent analysis of the data from the 27 states that received RSA (rehabilitation services administration) systems change demonstration grants on supported employment indicated that only about 11% of over 25,000 persons in supported employment had severe or profound mental retardation (Wehman, Kregel, & Shafer, 1989). This is quite a small number, considering that over 71% of the total supported employment population had a primary disability of mental retardation. The fact that over 54% of the persons with mental retardation had a classification of mild mental retardation is somewhat discouraging since these people technically should be served by more traditional rehabilitation methods.

There have been a few more encouraging descriptive reports from individual programs around the country. For example, Wehman et al. (1987) reported on the experiences of 21 persons with IQs below 40 who were working in jobs for at least minimum wage in mostly part-time, entry-level, service industry positions. A report from Madison, Wisconsin (Brown et al., 1987) on 33 graduates with severe intellectual disabilities (IQ range of 14–63) indicated that such persons could work in community-based jobs. However, most of these workers had a primary diagnosis of moderate mental retardation, and many were working less than 20 hours each week.

Although we know that superior demonstrations with this population exist, we do not have a systematic way of disseminating these results to persons working in programs across the country (Mank & Buckley, 1988). Currently, some states are working on making sure that good demonstrations are given adequate exposure and that policies in some states address specifically the issue of providing supported employment to persons with the most significant disabilities (Wehman, Kregel, & Shafer, 1989).

CRITICAL EMPLOYMENT VARIABLES

Despite the lack of data-based reports, several experts have written about factors that influence or hinder the employment of persons with very severe disabilities. Several of these papers specifically address supported employment (Bates, 1989; Brown et al., 1987; Mank & Buckley, 1988; Nisbet & Callahan, 1987; Rusch, Mithaug, & Flexer, 1986; Wehman & Moon, 1986). Table 1.2 lists variables that were discussed in the sources referenced above. As one may expect, there were many factors that were mentioned in several or all of the papers. The authors also agree that these factors must be addressed, and solutions must be sought when any one variable becomes a barrier. The remainder of Chapter 1 addresses issues that we feel most influence the employment of persons with severe mental retardation.

The Meaning and Value of Work

In the early 1980s there was some debate about wages for workers with severe disabilities (Bellamy et al., 1984; Brown et al., 1984). The concern was about whether produc-

Table 1.2. Critical employment variables

Meaning and value of work
Supported employment regulations
Staff resources
Transition and interagency coordination
Integration
Training in skills other than those specifically related to job performance
Transportation
Funding constraints and economic disincentives
Applied behavior analysis
Variety of work environments
Job development and modification techniques
Alternative job support strategies
Appropriate school vocational training programs
Family involvement

tivity and pay or integration was the most important outcome of work. However, most people realize now that real work cannot be based on any one particular variable, and what becomes meaningful employment for one person may be completely different for another. Bates (1989) and Ferguson and Ferguson (1986) eloquently said that work for people with the most severe disabilities cannot revolve around individual, clinical training issues but must be seen within the context of broader social, economic, and political concerns. While wages earned, hours worked, and some level of integration at the work site are certainly critical factors in employment, other factors such as simply being outside the home environment for short periods and acceptance by others in public work sites, regardless of productivity, make work meaningful for some citizens.

Constraints of Current Supported Employment Criteria

Many service providers have complained that supported employment according to federal definition (PL 99-506, the Rehabilitation Act Amendments of 1986) is impossible for people with severe or profound handicapping conditions because they cannot work at least 20 hours a week, they cannot earn a "living" wage, and they will forever need constant on-the-job training, which ties up already limited staff resources. While each of these arguments has some credibility, they cannot be used as reasons for *not* assisting a person with severe mental retardation in obtaining employment in the community.

The 20 Hours per Week Logic   One of the major criticisms heard from some service providers about supported employment has been the regulation that program participants must work 20 hours per week for their employment to be considered supported employment. For persons with very severe disabilities, for those who are school-age, or for those who do not wish to work 20 hours, this regulation has proven to be a hardship.

While some legitimate arguments can be made for lowering this figure to 15 hours or possibly increasing the amount of time an employee is allowed to work up to a 20-hour-per-week schedule, the reality is that in some programs a regulatory goal is probably essential. Without rules and guidelines, disposition of the funds associated with the program is difficult and this may compromise the integrity and intent of the program.

Persons with severe and profound mental retardation would benefit from an alteration in the rule because greater emphasis needs to be placed on giving them integrated work opportunities while in school. Also, for the most part, there are low perceptions of these individuals' ability to work full time; hence they may not ever receive an opportunity to work 20 hours or more. It is our belief that ultimately many persons with severe intellectual impairments can and should be able to work 20 hours per week or more, but they need the flexibility to work fewer hours initially and still receive training with supported employment funds.

A "Living" Wage   Very few people with severe and profound mental retardation will earn sufficient money from a job to independently support themselves. If, however, Congress moved the Substantial Gainful Activity (SGA) level up to $750 or $800 per month from the present $300, and if individuals could use this level as an income "floor," then this situation would be reversed. The increased level of minimum wage proposed in 1989 also is a step in the right direction.

For the most part it is likely that most people with severe mental retardation will continue to depend heavily on others who are nondisabled (i.e., family, friends, and paid caregivers) to assist them. Wages for real work are a way to: a) increase dignity and self-esteem, b) expand levels of discretionary income, and c) improve the opportunity to have some choices and greater control over one's life. For many persons with severe mental retardation, wage will *not* be the primary criterion for community-based work.

Continual On-the-Job Supervision   Another criticism of supported employment has been the necessity with some clients to provide continual supervision. Juhrs and Smith (1989), in describing the excellent program for adults with severe autism in Rockville, Maryland, indicate in their data that most individuals need one or two staff persons almost always present at the job site. They point out, however, that these clients will need this help in any setting whether it be sheltered work, day activity, or competitive employment, so why not provide it in an integrated paid employment setting?

The inability to fade employment specialist staff has been discussed for a long time, starting with our first writing on this topic (Wehman, 1981). Usually this problem is attributed to limited training of the client, poor job match, overprotectiveness of the employment specialist, or problems with the work supervisor at the job site. Another very real possibility, not discussed very much in the past, is that some clients have such extraordinary learning and behavior problems that significant staff withdrawal is unlikely. At this point, the issue becomes more of a public policy/cost-benefit one: does society value public dollars being expended heavily to promote integrated employment or somewhat less heavily for long-term segregated maintenance?

Finally, it must be remembered that complete supervision today at the job site does not necessarily mean supervision indefinitely. We are just beginning to learn about supported employment, and it may well be that after 1–4 years, frequent supervision will gradually turn into less frequent supervision. Individuals with severe mental retardation must be given a chance to show their capabilities after being excluded for so long.

Staff Resources in Employment Training Programs

Persons who have severe mental retardation or other severe or profound handicapping conditions need highly competent, specifically trained teachers, case managers, employment specialists, and in some cases, personal care managers. These persons, in turn, must help employers, co-workers, and the general public learn to accept the value and importance of workers with severe handicaps at community job sites. The fact is that most professionals in direct service delivery, training, or research positions do not really know what methods work best for helping people with severe disabilities reach their maximum employment potential. We do have evidence, however, that behavioral training strategies are effective in training for certain job acquisition and generalization skills and related social and community living skills.

We believe that these systematic instructional techniques (refer to Chapters 7, 8, and 9) must be implemented in order for employment to be successful. We also believe that instruction in using these methods must be provided to job trainers by persons who have actually performed training with this methodology at real employment sites. The cost and time that it initially takes for this kind of intensive staff development will pay off in the long run with less job turnover for staff and higher job retention for consumers.

It is also imperative that staff who work with persons with severe mental retardation have respect for the individuals whom they are assisting. People who are prejudiced for any reason or who have fear of failing with this responsibility cannot be expected to be role models in the community. If the staff of a program are not totally committed or believe for any reason that their work is really not important for the population they serve, the program will fail.

Table 1.3 provides staff development suggestions for enabling professionals to better serve persons with severe mental retardation.

Table 1.3. Staff development suggestions for serving persons with severe mental retardation at the job site

---

Only the most highly trained and motivated employment specialists should be at a job site with a worker with severe mental retardation. Pay such a person well!

Provide regular values clarification workshops for staff so that everyone can discuss and decide how they personally feel about individuals with handicaps and their civil rights.

Provide ongoing staff training in applied behavior analysis directed by an expert who has experienced success with these training techniques in community job sites.

Have every employment specialist spend time working alongside a competent, experienced professional who implements all phases of job-site training with individuals who have severe or profound mental retardation.

Have employment specialists spend time in the home of a worker with severe mental retardation to get to know the needs and desires of that person and his or her family.

Hold at least biweekly educational staff meetings in which all staff share information from current literature on services for persons with severe and profound handicaps.

Integration with Nondisabled Workers at the Job Site

Perhaps the major tenet of supported employment is its assertion that workers with severe disabilities must work alongside coworkers who do not have disabilities. Federal law states that no more than eight workers with handicapping conditions may work at a single work site when the program receives state/federal rehabilitation funds for supported employment. Some experts have most recently proposed that no more than two workers with disabilities should be in a supported employment situation (Brown, 1989). However, thus far research has not established which models or situations promote the greatest degree of, or most meaningful type of integration (Moon & Griffin, 1988; Shafer & Nisbet, 1988).

We believe that persons with severe mental retardation should work in situations where they can interact as much as possible with nondisabled coworkers and with the general public. We also think that the number of persons with disabilities at a specific site should be kept to a minimum, but more than one or two people can be appropriate under some conditions. Chapter 3 provides information on how several people with severe mental retardation who require continual training can work under the supervision of one employment specialist.

Funding Constraints and Disincentives

Almost all of the published research to date on supported employment has utilized cost figures for persons with mild and moderate mental retardation (e.g., Hill, Banks, Handrich, Wehman, Hill, & Shafer, 1987; Hill & Wehman, 1983). Persons with severe and profound mental retardation are much more expensive to place, train, and maintain. The range of costs are higher (Wehman, Kregel, & Shafer, 1989) and the initial costs to reach job stabilization (i.e., individual independence) are usually 50%–100% higher than the $3000–$4000 costs reported by many programs with clients who have milder disabilities (Wehman & Kregel, 1989). We do not see how persons with severe mental retardation can participate in supported employment fully without more money being allocated to them for services. Funding incentives will be needed for agencies (involved in vocational rehabilitation and at the local level serving persons with mental retardation) willing to take on these more difficult cases.

A problem of equal concern regarding job placement is the social security disincentives to work. Even though significant changes have been made to reduce these disincentives (e.g., loss of supplemented security income if one's earnings are too high) many families and their adult children are uncomfortable with risking total loss of benefits. We believe that until laws governing social security are changed, the fears and concerns of families must be respected. We have found that families respond well initially to part-time employment that does not affect benefits and then a gradual increase in work hours.

Formal Coordination between Service Providers (Transition)

Studies indicate that community-based vocational training during school years correlates positively with success in work during adulthood for persons with disabilities (Nisbet & Callahan, 1987; Wehman, Kregel, & Seyfarth, 1985). We also know that vocational training for those with the most severe disabilities may take more structured intervention over a longer period of time (Juhrs & Smith, 1989; Wehman, Parent, Wood, Kregel, & Inge, 1989). These two findings provide a rationale for formal, written agreements concerning the allocation of funds over a long period of time for the placement and training of persons with severe mental retardation, the delineation of who does what when, and the need to start the job training process during the school years. There are now a number of sources available that provide practical help in implementing transition and interagency coordination (Wehman, Moon, Everson, Wood, & Barcus, 1988).

Alternative Support Strategies

Persons with severe mental retardation or other very significant disabilities may need continual supervision in order to work in real jobs in the community. In other words, there may be no or at least only partial fading of supervision. Complete independence at the job site will not be the goal for these employees; thus the departure from earlier supported employment models (Wehman, 1981).

   The authors have found the job coaching method provided traditionally by rehabilitation or human service professionals to still be a viable means of providing placement, training, and continual follow-along to workers with severe mental retardation. Differences between the training for this population and for workers with less severe handicapping conditions include: the need for more intensive behavioral training (see Chapters 7–9); job modifications and more individualized placement strategies; and the use of a trainer to work at the job site at least part of the time for an indefinite period of time, such as is described in the cluster placement approach (see Chapter 3).

   Experts are now espousing a variety of other support strategies that do not involve the commitment of a professional job coach or employment specialist (Nisbet & Hagner, 1988). Some of these alternative support strategies include mentoring by a coworker, job sharing with a coworker, personal attendants, and using a training consultant to teach coworkers to provide assistance on a for-pay basis. Although we do not have replicable data indicating the success of these other models, we believe that a variety of untested support systems may be workable in our diverse business environments. It is the immediate responsibility of human service professionals and academicians involved in supported employment to test the viability of alternative strategies and record and disseminate the supporting data. In the meantime, it seems reasonable to continue using the professional employment specialist on a long-term basis to help persons with severe mental retardation get and keep employment.

Job Development and Modification Issues

Finding appropriate jobs for persons with severe mental retardation is a more complicated task than doing so for workers with less significant disabilities. It is much less a matter of finding a person for a certain job that already exists, and more a matter of searching for a position or sometimes creating a position *after* carefully analyzing the strengths and weaknesses of a particular person. Our experience has shown that some type of community-based assessment and short-term experience, such as that described in Chapter 5, is helpful in identifying possible jobs for someone with severe mental retardation.

It is also important to realize that since a worker with severe mental retardation may never be totally independent at a job site, the total work environment is a much more critical variable than with other supported employees. In the initial phases of job searching the employment specialist must look for a supportive and interactive atmosphere in which modifications and informal job sharing are possibilities. The complexity and continuity of job tasks must be much more carefully analyzed, and the stability of work force has to be examined. In the past we have written that high turn-over jobs (Wehman, 1981) may be best for supported employment positions, but these kinds of jobs may not be suitable for the consumer with the most severe disabilities. When a worker exhibits some socially inappropriate behaviors or has an unusual physical appearance, he or she needs a stable group of supervisors and coworkers who learn to interact with him or her over an extended period of time. Chapter 6 provides some suggestions for considering all these factors while looking for the right job.

Several logistical variables also become important in the job development process. Part-time jobs or job sharing may be much more appropriate for a person with severe or profound mental retardation. In that case it is critical to make certain that the maximum benefits and maximum pay are negotiated, since part-time employees often forfeit some extras. Other issues such as proximity to other supported employees (see Chapter 3) and transportation have to be decided on before placement is confirmed. The main difference in this decision-making process is that the employment specialist must assume that on-the-job support and reliance on someone else for transportation (as opposed, for example, to eventually learning to ride a city bus across town) will always be necessary. *Definitive answers about who will provide what indefinitely must be determined before placement.*

Systematic Behavioral Training

Although persons with severe mental retardation may never acquire 100% of all job skills in a particular environment or consistently work at the company production rate, these workers can acquire many skills and increase their production when they are taught with behavior analytic methodology. It has long been established that this methodology is effective in teaching complicated tasks to persons with severe handicaps in controlled environments such as sheltered workshops (Bellamy, Horner, & Inman, 1979; Gold, 1973). It has also been used in successfully training persons who have primarily moderate mental retardation in community-based jobs (Moon, Goodall, Barcus, & Brooke, 1986; Wehman, 1981). Although there are fewer examples in the literature of case studies and experimental studies involving specific behavioral interventions in community-based paid jobs, there are some to refer to (Wehman et al., 1987). We know that behavioral training can be used to teach job-specific skills (Test, Grossi, & Keul, 1988); incidental behaviors related to achieving independence (Wacker et al., 1986); social skills (Breen, Haring, Pitts-Conway, & Gaylord-Ross, 1985); generalization of learning (Horner, Eberhard, & Sheehan, 1986); and self monitoring on the job (Brooke & Shafer, 1985). Chapter 4 and Chapters 7–9 provide much more detail on how to use behavioral training strategies to teach a variety of job-specific and job-related skills to persons with severe mental retardation or other significant developmental disabilities.

Family Involvement

Perhaps the single most critical factor in a placement is the support and attitude of the family. A supportive family usually will help compensate significantly for whatever deficiencies there are in the training program, the worker's skill repertoire, and even the local economy. Supportive family members can help in job identification, help improve work habits, and be a major source of accurate information about the person's interests and capabilities. The family can help arrange transportation, be flexible in accommodating work schedules, and be supportive of the professional staff person training the individual at the job site.

We believe that the family is the major resource that is being either overlooked or not fully utilized in the integrated employment process. The major requirement for overcoming this deficiency is to involve families in the vocational planning process much earlier in the client's life than is done now (9–14 years of age as opposed to 20–25 years of age). Approximate vocational preparation and paid job placements in the community for transition-age students is the best thing we know of to make believers out of families.

Individual Characteristics of Persons with Severe Handicaps

Persons with severe mental retardation often include a broad range of individuals who have been labeled "trainable," "severely/profoundly retarded," "deaf-blind," "autistic," or "multihandicapped." The common characteristic that each category has is a combination of substantial physical, cognitive, and/or behavior problems that significantly impair learning. We have found the behavioral characteristics mentioned below to have a particular effect on job success and to be areas that must be addressed in order for employment to become a reality for more citizens with severe mental retardation.

Chronological Age and Gender   Generally speaking, there is no inherent reason why chronological age or gender of a person should affect the likelihood of getting employed or staying employed. Age or gender should not, in and of themselves, be discriminating factors. However, the reality is different. It is a fact that *younger* adults with severe handicaps are more likely to be placed than older adults. Younger people have spent less time either sitting at home with nothing to do, or they may have attended segregated day programs for 15–20 years rather than 25–35 years. Typically they are physically stronger, more motivated, and in some cases have had better school vocational training programs. A challenge for all of us is to find appropriate jobs for older persons with severe handicaps.

It has been shown that men with signficant levels of mental retardation are more likely to be competitively placed than women (Hill, Hill, Wehman, Banks, Pendleton, & Britt, 1985). Thus, out of every three placements within a sample of 214 persons with mental retardation, two were men. This finding has been frequently corroborated anecdotally in other local programs. Why is this the case? It would appear that many of the placement staff and/or hiring businesses feel that men can more capably handle entry level service jobs than women. Many of these jobs do require physical strength, but it would clearly be wrong to assume that only men can function in these positions. Professionals involved in job placement must rid themselves of gender stereotyping and then help employers to do the same! We must also find a better variety of jobs and stop trying to fit everyone into the service industry.

Social Behavior   A frequent characteristic of persons with severe intellectual handicaps is unacceptable social behavior. On the one hand, this may take the form of a behavioral excess such as stereotypic (nonfunctional) body rocking behavior, strange shrieking, or hugging strangers on the street. A social behavior deficit, on the other hand, may involve socially withdrawn behavior, being unresponsive to greetings, or not exhibiting awareness of other people in the environment. Inappropriate social behavior often can be modified by an improvement in the quality and consistency of instructional procedures. We have found that these behaviors often decrease or completely stop once a person gets a job, simply because that person is enjoying himself or herself more, is stimulated by something more appropriate, and just does not have time to engage in inappropriate behaviors. We have also found employers and the general public to be more accepting of some behavioral differences that family members and human service professionals cannot overlook. In other words, the elimination of all inappropriate behaviors except, perhaps, injury to others, is *not* a prerequisite to job placement.

Communication Skills   Persons with severe and profound mental retardation usually are nonverbal. Furthermore, they may also be unable to communicate using manual devices such as communication boards or Blissymbols. Signing systems may be an effective alternative but do not tend to be very useful at job sites since so much of the public does not know these languages. However, whatever the language program devised, the fact remains that communication skills in workers with severe mental retardation usually are grossly delayed, further contributing to the problems in career and vocational progress. We have found that many workers can develop, with the help of an employment specialist, a unique communication system for a particular job site so that supervisors and coworkers can at least communicate basic needs and desires.

Personal Care   The ability to care for oneself independently often is taken for granted. Independent grooming, eating, dressing, and toileting are presumed to be skills easily acquired at a young age. Proficiency in these skills is not easily attained for persons with severe handicaps. In fact, for many students these skills alone are major instructional objectives for long time periods. An excellent feature of supported employment is the opportunity for a worker to continue developing these skills *during* employment instead of *before* employment. The major area in which independence must be achieved is toileting.

Mobility and Travel Skills   Moving about within a school, neighborhood, or home is a skill that is critical to being independent. One must have the physical means to move about and also usually must have the cognitive understanding and memory to follow guidelines and instructions. Unfortunately, most students with severe handicaps may never be totally independent travelers because they lack one or the other of these abilities. Educators frequently contribute to this deficit by providing training only within the classroom and not allowing practice sessions in the natural environment of the community. An excellent supported employment program will be reflected by specific training and practice in mobility and travel during employment training. If a worker cannot learn to travel on community transportation, then family, friend, and volunteer sources that do not require independence must be tapped. This is a particularly crucial issue that has to be resolved on an individual basis with the help of all available resources.

Academic and Cognitive Behaviors   As one might expect, persons with severe intellectual handicaps usually exhibit very limited proficiency in reading, computation, and writing skills. Furthermore, the usefulness of these skills for these persons in future employment is less clear. It is clear, however, that there is substantial time spent in teaching nonfunctional skills at the expense of higher utility, nonacademic skills such as crossing a street independently or punching in and out on a timecard. As a student progresses through school, more and more attention must be focused upon life skills that are critical for survival in work environments, and most of these skills are *not* academic!

Appropriate School Training Programs

The better the training program and quality of setting that a student was in before placement, the greater the likelihood of the student getting and keeping employment. While the assumption of supported employment is that training continues at the job site once the placement is made (Wehman & Moon, 1988), this assumption in no way detracts from the utility and validity of an excellent school training program. The question is: what constitutes an excellent training program and setting? We think a real life *functional curriculum* (Wilcox & Bellamy, 1982), *community-based instruction* (Falvey, 1986), and *schools integrated with nonhandicapped youth* (Gaylord-Ross, 1989) are the cornerstones of an excellent training program for integrated employment. Below is a brief description of five guidelines that are associated with these cornerstones and that reflect all areas of community living, not just work.

Age-Appropriate Curriculum Materials   A primary consideration in educational and vocational programming for youth with severe handicaps is the development and utilization of curricular materials and activities that are consistent with a student's chronological age. Classrooms and other instructional settings also should reflect the chronological age of the students being served. The furniture, physical arrangement, bulletin boards, and other characteristics of the physical environment must be carefully evaluated according to the age-appropriate standard. Although Mickey Mouse and Peter Rabbit may belong in preschool or primary classrooms, they are not appropriate in the secondary class, regardless of the students' level of functioning. Both classroom decor and educational activities in a secondary classroom should reflect an emphasis on preparation for adult living in the least restrictive environment.

Interactions with severely handicapped students should be representative of interactions with any individual within a similar chronological age group. As we do not refer to nonhandicapped 18- to 21-year-olds as kids or children, neither should we refer to moderately and severely handicapped 18- to 21-year-olds as such. They, too, deserve to be referred to with dignity as "young man" or "young woman" or, at least, the somewhat ageless label "student." Similarly, the practice of delivering physical affection in the form of hugs and kisses or praise such as "good boy" or "good girl" is not appropriate for persons in the adolescent or adult age group.

At all ages, an active effort should be made to identify chronological age–appropriate objectives and materials. Although this emphasis may be extremely challenging for specific students, it is consistent with the philosophy of normalization and with the desire to promote community participation with individuals who do not have disabilities (Brown, Branston, Hamre-Nietupski, Pumpian et al., 1979).

Consider the consequences of choosing to ignore the importance of age-appropriateness. When parents, community residents, administrators, vocational rehabilitation counselors, and others view 20-year-old John playing with Tinker Toys during the middle of the day, what conclusion will they draw? Of course, they will surmise that John is a toddler and thus not competent enough to perform skills in the community, at home, or in a vocational setting. This mindset makes it exceptionally difficult to persuade these key individuals that John has viable training potential.

Functional Activities   Once specific age-appropriate objectives are selected, functional teaching activities and materials should be developed. Functional teaching activities are instructional programs that involve skills of immediate usefulness to students and employ teaching materials that are real rather then simulated. For example, a student should be taught to match or sort colors by using different colored clothing items rather than by using different colored blocks.

An endless number of examples of nonfunctional activities frequently used in the classroom can be cited. This proliferation of nonfunctional activities can be traced to several possible origins. First, the deluge of commercial materials that have appeared in recent years has influenced teachers of students with severe handicaps in their choice of materials and accompanying activities. Second, there is a belief among many educators that traditional nonfunctional activities are necessary for the child's readiness for more complex activities. This philosophy accounts, in part, for the reason that 20-year-old students have acquired isolated skills that have no apparent functionality, such as stacking rings on a post, when they still are unable to stack dishes properly.

Instruction Outside the Classroom As a part of each student's schedule, instruction outside the classroom should be included. Instruction on using the toilet, eating, community mobility, and countless other behaviors must be conducted in the environments in which these skills are typically expected to occur. If our goal is to see individuals function as fully in jobs and other community life as possible, educators must seriously question the strict reliance on the "classroom only" training model. This model has been tried for several years and has been found to be seriously lacking because it does not facilitate generalization of skills. As an alternative, a classroom/community service delivery model seems to be viable for students with severe handicaps. In this model students are taught in a variety of different community settings, and skill acquisition is verified in the natural environments where the skills are required.

Integrated Therapy Additional components of a student's program schedule often included a variety of ancillary services (e.g., physical therapy, speech therapy, and occupational therapy). The traditional method of delivering these services is to remove the individual from the ongoing classroom activities and provide the special service in an isolated therapy room. The individual therapy sessions typically last between 10 and 30 minutes and are conducted one to three times a week. With moderately and severely handicapped individuals, short therapy sessions that occur frequently may be insufficient to effect significant behavior change.

The integrated therapy model, also known as the transdisciplinary model, is an effective and efficient model for delivering special services to moderately and severely handicapped students. In this model, the specialist is involved extensively in an in-service role, teaching classroom teachers, aides, and parents how to conduct therapeutic activities and integrate them into regularly scheduled events. For example, a speech therapist may provide directions to classroom personnel and parents regarding how to encourage spontaneous requests during snack and meal time. By teaching a variety of persons to implement needed special programs and by integrating these activities throughout a student's day, skill development may be enhanced. These therapies can often be developed in such a way that they can take place on a job as has been done for students with cerebral palsy (Wehman, Wood, Everson, Goodwyn, Conley, 1988).

Interaction with Nonhandicapped Individuals Public Law 94-142 requires that all handicapped individuals be provided with a free, appropriate education in the least restrictive environment. The intent of this law is that handicapped persons must be educated with nonhandicapped individuals to every extent possible (McDonnell & Hardman, 1989). For persons with mild handicaps, this may involve mainstreaming into some regular classrooms, whereas for the students with moderate and severe handicaps, this may involve the location of self-contained classes in age-appropriate regular public schools. As seen in San Francisco, Syracuse, and other places, children with very severe handicaps are also beginning to go into regular classes as well (Sailor et al., 1988). Brown and his associates (1989) argue vociferously for the use of the "home school" in which students with severe handicaps go to their neighborhood school. They also argue for placement into regular classes.

Interactions with nonhandicapped persons take many forms and are of varying degrees. Brown, Branston, Hamre-Nietupski, Johnson et al. (1979) delineated the following levels of interaction: 1) proximal, 2) helping, and 3) reciprocal. At a minimum, students with moderate and severe handicaps and nonhandicapped students should be involved in proximal interactions. Proximal interactions are those that place students with moderate and severe handicaps and nonhandicapped students together in common locations. For example, riding the school bus, attending school assemblies, and eating lunch are all activities that can be engaged in together when moderately and severely handicapped students are located in proximity to their nonhandicapped peers. Helping interactions are those in which the nonhandicapped students assist handicapped students in various activities such as moving to and from activities, feeding, dressing, and playing games. These helping interactions can be informal and unstructured or can be more systematic in nature (e.g., tutorial interaction). The third type of interaction identified by Brown, Branston, Hamre-Nietupski, Johnson et al. (1979) is the situation in which the handicapped and nonhandicapped students receive some reciprocal benefit from being with each other. Playing a mutually enjoyable game and voluntarily attending a social event together are examples of reciprocal interactions.

Interactions between handicapped and nonhandicapped persons may benefit both participants in a variety of ways. More in-service efforts should be directed toward preparing employers, co-workers, regular educators, and students for increasing interactions with moderately and severely handicapped students. As school-based interactions are established, there will be greater opportunity for meaningful interactions to occur within work settings, neighborhoods, and other community settings. The long-term impact of these interactions may be significant improvements in the quality-of-life experienced by young people with severe handicaps.

CONCLUSIONS

Obviously, there can be almost innumerable barriers to employment for persons with severe mental retardation. All, however, can be overcome when the worker, his or her family, and the employment training specialists are willing to give the job everything they have. In the long run, even if a particular job does not work out, it can be viewed as a resumé building experience in which the worker's skills were acquired, preferences were expressed, and strengths and weaknesses were confirmed. There is no reason why employees with severe mental retardation cannot be part of America's mobile work force!

The time has come for us to be more creative, to be more risk taking in our efforts to help all citizens find meaningful work. We have to find *multiple* solutions to the issues discussed in this chapter by creating a variety of employment options. There are guidelines now for us to work within and, certainly, for us to eventually change. There are no right or wrong guidelines for helping people get and keep employment.

REFERENCES

Bates, P. (1989). Vocational training for persons with profound disabilities. In F. Brown & D.H. Lehr (Eds.), *Persons with profound disabilities: Issues and practices* (pp. 265–294). Baltimore: Paul H. Brookes Publishing Co.

Bellamy, G.T., Horner, R., & Inman, D. (1979). *Vocational habilitation of severely retarded adults: A direct service technology.* Baltimore: University Park Press.

Bellamy, G.T., Rhodes, L.E., Wilcox, B., Albin, J.M., Mank, D.M., Boles, S.M., Horner, R.H., Collins, M., & Turner, J. (1984). Quality and equality in employment services for adults with severe disabilities. *Journal of The Association for Persons with Severe Handicaps, 9,* 270–277.

Breen, C., Haring, T., Pitts-Conway, V., & Gaylord-Ross, R. (1985). The training and generalization of social interaction during breaktime at two job sites in the natural environment. *Journal of The Association for Persons with Severe Handicaps, 10,* 41–50.

Brooke, V., & Shafer, M., (1985). Behavioral training strategies in competitive employment. In S. Moon, P. Goodall, & P. Wehman (Eds.), *Critical issues related to supported competitive employment* (100–128). Richmond: Virginia Commonwealth University, Rehabilitation Research and Training Center.

Brown, L. (1989, April). *Integrated employment for persons with severe handicaps.* Keynote presentation at the Virginia Commonwealth University, Rehabilitation Research and Training Center (VCU-RRTC) symposium on Supported Employment, Virginia Beach.

Brown, L., Branston, M.B., Hamre-Nietupski, S., Johnson, F., Wilcox, B., & Gruenewald, L. (1979). A rationale for comprehensive longitudinal interactions between severely handicapped students and nonhandicapped students and other citizens. *AAESPH Review, 4*(1), 3–14.

Brown, L., Branston, M.B., Hamre-Nietupski, S., Pumpian, I., Certo, N., & Gruenewald, L. (1979). A strategy for developing chronological age-appropriate and functional curriculum content for severely handicapped adolescents and young adults. *Journal of Special Education, 13*(1), 81–90.

Brown, L., Rogan, P., Shiraga, B., Zanella Albright, K., Kessler, K., Bryson, F., VanDeventer, P., & Loomis, R. (1987). A vocational follow-up evaluation of the 1984–1986 Madison Metropolitan. School District graduates with severe intellectual disabilities. *A Research Monograph of The Association for Persons with Severe Handicaps, 2*(2).

Brown, L., Shiraga, B., York, J., Kessler, K., Strohm, B., Rogan, P., Sweet, M., Zanella, K., VanDeventer, P., & Loomis, R. (1984). Integrated work opportunities for adults with severe handicaps: The extended training option. *Journal of The Association for Persons with Severe Handicaps, 9*(4), 262–269.

Falvey, M.A. (1986). *Community-based curriculum: Instructional strategies for students with severe handicaps.* Baltimore: Paul H. Brookes Publishing Company.

Federal Register. August 14, 1987. Washington, DC: Government Printing Office.

Ferguson, D.L., & Ferguson, P.M. (1986). The new victors: A progressive policy analysis for work reform for people with very severe handicaps. *Mental Retardation, 24,* 331–338.

Gaylord-Ross, R. (1989). *Integration strategies for students with handicaps.* Baltimore: Paul H. Brookes Publishing Co.

Gold, M. (1973). Research on the vocational habilitation of the retarded: The present, the future. In N. Ellis (Ed.), *International review of research in mental retardation* (Vol. 6). New York: Academic Press.

Hill, M.L., Banks, P.D., Handrich, R.R., Wehman, P.H., Hill, J.W., & Shafer, M.S. (1987). Benefit-cost analysis of supported employment for persons with mental retardation. *Research in Developmental Disabilities, 8*(1), 71–89.

Hill, J.W., Hill, M., Wehman, P., Banks, P.D., Pendleton, P., & Britt, C. (1985). Demographic analyses related to successful job retention for competitively employed persons who are mentally retarded. In P. Wehman & J.W. Hill (Eds.), *Competitive employment for persons with mental retardation: From research to practice* (pp. 65–93). Richmond: Virginia Commonwealth University, Rehabilitation Research and Training Center. Monograph Vol. 1.

Hill, M., & Wehman, P. (1983). Cost benefit analysis of placing moderately and severely handicapped individuals into competitive employment. *Journal for The Association of the Severely Handicapped, 8,* 30–38.

Horner, R.H., Eberhard, J., & Sheehan, M.R. (1986). Teaching generalized table bussing. The importance of negative teaching examples. *Behavior Modification, 10,* 457–571.

Juhrs, P., & Smith, M. (1989). Community-based employment for persons with autism. In P. Wehman & J. Kregel (Eds.), *Supported employment for persons with disabilities.* New York: Plenum Press.

Mank, D., & Buckley, J. (1988). Supported employment for persons with severe and profound mental retardation. In P. Wehman & M.S. Moon (Eds.), *Vocational rehabilitation and supported employment* (pp. 313–324). Baltimore: Paul H. Brookes Publishing Co.

McDonnell, A., & Hardman, M. (1989). The desegregation of America's special schools: Strategies for change. *Journal of The Association for Persons with Severe Handicaps, 14*(1), 68–75.

Moon, S., Goodall, P., Barcus, M., & Brooke, V. (1986). *The supported work model of competitive employment for citizens with severe handicaps: A guide for job trainers* (rev. ed.) Richmond: Virginia Commonwealth University, Rehabilitation Research and Training Center.

Moon, M.S., & Griffin, S.L. (1988). Supported employment service delivery models. In P. Wehman & M.S. Moon (Eds.), *Vocational rehabilitation and supported employment* (pp. 17–30). Baltimore: Paul H. Brookes Publishing Co.

Nisbet, J., & Callahan, M. (1987). Achieving success in integrated workplaces: Critical elements in assisting persons with severe disabilities. In S.T. Taylor, D. Biklen, & J. Knoll (Eds.), *Community integration for people with severe disabilities* (pp. 184–201). New York: Teachers College Press.

Nisbet, J., & Hagner, D. (1988). Natural supports in the workplace: A reexamination of supported employment. *Journal of The Association for Persons with Severe Handicaps, 13*(4), 260–267.

Rusch, F.R., Mithaug, D.E., & Flexer, R.W. (1986). Obstacles to competitive employment and traditional program options for overcoming them. In F. Rusch (Ed.), *Competitive employment issues and strategies* (pp. 7–22). Baltimore: Paul H. Brookes Publishing Co.

Sailor, W., Gee, K., Goetz, L., & Graham, N. (1988). Progress in educating students with the most severe disabilities: Is there any? *Journal of The Association for Persons with Severe Handicaps, 13*(2), 87–99.

Shafer, M., & Nisbet, J. (1988). Integration and empowerment in the workplace. In M. Barcus, S. Griffin, D. Mank, L. Rhodes, & S. Moon (Eds.), *Supported employment implementation issues* (pp. 45–72). Richmond: Virginia Commonwealth University, Rehabilitation Research and Training Center.

TASH Subcommittee on Services for Students with Multiple and Profound Handicaps. (1987). Chicago.

Test, D.W., Grossi, T., & Keul, P. (1988). A functional analysis of the acquisition and maintenance of janitorial skills in a competitive work setting. *Journal of The Association for Persons with Severe Handicaps, 13*(1), 1–7.

Wacker, D.P., Berg, W.K., Visser, M.B., Egan, J.E., Berrie, P., Ehler, C., Short, B., Swatta, P., & Tasler, B. (1986). A preliminary evaluation of independence in a competitive employment setting. *Journal of The Association for Persons with Severe Handicaps, 11*(4), 246–254.

Wehman, P. (1981). *Competitive employment: New horizons for severely disabled individuals.* Baltimore: Paul H. Brookes Publishing Co.

Wehman, P. (1988). Supported employment: Toward zero exclusion of persons with severe disabilities. In P. Wehman & M.S. Moon (Eds.), *Vocational rehabilitation and supported employment* (pp. 3–16). Baltimore: Paul H. Brookes Publishing Co.

Wehman, P., Hill, J.W., Wood, W., & Parent, W. (1987). A report on competitive employment histories of persons labeled severely mentally retarded. *Journal of The Association for Persons with Severe Handicaps, 12*(1), 11–17.

Wehman, P., & Kregel, J. (Eds.). (1989). *Supported employment for persons with disabilities.* New York: Plenum Press.

Wehman, P., Kregel, J., & Seyfarth, J. (1985). A follow-up of mentally retarded graduates' vocational and independent living skills. *Virginia Rehabilitation Counseling Bulletin, 29*(2), 90–99.

Wehman, P., Kregel, J., & Shafer, M. (1989). *Emerging trends in the national supported employment initiative: A preliminary analysis of twenty-seven states.* Richmond: Virginia Commonwealth University, Rehabilitation Research and Training Center.

Wehman, P., & Moon, S. (1986). Critical values in employment programs for persons with developmental disabilities: A position paper. *Journal of Applied Rehabilitation Counseling, 18*(1), 12–16.

Wehman, P., & Moon, M.S. (Eds). (1988). *Vocational rehabilitation and supported employment.* Baltimore: Paul H. Brookes Publishing Co.

Wehman, P., Moon, M.S., Everson, J.M., Wood, W., & Barcus, J.M. (1988). *Transition from school to work: New challenges for youth with severe disabilities.* Baltimore: Paul H. Brookes Publishing Co.

Wehman, P., Parent, W., Wood, W., Kregel, J., & Inge, K. (1989). Supported employment for persons with severe and profound retardation. In P. Wehman & J. Kregel (Eds.), *Supported employment for persons with disabilities.* New York: Plenum Press.

Wehman, P., Wood, W., Everson, J.M., Goodwyn, R., & Conley, S. (1988). *Vocational education for multihandicapped youth with cerebral palsy.* Baltimore: Paul H. Brookes Publishing Co.

Wilcox, B., & Bellamy, G.T. (1982). *Design of high school programs for severely handicapped students.* Baltimore: Paul H. Brookes Publishing Co.

SUPPORTED EMPLOYMENT PERFORMANCE OUTCOMES FOR PERSONS WITH SEVERE MENTAL RETARDATION

2

Supported employment has begun to make a major difference in the work histories and vocational outcomes of thousands of persons with mental retardation and other developmental disabilities (e.g., Kiernan & Schalock, 1989; Rusch, 1986; Wehman, Kregel, & Shafer, 1989; Wehman & Moon, 1988). Unfortunately, persons with severe and profound levels of mental retardation are participating to a very limited extent. In a survey of the 27 states that receive supported employment systems change grants from the U.S. Department of Education, it was found that only 11.2% of the over 25,000 disabled participants in supported employment were identified as having severe mental retardation (Wehman et al., 1989).

There is relatively little literature available to document the competitive and other nonsheltered employment capabilities of this group. Wehman, Hill, Wood, and Parent (1987) reviewed 21 cases of persons with severe mental retardation who were in competitive employment. They found that 55% were retained after 6 months. Rhodes and Valenta (1989) report that nine persons with measured intelligence under 40 worked in a sheltered enclave for a company in Seattle, Washington. These workers had accumulated well over $150,000 in wages. Wehman and his colleagues (Wehman, Parent, Wood, Kregel, & Inge, 1989) report four case studies of persons with severe mental retardation and autism working successfully. Similarly, Juhrs and Smith (1989) report on over 50 persons with severe autism working in paid community employment. In two latter papers, it was indicated that large amounts of staff intervention time were critical to ensure placement and retention.

To our knowledge there are minimal data, other than case study information, that present the integrated employment capabilities of persons with severe mental retarda-

This chapter was co-authored with John Kregel, Ph.D., Director of Research at the VCU Rehabilitation Research and Training Center.

tion. For the most part, programs are reporting employment outcome data that focus primarily on individuals with mild and moderate mental retardation (Rusch, 1986), that is, persons with measured intelligence ranges from 40 to 70. Clearly, many if not most of these people are benefiting from a transitional or supported employment model of placement. However, the questions remain: are persons with severe and/or profound mental retardation (as measured by a standardized intelligence test) capable of working in supported employment? What data are available?

In order to answer these questions and study the vocational outcomes of persons with severe mental retardation, this chapter undertakes a descriptive analysis of 141 placements made with persons identified as having severe or profound mental retardation. Data were collected on these persons since the date of their first supported employment placement, which in some cases was as early as 1978. The sources of the data are: 1) university demonstration projects from Virginia Commonwealth University, 2) the Virginia state system for supported employment, 3) the North Dakota state system, 4) the Nevada state system, 5) school programs in LaCanada, California, and 6) five model school systems in Florida. What follows is a description of the data management system.

THE EMPLOYMENT DATA MANAGEMENT SYSTEM

A comprehensive information management system has been developed to monitor the employment outcomes of target employees participating in supported employment programs in Virginia and other states. First developed as a research data-base to evaluate the results of demonstration programs operated by Virginia Commonwealth University, the Supported Employment Information System (SEIS) has expanded to track the progress of the large number of local community-based employment programs begun between 1985 and 1988 as a result of the Virginia supported employment initiative.

The present system represents a cooperative effort of the Department of Rehabilitative Services (DRS); the Office of Supported Employment in the Department of Mental Health, Mental Retardation, and Substance Abuse Services (DMHMRSAS); the Virginia Commonwealth University, Rehabilitation Research and Training Center (VCU-RRTC); and 46 local programs vendored by DRS to provide supported employment services. The Department of Rehabilitative Services provides administrative leadership in the design and implementation of the system. Vendor agreements with local service providers require the submission of data to the system as a condition for receiving reimbursement for services. The VCU-RRTC, through a contract with DRS, is responsible for system maintenance, data analysis, and the preparation and dissemination of monthly and quarterly reports. Regional consultants from the Office of Supported Employment serve as liaisons between local providers and the RRTC, training local providers in the use of the system, assisting in the collection of data, and interpreting technical reports for local agencies and employment specialists.

Purpose of the SEIS

The SEIS has been designed to serve several distinct purposes. At the state level, aggregate information is used by DRS and DMHMRSAS to document the scope and effectiveness of supported employment, communicate the results of the supported employment initiative to state agencies and legislators, provide an empirical basis for policy formulation and program management, and detect trends and emerging issues to be addressed as the supported employment initiative evolves over time.

At the local program level, the system allows program administrators to track the growth and progress of their programs on a quarter to quarter basis and to compare the outcomes of their efforts to state and regional averages. Specialized reports, such as the Monthly Intervention Report, are designed as management tools that allow administrators to monitor specific aspects of programs. The Regional Consultants from the Office of Supported Employment make extensive use of the system when providing feedback to local agencies and designing technical assistance activities.

Data from Nevada, North Dakota, and other local programs listed earlier are mailed to VCU quarterly. These data are then analyzed and summarized along with the data from the 46 vendors in Virginia. These are the data used to screen persons with severe and profound mental retardation for analysis.

Since extensive data are continuously collected on each target employee, as opposed to use of aggregated program data, the SEIS is also used to evaluate the effect of supported employment participation on individual target employees. The system is sensitive to subtle changes in an individual's employment situation. Each target employee can be monitored on a monthly and quarterly basis to guarantee that the individual benefits maximally from the services received from the supported employment program.

Overview of the Data Management Process

The SEIS consists of over 200 data elements, organized into nine data collection forms. The system provides detailed information on target employee demographic and functional characteristics, consumer assessment information, the results of job analyses, comprehensive data on the types of jobs performed by employees, the amount and type of services provided by the supported employment program, supervisors' evaluations of the target employees' work performance, and complete information regarding employment retention and reasons for job separation. Some data elements are collected one time only, others are collected at regular 3- or 6-month intervals, and still others are collected on a continuous, daily basis.

Data forms are submitted on a prescribed schedule to VCU. The schedule for data completion is based on a consumer's date of placement rather than a specific calendar month. This enables data collection to be dispersed over a lengthy period of time instead of requiring extensive data collection at the end of each fiscal quarter. Instead of forcing employment specialists to collect and sort large amounts of data several times a year, data collection becomes a component of the employment specialists' daily routine.

Once data are received by VCU, a data management specialist reviews each form for completeness, accuracy, and consistency with previously submitted data. The data management specialist contacts local programs to clarify and obtain missing data, then codes each form for data entry and analysis.

Summary reports are returned to state agencies and local programs on a monthly and quarterly basis. All SEIS participants receive aggregated statewide reports that contain both numerical tables and graphic depictions of data. Regional consultants receive both statewide and regional aggregate reports to allow them to compare local programs within their specific region. Each of the 46 local providers receives a quarterly report that details the outcomes of its own agency. All quarterly reports contain complete information on the immediate quarter, as well as cumulative information, to allow all local programs to monitor the results and growth of an individual program over time.

RESULTS

Consumer Demographic and Placement Outcomes

A total of 109 individuals were reported with a mean age of 28.2 years and an age range of 17–53. The mean level of measured intelligence (IQ) (usually assessed by the Stanford-

Binet Intelligence Scale) of all of these consumers referred for employment is 30.3, with a range of 17–39. The mean IQ of working consumers was 30.4 as of December 31, 1988. There were a total of 141 placements made to date, with 72 persons working in the most recent reporting period of October to December, 1988. A total of $496,482 has been earned cumulatively by persons in these 141 placements. (See Tables 2.1 and 2.2.)

Table 2.3 shows that 78.4% or 80 of the placed consumers received Supplemental Security Income at referral and another 22 persons received Disability Income. Almost two-thirds received government medical insurance. Table 2.4 indicates that all persons were in supervised living situations. Almost half were living with their parents.

One measure of effort and time spent on the job placement and retention of these individuals is the cumulative recording of hours spent by staff. In Table 2.5 the percent of time and hours is presented. Fifty-six percent of all the time was actually spent right at the job site providing training, counseling, and support for the consumer with severe mental retardation.

Table 2.6 shows the level of integration opportunity available between consumers with severe mental retardation and nonhandicapped co-workers. In almost 75% of all cases there were frequent to moderate levels of interaction.

Table 2.7 indicates that 93 or 66% of all the placements were in competitive employment with long-term job coach support. Approximately one out of five or 20.6% were involved in sheltered enclaves within industry. The highest mean wage was $3.63 per hour within the supported competitive employment model.

Table 2.8 provides an overall summary of the wages earned and hours worked for all of the 141 placements. The mean hours worked per week was 22 hours, and mean weeks employed of all placements was 47 weeks. The average placement to date has earned $3,521 total. The lower half of Table 2.8 indicates the breakdown of what number of persons worked what hour totals per week. Over 75% worked more than 20 hours per week.

The type of work performed is reflected in Table 2.9, which shows that food services (32.6%) and cleaning/custodial services (44%) were by far the largest sources of employment. Laundry, assembly, and stock work provided for approximately another 20% of the jobs.

Table 2.1. Consumer age and IQ statistics

Item	Consumer reported	Mean	Range
Age of all consumers at time of referral	163	28.2	17–53
Age of consumers at time of discharge	25	28.6	20–55
Current age of consumers working as of 12/31/88	69	31.8	19–55
Current age of consumers in referral pool	69	28.3	19–53
IQ of all consumers ever referred	163	30.3	17–39
IQ of consumers working as of 12/31/88	69	30.4	17–39
IQ of consumers in referral pool	69	30.2	17–39

Table 2.2. Employment outcomes

Outcome measure	Cumulative totals
Consumers working in jobs (any time during quarter)	109
Placement into jobs (includes first, concurrent, and subsequent placements)	141
Referrals to providers (consumers considered for placement or services)	163
Cumulative gross wages earned (by all consumers)	$496,482

Table 2.10 shows the fringe benefits associated with the placements. Almost 50% (62) of the placements had *no* fringe benefits. Less than 20% had either sick leave or medical insurance and approximately one-fourth of all placements had paid vacation.

Table 2.11 indicates that a total of 66 separations from work have occurred, with 39.4% being resignations by the worker with severe mental retardation. An exactly equal number of employees have been terminated by the company that hired them. A large number of reasons were given for job separation, as shown in Table 2.12. The leading reason for cessation of employment was the economic situation, followed by the persons not wanting to work, need for continual prompting at the job, taking a better job, aberrant behavior, and low quality work.

Finally, Table 2.13 shows the job replacement and changes that have occurred over time. After 2 years, 17 of 25 possible clients were still in their first jobs. After 12 months, 53 (or 81.5%) were still in the initial jobs.

DISCUSSION OF OUTCOMES

The results of this analysis may be viewed from several different perspectives. First, the data presented unequivocally document that individuals with severe or profound mental retardation, previously viewed as incapable of community-based employment, can earn meaningful wages in integrated employment settings through participation in local supported employment programs. The success of small numbers of individuals with severe disabilities in university-based supported employment demonstration programs has been documented frequently in the past. However, to our knowledge, this is the first report of a fairly large (109) group of individuals, consisting exclusively of persons with severe

Table 2.3. Government benefits received at referral by placed consumers

Government benefits	Cumulative number	Total %
Social Security Income	80	78.4
Social Security Disability Income	22	21.6
Medicaid	53	52.0
Medicare	14	13.7
Food stamps	8	7.8
Welfare	3	2.9
Other aid	11	10.8
Not reported	7	—

Table 2.4.   Residential situation for consumers at first placement

Residential situation	Cumulative number	Total %
Independent	0	0.0
Supported living arrangement	3	3.1
Sponsored placement (foster care)	3	3.1
Domiciliary care apartment	7	7.1
Supervised apartment	6	6.1
Parents	48	49.0
Other relatives	2	2.0
Group home/halfway house	25	25.5
Other situation	4	4.1
Not reported	11	—
Total	109	100.0

or profound mental retardation, participating in supported employment through local community-based service agencies, as opposed to research programs affiliated with universities.

When viewed collectively, the outcomes achieved by the individuals represented in the data are substantial. The overwhelming majority of individuals are served in the individual placement model, implying that individuals are able to become fully competent, independent members of the workforce after intensive initial training. The average consumer in the analysis had been employed almost a year (47 weeks) and had earned an annual salary of slightly over $3,500. This represents a 300% increase over what these same consumers made in the year prior to their referral to the supported employment program (Kregel & Wehman, 1989).

Another important finding is that the individuals were generally able to retain their jobs for extended periods of time. Retention rates for the individuals in the analysis for the first 2 years of employment were as follows: 80% employed at 6 months after

Table 2.5.   Staff intervention hours provided by category

Intervention time category	Cumulative time (in hours)	Total %
Active time at job site	11090:25	56.0
Inactive time at job site	2985:52	15.1
Travel and transport time	2453:48	12.4
Consumer training time	512:51	2.6
Consumer program development	689:11	3.5
Direct employment advocacy	891:01	4.5
Indirect employment advocacy	815:33	4.1
Consumer screening and evaluation	351:29	1.8
Undifferentiated time not categorized[a]	1644:34	—
Total	21434:44	100.0

[a]Some intervention time provided prior to 8/83 was not differentiated into categories. This time is not included in the computation of percentages.

Table 2.6. Level of integration in the workplace

Level of integration	Cumulative number	Total %
Complete segregation	1	0.8
General physical separation	13	10.1
No work-related interaction	19	14.7
Moderate level of work-related interaction	58	45.0
Frequent work-related interaction	38	29.5
Not reported	12	—
Total	141	100.0

initial placement, 69% employed at 12 months, 59% employed at 18 months, and 61% employed at 24 months. In interpreting this information, one should note that not all individuals in the analysis had had the opportunity to work for 24 months, which causes slight variation in the retention totals. These figures compared very favorably with retention rates found for individuals with moderate mental retardation and mild/borderline mental retardation who were placed into employment by the same local programs that served the individuals in the present analysis (Shafer, Kregel, & Banks, 1989). In short, the data reported above show that individuals with severe or profound mental retardation, over half of whom had earned nothing in the year prior to referral to supported employment, can obtain employment in a variety of community-based settings. Furthermore, they are able to earn wages several times greater than they had earned in their previous setting, and retain their jobs for extended periods of time, meeting or exceeding the retention rates of other supported employment participants.

However, a close inspection of the qualitative nature of the employment outcomes reported reveals some serious causes for concern. The consumers in the analysis were earning only $3.22 per hour. Only 15% received fringe benefits such as sick leave or medical insurance. Over one-fourth experienced no work-related interaction with co-workers while on the job. These findings call into question the quality of the employment experiences of the participants and whether they were benefiting maximally from supported employment.

Table 2.7. Type of employment program and wages

Type of employment program	Cumulative number	Total %	Hourly mean wages	Range
Entrepreneurial	8	5.7	$0.85	0.62–1.50
Mobile work crew	6	4.3	$3.13	1.29–4.91
Enclave	29	20.6	$2.70	0.73–5.00
Supported job	5	3.5	$2.60	1.68–4.61
Supported competitive	93	66.0	$3.63	3.35–5.21
Total	141	100.0		

Table 2.8.   Wages earned and hours worked for placed consumers

Item	Positions reported	Mean	Range
Hourly wage	141	$3.22	$0.62–$5.21
Hours worked per week	141	22	3–40
Total weeks employed	141	47	1–532
Cumulative wages per year	141	$3,521	$67–$44,482

Hours worked per week	Cumulative number	Total %
Less than 20 hours	33	23.4
20–30 hours	85	60.3
30–40 hours	23	16.3
Total	141	100.0

Comparative Review of Outcomes

In order to obtain a fuller understanding of the employment outcomes achieved by the group of consumers with severe or profound mental retardation, it is useful to compare the outcomes achieved by these individuals with the outcomes of other supported employment participants. Wehman, Kregel, and Banks (1989) summarized the results of a 10-year university demonstration program that placed 255 individuals into competitive employment from 1978 to 1988. The primary disability of all individuals in this analysis was mental retardation, with consumers placed having a mean IQ score of 51, and over half being classified as having moderate mental retardation. Another study that may be used for contrast purposes (Kregel, Wehman, Revell, & Hill, in press) examined the employment outcomes of 944 individuals served by local supported employment programs in Virginia. In this study, consumers with mental retardation accounted for 83.1% of all placements, with other consumers possessing primary disabilities such as long-term mental illness, cerebral palsy, and traumatic brain injury.

Contrasting the results of these two studies with the present analysis will illuminate key differences in the outcomes experienced by workers with severe or profound

Table 2.9.   Type of work

Type of work	Cumulative number	Total %
Food services	46	32.6
Janitorial/custodial	62	44.0
Unskilled labor	1	0.7
Bench work/assembly	15	10.6
Laundry	6	4.3
Stock clerk/warehouse	7	5.0
Transportation	2	1.4
Clerical/office work	1	0.7
Groundskeeping	1	0.7
Total	141	100.0

Table 2.10. Fringe benefits of job placements

Fringe benefits	Cumulative number	Total %
Sick leave	20	15.2
Medical insurance	21	15.9
Paid/vacation	36	27.3
Dental insurance	7	5.3
Employee discounts	21	15.9
Free/discounted meals	40	30.3
Other benefits	6	4.5
No fringe benefits	62	47.0

mental retardation as opposed to those achieved by other supported employment participants. In several instances the outcomes of the individuals with severe or profound mental retardation meet or exceed those of other individuals. On several key outcome measures, however, the individuals are severely lacking when compared with other supported employment participants. Specific areas for comparison include type of employment model, wages, hours worked, fringe benefits, type of job, level of integration, job retention, and type and reason for separation. Each of these outcome measures is discussed below.

Type of Employment Model While the majority of consumers in the present analysis (66%) were placed in the individual supported competitive employment model, individuals with severe or profound mental retardation appear more likely to be placed into group options than other individuals. For example, in the Kregel et al. (in press) study, 83.9% of all consumers were served in the individual placement model. While percentages for mobile work crews and small business options were roughly equivalent, individuals with severe or profound mental retardation were far more likely to be placed in these options. Although the individual placement model is generally viewed as the most normalizing of all the service delivery models (Rehab Brief, 1986), the enclave model may be an appropriate placement for many individuals if other factors, such as wages and level of integration, are carefully considered.

Hourly Wages The hourly wages earned by individuals with severe or profound mental retardation are roughly equivalent to those earned by other supported employment participants. The hourly wage for consumers in the individual placement model in the present analysis was only slightly lower than that reported in the Kregel et al. (in press) study ($3.63 versus $3.79 per hour). Wages for individuals in group employment options met or exceeded those found in the other studies. When interpreting these data, it should be noted that a significantly greater number of individuals with severe or pro-

Table 2.11. Type of separation from employment

Separation type	Cumulative number	Total %
Resigned	26	39.4
Laid off	14	21.2
Terminated	26	39.4
Total	66	100.0

Table 2.12.   Reason for separation from employment

Separation reason	Cumulative number	Total %
Economic situation	12	18.2
Does not want to work	5	7.6
Continual prompting needed	5	7.6
Took better job	5	7.6
Aberrant/bizarre behavior	5	7.6
Low quality work	5	7.6
Insubordinate behavior	4	6.1
Poor job match	4	6.1
Other reasons	4	6.1
Employer uncomfortable	3	4.5
Transportation problem	2	3.0
Slow work	2	3.0
Poor attendance/tardiness	2	3.0
Poor work attitude	2	3.0
Seasonal lay off	2	3.0
Moved away	1	1.5
Parent/guardian initiated	1	1.5
Parental interference	1	1.5
Medical/health problem	1	1.5
Total	66	100.0

found mental retardation work in group employment options. Group employment options provide substantially more limited opportunities than those provided in the individual placement model, thereby reducing the overall amount of wages earned by these individuals. The *combined* hourly wage for individuals in all models in the present analysis was $3.22, compared with a combined hourly wage of $3.56 reported by Wehman, Kregel, and Banks (1989), and $3.64 reported by Kregel et al. (in press). While some professionals and advocates would argue that these wage levels are far too low and prohibit individuals from achieving economic self-sufficiency, this concern appears to be a problem that applies to all supported employment programs. When the type of placement option is accounted for, the data show that persons with severe or profound mental retardation do not earn substantially lower hourly wages than other supported employment participants.

Table 2.13.   Number of different jobs held by individuals at various times after placement by providers

Number of jobs	3 Months		6 Months		9 Months		12 Months		18 Months		24 Months	
	N	%	N	%	N	%	N	%	N	%	N	%
One job	96	95.0	80	90.9	67	87.0	53	81.5	31	72.1	17	68.0
Two jobs	5	5.0	6	6.8	9	11.7	8	12.3	8	18.6	3	12.0
Three jobs	0	0.0	2	2.3	1	1.3	4	6.2	4	9.3	5	20.0
Total	101	100.0	88	100.0	77	100.0	65	100.0	43	100.0	25	100.0

Day 1 begins at the date of first placement.

Hours Worked Per Week   While individuals with severe or profound mental re-tardation show no difference in the hourly wages earned, they do tend to work slightly fewer hours per week than other supported employment participants. The individuals in the present analysis averaged 22 hours of employment weekly as compared with 26 and 28 hours per week in the contrast studies. The individuals with severe or profound mental retardation were also far more likely to work less than 20 hours per week. The reasons for this discrepancy are unclear. For example, individuals with severe or profound mental retardation may work fewer hours per week because of chronic medical conditions that interfere with their ability to work, or may desire fewer hours of employment, or employment specialists may have difficulty finding appropriate jobs for them that provide a greater number of hours of work per week.

Fringe Benefits   Important employment outcomes frequently not emphasized in the supported employment literature are the fringe benefits received by consumers in their integrated employment placements. The type and amount of fringe benefits received by consumers is an important element of the overall quality of the job. There appear to be substantial differences between the amount and type of fringe benefits received by individuals with severe and profound handicaps and other supported employment participants. For example, individuals with severe or profound mental retardation are only half as likely to receive sick leave or medical insurance and are far less likely to receive other fringe benefits such as paid vacations. In fact, almost half of the individuals with severe or profound mental retardation were receiving no fringe benefits at all, compared with less than a third of all supported employment participants in the Kregel et al. (in press) study. A poorer likelihood of receiving fringe benefits is another factor that can be attributed to the larger number of individuals with severe or profound mental retardation who are served through group employment options.

Type of Job   When compared with other supported employment participants, individuals with severe or profound mental retardation appear to be slightly more likely to work in custodial or bench work/assembly positions and less likely to work in food service positions. For the most part, however, the types of positions obtained by the consumers in the present analysis roughly paralleled those of the contrast studies, suggesting that the *general* type of job obtained for a supported employment participant is based more on an analysis of the local labor market than a conscious decision to place individuals with specific functioning levels into certain types of positions.

Level of Integration   Integration (i.e., physical proximity and social interaction with others) is a primary value of the supported employment initiative. A comparison of the level of integration achieved by the consumers in the present analysis with those in the Kregel et al. (in press) study shows that individuals with severe or profound mental retardation were substantially more likely to be placed into positions that did not provide them an opportunity to engage in work-related interaction with others. One-fourth of the individuals in the present analysis experienced no work-related interaction or experienced general physical separation while at the job site, compared with only 16% of all supported employment participants in Virginia. Furthermore, only 29.5% experienced *frequent* work-related interactions, compared with 42.9% of all other participants. Since integration is so central a value to the entire supported employment concept, the causes of the apparent lack of integration should be examined carefully. Future analyses should attempt to determine whether this lack of integration is a function of the specific employment settings into which individuals with severe or profound handicaps are placed, or if group employment options, such as enclaves and work crews, inherently provide a limited amount of integration. Although the data above raise an important concern, it should be noted that most of the individuals in the present analysis entered supported employment directly from totally segregated, sheltered environments where they experienced no integration at all.

Employment Retention   As previously noted, it was found that individuals with severe or profound mental retardation were able to retain employment to the same degree as all other supported employment participants. In a detailed statistical analysis of employment retention among individuals exclusively served in the individual placement model, Shafer et al. (1989) found little difference between the retention rates of individuals with moderate or severe mental retardation and individuals with borderline or mild mental retardation. Similarly, no statistically significant differences were found between individuals with severe mental retardation in the present analysis and those in contrast studies. In fact, individuals with severe or profound mental retardation possessed slightly higher retention rates at each of the 6-, 12-, 18-, and 24-month measurement periods.

Type and Reason for Separation   No substantial differences were found in a comparison of the type of separation from employment (i.e., resignation, termination, lay-off) between the present analysis and either of the contrast studies. Slight differences emerged when the reasons for separation provided by employment specialists were examined. Individuals with severe or profound mental retardation appear slightly *more likely* to have been separated due to factors such as low work quality, aberrant or inappropriate behavior, and the need for continual prompting, and *less likely* to be separated due to factors such as poor work attitude or poor attendance/tardiness. These results should be viewed as very preliminary in nature, as the number of individuals in several of these categories is quite small.

CONCLUSION

The purpose of this chapter is to present data that show the employment outcomes associated with persons who have measured intelligence in the level of severe mental retardation. Clearly, progress has been made in the 1980s, but much work is left to be done. Specifically, service providers must develop greater skill levels in utilizing behavioral training technology at the job site. Also, greater care must be taken in selecting jobs that enhance client satisfaction and at the same time are consistent with the client's capability.

REFERENCES

Juhrs, P.D., & Smith, M.D. (1989). Community-based employment for persons with autism. In Wehman & Kregel (Eds.), *Supported employment for persons with disabilities* (pp. 163–176). New York: Plenum.

Kiernan, W.E., & Schalock, R.L. (1989). *Economics, industry and disability: A look ahead.* Baltimore: Paul H. Brookes Publishing Co.

Kregel, J., & Wehman, P. (1989). *Supported employment: promises deferred for persons with severe handicaps.* Manuscript submitted for publication.

Kregel, J., Wehman, P., Revell, W.G., & Hill, W. (in press). Supported employment in Virginia 1980–1988. In F.R. Rusch (Ed.), *Supported employment: Issues and strategies* (2nd ed.).

Rehab Brief (1986). *Supported employment. 10* (1). Washington, D.C.: U.S. Department of Education, National Institute on Disability and Rehabilitation Research, Office of Special Education and Rehabilitation Services.

Rhodes, L.E., & Valenta, L. (1989). Industry-based supported employment: An enclave approach. In P. Wehman & J. Kregel (Eds.), *Supported employment for persons with disabilities* (pp. 53–68). New York: Plenum.

Rusch, F.R. (1986). *Competitive employment issues and strategies.* Baltimore: Paul H. Brookes Publishing Co.

Shafer, M.S., Kregel, J., & Banks, P.D. (1989). *Employment retention and career movement among individuals with mental retardation working in supported employment.* Unpublished manuscript, Virginia Commonwealth University, Rehabilitation Research and Training Center, Richmond, VA.

Wehman, P., Hill, J.W., Wood, W., & Parent, W. (1987). A report on competitive employment histories of persons labeled severely mentally retarded. *Journal of The Association for Persons with Severe Handicaps, 12*, 11–17.

Wehman, P., Kregel, J., & Banks, D. (1989). Competitive employment for persons with mental retardation: A decade later. In P. Wehman & J. Kregel (Eds.), *Supported employment for persons with disabilities* (pp. 97–114). New York: Plenum.

Wehman, P., Kregel, J., & Shafer, M.S. (1989). *Emerging trends in the national supported employment initiative: A preliminary analysis of twenty-seven states.* Richmond, VA: Virginia Commonwealth University Rehabilitation Research and Training Center.

Wehman, P., & Moon, M.S. (1988). *Vocational rehabilitation and supported employment.* Baltimore: Paul H. Brookes Publishing Co.

Wehman, P., Parent, W., Wood, W., Kregel, J., & Inge, K. (1989). The Supported work model of competitive employment: Illustrations of competence in workers with severe and profound handicaps. In P. Wehman & J. Kregel (Eds.), *Supported employment for persons with disabilities* (pp. 19–52). New York: Plenum.

DEVELOPMENT OF A CLUSTER OR DISPERSED GROUP JOB PLACEMENT FOR TRANSITION-AGE WORKERS WITH SEVERE MENTAL RETARDATION

3

Supported employment has greatly changed the employment outcomes for many individuals with mental retardation. It has provided paid work within integrated community work environments for a group of persons who previously were considered unemployable (Lattuca, Venne, & Campbell, 1989). A variety of supported employment options have made this transition to paid employment possible. These options include the individual placement model (Wehman, Hill, Hill, Brooke, Pendleton, & Britt, 1986), industry-based enclaves (Rhodes & Valenta, 1985b; Rhodes & Valenta, 1985a), mobile work crews (Bourbeau, 1985), and small businesses (O'Bryan, 1985).

Unfortunately, however, many persons with the most severe disabilities continue to be excluded from supported employment (Wehman, Kregel, & Shafer, 1989). These individuals often are considered too difficult to place due to severe mental retardation; presence of interfering, challenging behaviors; and/or secondary physical disabilities. They usually display a slower rate of skill acquisition and little adaptability to change (Rhodes & Valenta 1985b).

One supported employment option for providing the long-term support needed by individuals with severe disabilities is the enclave model. This is defined as a group of individuals with handicaps working with ongoing support within a regular business or industry (Rhodes & Valenta, 1985b). The ongoing support usually is provided by a host agency that operates supported employment programs. This agency actually employs the workers and contracts with the business or industry to provide the labor force (Lattuca et al., 1989). The workers with disabilities usually are paid subminimum wages based on their production.

Rhodes and Valenta (1985b) have outlined the process that they found useful for establishing an enclave in industry. In their enclave, eight individuals worked on an enclave line doing subassemblies of, for example, defibrillator components such as chest paddles for electrodes, wire harnesses, and battery support harnesses. These tasks represented the same type and variety of work performed by other company employees. Ongoing supervision was provided by a nonprofit organization, Trillium Employment Services, which was started in order to implement the enclave option in industry. Workers were hired through Trillium and were paid subminimum wages based on their production. The average wage earned by an individual in the enclave was $323 per month.

Group placements such as an enclave have proved to be a viable employment option for individuals with severe disabilities. In January, 1988, the Supported Employment Project for Youth with Severe Disabilities at Virginia Commonwealth University began the process of establishing an enclave for a group of school-age individuals who required long-term, ongoing job-site support. These young people, for a variety of reasons, had been unable to work successfully in individual placements that required them to work at least 20 hours per week. A number of issues were raised related to designing a group placement that would provide maximum benefits to these workers. Some of these included: 1) the type of work targeted, 2) physical work space, 3) work routines, 4) worker personnel status, 5) pay and benefits, 6) staff supervision and support, and 7) selection and number of employees. Rhodes and Valenta (1985a) suggested that these variables could be placed on a continuum of least to most desirable characteristics. For example, the most desirable work to be targeted would be those job duties typically performed by other employees in the agency. The least desirable would be work that was not performed by co-workers. Later in this chapter, under "Development Issues for Group Placements," each characteristic is discussed based on the issues raised by the Supported Employment Project for Youth with Severe Disabilities. Several philosophical issues must also be addressed concerning a group placement, since there is some debate about its appropriateness.

PHILOSOPHICAL CONCERNS ABOUT GROUP PLACEMENTS

Some experts on employment for persons with the most severe disabilities have stated that all group placements are undesirable. For example, Dr. Lou Brown from the University of Wisconsin has said that no more than two persons with disabilities should ever work at the same site (Brown, RRTC Symposium on Supported Employment, April 14, 1989). Others have stated that individual work arrangements are more "normal," usually pay more, and probably are more likely to promote integration (Moon & Griffin, 1988) than group placement options. Although we agree that individual placements should be the goal for all persons who want paid employment, we must also admit that we currently do not know how to accomplish this for everyone.

There is no single criterion by which to judge the appropriateness of a job placement. To a large degree, it depends on the experiences and choices of the consumer and his or her family. The age of the consumer also will make a difference in the type of placement made. For example, a group placement is more common for high school and college-age workers who are looking for various experiences or seasonal, usually summer, jobs. Occasionally, a combination of consumer and family priorities in addition to the service provider cooperations may determine whether a group placement is desirable. Does the consumer want higher pay or more opportunities to socialize with people who do not have disabilities? Is the group or person providing initial placement and training required to have persons work on the average of 20 hours each week in order to receive federal and state rehabilitation supported employment funds? The authors do not believe that anyone can arbitrarily judge the rightness or wrongness of community-based employment as long as it provides dignity to the consumers, as much pay as anyone would make for that job, and the chance to interact with persons who are *not* family or human service professionals, and persons who do not have disabilities.

Historically, there have been three great disadvantages to enclaves, work crews, and small businesses that employ primarily workers with disabilities. First, people employed in these models have tended to make less than minimum wage. Second, because workers have performed most job duties as a group, they have spent much of the work-day isolated from the general public with other workers who have disabilities. Third, the authors feel that many consumers who have been placed in group placements to date have been capable of eventual job independence. The type of model proposed in this chapter, in our opinion, avoids to some extent these pitfalls because it is based on the following philosophical tenets:

> Any person working in a group should perform the same job duties as other workers at the site and perform them side by side with other workers in the same environment.
>
> Workers with handicaps should be hired for the regular wage and regular company benefits.
>
> As few workers with handicaps as possible should be at a site at the same time during a given work shift.
>
> Very young workers without a work history or workers who have been unsuccessful in several individual placements are best potential employees for group models.
>
> Workers in group situations should be trained to the greatest degree possible and encouraged to advance to an individual job placement in which they ultimately can work without the assistance of an employment specialist.

DEVELOPMENT ISSUES FOR GROUP PLACEMENTS

Type of Work Targeted

Once the decision is made to develop a group placement that will provide continual on-site supervision, the type of work to be targeted should reflect standard job duties performed by coworkers who do not have disabilities. It is recommended that the employment specialist who will later supervise the group placement be responsible for completing the job development. A community job market screening (Moon, Goodall, Barcus, & Brooke, 1986) may be used to target potential jobs in the community that would be appropriate for individuals with severe mental retardation. The jobs most appropriate for selection are entry level positions that have consistent work routines and minimal task changes. It also may be useful to identify several candidates for the group placement prior to job development. By knowing the consumer characteristics at the time of job development, the employment specialist will be able to target potential work in the community more efficiently. More specific information on the selection of a group placement site can be found under the "Job Development" section of this chapter.

Physical Work Space

The ratio of nondisabled coworkers to employees with disabilities should be considered carefully in development of a group placement. Therefore, a primary objective for selecting a group job-site must be integration of the employees throughout the physical work space. For example, individuals with disabilities should be assigned job duties that are not executed in the same immediate work areas. Doing so necessitates identification of a work environment in which the group supervisor can quickly navigate while allowing the employees to work side by side with nondisabled coworkers. It is suggested that physical proximity to coworkers who do not have disabilities may promote integration at the work site and be less stigmatizing to employees with disabilities than sites that group disabled workers in one location.

Work Routines

In order to meet the requirements of supported employment, a group placement must provide at least 20 hours of work per week for each employee. If the decision is made to provide part-time work opportunities for individuals with severe handicaps, sites that allow for part-time employment should be targeted. In addition, the employment specialist should advocate for regular breaks and lunch times to allow for coworker interactions during normally occurring times for socialization.

The requirement of part-time employment may be an asset for job-site development of a group placement. Employers may be willing to split one full-time position into two part-time positions. Dividing job duties between two individuals would help keep work routine changes to a minimum. For example, the job duties for one full-time position might include sweeping and mopping the floor, cleaning the bathrooms, and emptying ashtrays and trash cans. The supervisor might be willing for one individual to see to the floors and trash during one part-time shift, while the other cleaned and monitored the bathrooms during another part-time shift.

By beginning the placement with one to two task responsibilities per worker, the employment specialist could ensure that intensive training was provided at all times and that the work was completed to the supervisor's satisfaction. However, it should be noted that as a worker becomes competent, additional job duties should be negotiated with the employer to provide more responsibility and variety. In addition, the workers could eventually learn each others' job duties to be able to rotate responsibilities and possibly prevent task boredom.

Personnel Status, Pay, and Benefits

The most desirable personnel status, pay, and benefits for employees working in group options would be the same as those available to their coworkers. This means that the employer selected should place the individuals with disabilities on the regular company payroll, pay at least minimum wages, and provide standard company benefits. This is significantly different from the enclave situation described earlier in which the enclave workers were hired by the supported employment company and paid subminimum wages on a contract basis.

Staff Supervision and Support

Supervision in a group placement model is provided by an employment specialist for all hours that the workers are at the job site and for as long as necessary. In negotiating with potential employers, the employment specialist should make it clear that he or she would be responsible for all training and supervisory needs of the employees. In addition, the employment specialist should explain that he or she would pace his or her distance from the employees, based on individual worker need. Completion of all work duties would be guaranteed, and the employment specialist would be responsible for meeting production standards to the employer's satisfaction. It should also be established whether or not the employment specialist would be responsible for completing the job duties of any worker who was sick or on vacation. Of course, the employment specialist can fade from the job site eventually, if possible. The point of a group placement, though, is to meet the needs of persons who may not be able to achieve vocational independence.

Selection of Employees

Several criteria for acceptance into a group referral pool should be considered. First, an individual would have severe disabilities with little or no work history. We believe that a group situation is a good first job for school-age persons who need experience and a high degree of supervision. Group placement also is appropriate for young adults because it may allow them to try a variety of job duties while receiving both training and pay.

Consideration also must be given to those individuals who have problem behaviors, a history of slow skill acquisition, or who exhibit little adaptability to change. In addition, individuals who have repeatedly been unsuccessful in individual supported employment positions may be given priority status.

It is recommended that a heterogeneous grouping of individuals comprise the group model rather than a grouping of individuals with similar behavioral characteristics. In a group of workers whose skill abilities vary, individual strengths and weaknesses can complement each other, thereby facilitating supervisory responsibilities, as well as ensuring that the jobs are completed to company standards. However, employment specialists should be careful not to place individuals in a group when individual placement is possible and has not been attempted first.

Summary

A desirable group placement consists of individuals who have severe disabilities. These workers are hired directly by the employer, paid at least minimum wages, work at least part time, and complete regular job duties performed by nondisabled coworkers. All work is performed alongside coworkers who do not have disabilities. Group employees with disabilities should never perform identical duties in a segregated arrangement.

After consideration of these criteria, the term enclave does not appear appropriate for the type of group placement described. Instead, the objectives outlined define a group of individuals working in a cluster or dispersed arrangement. They may be at a single job site performing a variety of jobs or at different sites that are clustered, that is, close together. Table 3.1 shows a summary of cluster placement characteristics. The section following Table 3.1 outlines the development of a cluster placement at a local mall food court.

DEVELOPMENT OF THE CLUSTER PLACEMENT

Job Development

Job development for the cluster placement model developed by the Supported Employment Project for Youth with Severe Disabilities followed the same process outlined by Moon et al. (1986), which was designed for the individual placement model of supported employment. Leads for potential sites were obtained from the classified ads, word of mouth from other employment specialists, and cold calls placed by the employment specialist to canvass various neighborhoods of the city. The majority of the jobs available were custodial positions in local hospitals, hotels, and a mall. It was quickly determined that the hospital positions were not appropriate for the cluster placement since a great

Table 3.1.   Characteristics of cluster placements

Characteristics	Outcome
Type of work targeted	Employment performing standard job duties for all company employees
Physical work space	Dispersement throughout the job site working side by side with nondisabled coworkers
Work routines	Minimum of 20 hours per week with one to three task responsibilities per worker
Personnel status, pay, benefits	Employee at the job site with minimum wages and standard company benefits
Staff support and supervision	Continuous on-site supervision and training by an employment specialist
Selection of employees	Targeted employment for individuals with severe mental retardation who have no work history or have a previous history of failure in the individual placement model

deal of judgement was required in working with the patients during cleaning of hospital rooms. The employment specialist pursued several housekeeping positions in local hotels with the idea that several individuals could be dispersed across a floor of the hotel for the cluster placement. After completing a job analysis form (Moon et al., 1986) and working two different housekeeping positions, the employment specialist determined that the production rate of eight rooms in 4 hours per worker was not feasible for the consumers in the group referral pool. Figure 3.1 shows the community job market screening form used to develop this placement.

Identification of the job site for the cluster placement was made by an employment specialist who was doing job development for the individual placement model of supported employment. She had been making cold calls at a local mall and had identified a full-time position in the mall's food court. The job supervisor was not interested in the individual placement model but stated that he would be interested in discussing the concept of employing individuals with disabilities if a full-time supervisor were provided. At the time of initial contact, the rate of employee turnover was approximately 65%. Figure 3.2 shows the employer contact sheet, and Figure 3.3 the initial employer interview form that was completed for the mall position.

Upon observation, it was determined that the mall's food court could meet the requirements of dispersing workers throughout the physical work space, while allowing the employment specialist easy access to the individuals. The food court area was 5,700 square feet in size, with a seating capacity of 484 customers. There were 10 food service businesses, including a pizza restaurant, hamburger restaurant, Mexican food stand, and yogurt specialty stand situated around the perimeter of the food court. The mall's only restrooms were located within this area down a hallway approximately 15 feet long, as was a small kitchen used to clean and sanitize food trays. Approximately 45 individuals worked in this area for the various food vendors and in maintenance positions for the food court. Figure 3.4 shows a diagram of the food court area.

It was agreed during the initial employer interview that two individuals would split the full-time position of restroom attendant in the mall's food court, with one working 4 hours in the morning and one working 4 hours in the afternoon, Tuesday through Saturday. They would be employed by the mall management and would receive the same wages and benefits available to other part-time workers. The employer agreed that two to four additional workers would be added to the cluster as the employees learned their

VIRGINIA COMMONWEALTH UNIVERSITY
REHABILITATION RESEARCH AND TRAINING CENTER

COMMUNITY JOB MARKET SCREENING FORM

Date completed: _____   **Completed by:** _____

1. GENERAL SCREENING

List job openings that occur frequently (from classified advertisements, employment service listings, public service advertisements):

Job title/Type of work	General requirements
Custodian/mall maintenance	*none*
Hospital janitor/clean hospital rooms	*none*
Spice container packers	*none*
Housekeepers/clean hotel guest rooms	*none*
Kitchen utility/food service	*none*
Custodian/grocery store stocker/baggers	*none*

2. SPECIFIC SCREENING

List potential appropriate companies or industries in this community to contact for job openings.

Current

Company/contact person	Type of Work	Address/telephone
Mall food court	*bathroom maintenance*	
	dishwashing	
	trash disposal	
	table busing	
Local hospital	*cleaning hospital rooms*	
Large spice factory	*packaging spices*	
Hotel chain	*cleaning guest rooms*	
Fast food restaurant	*pot scrubbing*	
	dishwashing	
	floor maintenance	
Local grocery chain	*bagging groceries*	
	stocking shelves	
	cleaning parking lot	

Developing

Company/contact person	Type of work	Address/telephone
Mall food court		
Large spice factory		
Hotel chain		

Figure 3.1. Community job market screening form for development of a cluster placement.

job responsibilities and as other positions became available in the food court area. The process of job development for the cluster placement required approximately 3 months.

VIRGINIA COMMONWEALTH UNIVERSITY
REHABILITATION RESEARCH AND TRAINING CENTER

EMPLOYER CONTACT SHEET

Date of initial contact: *3-24*

Initiated by:

Method: phone   visit   letter

Name of company:

Address:

Telephone:

Name of contact person:

Title: Food Court Maintenance Supervisor

General response: __X__ Interested   __X__ Position available
                    _____ Not interested   _____ Not available
                                                    _____ Not appropriate

Comments: *Job lead was passed on by another employment specialist who was look-*
ing for an individual placement position. The supervisor reported that he would be
interested in hiring someone only if the agency provided supervision on a full-time
basis. Contact by telephone determined that the current position is restroom atten-
dant. Initial visit for the next day was confirmed. At initial visit the idea of establishing a
cluster placement was discussed. Mr. (   ) was very open and responsive to the
idea! He is willing to split the full-time bathroom attendant position into part-time for
two individuals. He is also willing to discuss giving additional positions to the project at
a later date. Appears very interested in the Targeted Jobs Tax Credit. Would like to meet
two workers on Tuesday. Job analysis form was completed as well as sequence of job
duties.

(Further contact with company can be recorded on the reverse side.)

Figure 3.2.   Employer contact sheet for mall cluster placement.

Table 3.2 shows the benefits for part-time nondisabled workers that were also received
by the cluster employees.

Job Placement and Training

Two young women were taken for job interviews with the food court supervisor after the
initial agreement had been made to begin the cluster placement. Both of these individuals
had participated in situational assessments, and the employment specialist had used the
assessments to match them to the position at the mall. Chapter 5, on situational assessment, and Moon et al. (1986) review the job matching process.

The young woman selected for the morning hours was 19 years old and had Down
syndrome, with an IQ of less than 29. She was described as having a poor attention span,
poor visual perception skills, poor fine motor skills, difficulty performing tasks in sequence, and a speech impairment. A recent psychological report stated that she had the
social skills of a 2-year-old. She had been in a segregated school program for 12 years and

VIRGINIA COMMONWEALTH UNIVERSITY
REHABILITATION RESEARCH AND TRAINING CENTER

EMPLOYER INTERVIEW FORM

Company: *Mall*　　　　　　　　　　Date: *3-29*

Address:　　　　　　　　　　　　　Telephone:

Person interviewed: *Mr. (   )*
Title: *Food Court Maintenance Supervisor*

Job title: *Restroom attendant*　　　　Rate of pay: *4.15/hour*

Work schedule: *Tuesday–Saturday 8:00–4:00*

Company benefits: *2 weeks of annual leave after 1 year of employment; 6 paid holidays including New Year's Day, Memorial Day, Independence Day, Labor Day, Thanksgiving Day, and Christmas Day; 1 paid day of funeral leave for immediate family member; 3 days of sick leave per year; annual bonus at Christmas, which may equal 1 week's pay.*

Size of company (or number of employees): *18 in food court maintenance*

Volume and/or pace of work: *Overall the pace is steady to slow. There may be some periods of time when the pace is fast . . . mostly during holidays and Saturdays.*

Number of employees in this position: *One for maintaining both restrooms*

Written job description available? *no*
Description of job duties: *(Record on Sequence of Job Duties Form)*
Availability of supervisor: *The supervisor is in immediate area but is not interested in providing more than 10% of his time to supervision of the cluster placement employees.*
Availability of coworkers: *There are approximately 10 coworkers in the food court area.*

Orientation skills needed (size and layout of work area): *The food court is 5,700 square feet. The restroom attendant position requires minimal orientation skills, since the individual will be in one small area, except during break times.*

What are important aspects of the position:
Speed _____ vs. Thoroughness __X__ Judgment _____ vs. Routine __X__
Teamwork _____ vs. Independence __X__ Repetition _____ vs. Variability _____

Other: *Neat appearance is a must . . . uniform is required and provided by the mall management. The uniforms will be cleaned weekly by mall.*

What are the absolute don'ts for employee in this position: *Stealing, drinking, excessive absences*

Describe any reading or number work that is required: *None*

What machinery or equipment will the employee need to operate: *Minimal . . . use of a mop and broom*

Atmosphere:　__X__ Friendly, cheerful　　　　　_____ Aloof, indifferent
　　　　　　　__X__ Busy, relaxed (sometimes)　　_____ Busy, tense
　　　　　　　__X__ Slow, relaxed (mostly)　　　　_____ Slow, tense
　　　　　　　_____ Structured, orderly　　　　　_____ Unstructured

Comments: *Excellent benefits; management is very positive; coworkers are friendly; regular merit raise after 90 days; good opportunity for social integration during breaks; opportunity for skill development in other areas of the mall.*

Figure 3.3.　Employer interview form used with mall supervisor.

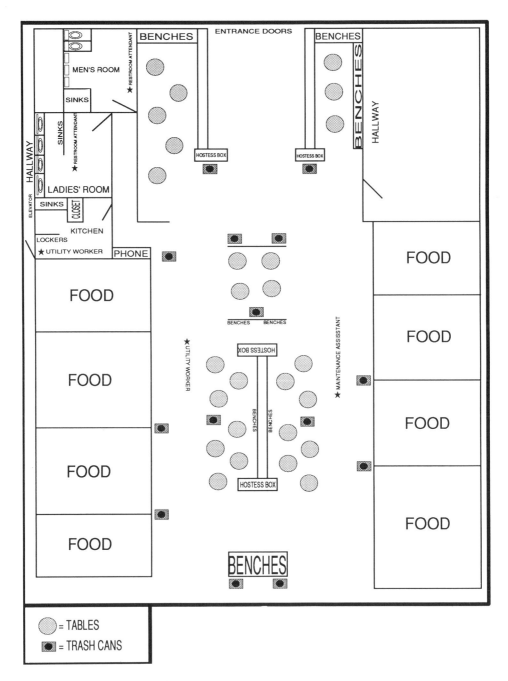

Figure 3.4.   Mall food court diagram.

did not have any work experience. Her teachers strongly recommended employment in the cluster placement versus an individual competitive employment placement.

The second young woman was 22 years old and had severe mental retardation, with an IQ of 34. She spoke in unclear sentences and often repeated what was said to her, rather than initiating conversation. She was described as being withdrawn and insubordinate. Her mother reported having problems with her disappearing with strange men for

Table 3.2.   Benefit package for cluster placement employees

Wages
  $4.15 per hour starting wage
  $4.50 per hour after 90-day probationary period
Vacation/annual leave
  2 weeks paid vacation after 1 year of employment
  3 weeks paid vacation after 3 years of employment
Sick leave
  3 days of paid sick leave per year after completion of the initial probationary period
  Payment for unused sick leave days at the end of each calendar year
Funeral leave
  1 day paid leave for death of an immediate family member
Holidays
  Six paid holidays paid after 60 days of employment:

New Year's Day	Labor Day
Memorial Day	Thanksgiving Day
Independence Day	Christmas Day

Bonus
  Christmas bonus, which has been as much as 1 week's wages

days at a time. Approximately 7 months prior to the mall placement, she had been placed by the project in an individual supported employment job at a local fast food restaurant. Duties had included washing and putting away dishes and emptying the trash. During this employment period, she had an episode of disappearing for 2 days and was described by the management as insubordinate. She was fired 5 months into employment for several incidents of refusing to work. This young woman was selected for cluster placement based on this work history and the recommendation of her mother and teachers.

The date for placement was scheduled for 1 week after the employee interviews to allow time for the employment specialist to arrange for transportation, notify social security, complete the paper work for the Targeted Jobs Tax Credit, and to complete preliminary task analyses. The morning employee would be responsible for doing a detailed cleaning of the men's and women's restrooms, including cleaning the toilets, sinks, floors, emptying the trash, and supplying the paper products. The afternoon employee's responsibilities would focus primarily on spot cleaning and making sure that the paper products were supplied. Both positions were slow paced and allowed time for intensive systematic instruction across all job duties from the first day of work. A system of least prompts (Moon et al., 1986) was used for both workers. Table 3.3 shows a sequence of all food court job duties performed by the cluster workers; Table 3.4 shows a sample task analysis used during training.

Approximately 2 months after the initiation of the placement, an additional part-time position was offered to the employment specialist. The individual filling the afternoon restroom attendant position had been helping a coworker, a utility worker, to clean trays and had reached skill acquisition of that task. When the utility worker resigned, the supervisor suggested that the cluster employee assume the responsibility of cleaning the trays. The job duties involved are outlined in Table 3.3.

This change in job duties allowed the addition of the new afternoon worker who assumed the restroom attendant job duties. This young woman was 22 years old and had severe mental retardation, with an IQ of 33. In addition, she had a seizure disorder and cerebral palsy, which was evident in a slow awkward gait and an inability to use one hand.

Table 3.3.   Sequence of job duties

Position #1: Restroom attendant

8:00 A.M.	Punch in
8:00– 8:05	Put out "no entry" signs
8:05– 8:20	Gather supplies
8:20– 9:00	Clean men's restroom
9:00– 9:45	Clean women's restroom
9:45–10:00	Clean phones and water fountain
10:00–10:15	Break
10:15–noon	Spot clean restrooms
Noon	Punch out

Position #2: Maintenance Assistant

11:30 A.M.	Punch in
11:30–11:40	Gather supplies
11:40–noon	Clean toilets
Noon–12:15	Clean sink
12:15–12:30	Clean mirrors
12:30– 2:00	Mop floor, sweep floor, wipe sinks, check toilet paper as needed
2:00– 2:15	Break
2:15– 3:00	Mop floor, sweep floor, wipe sinks, check toilet paper, empty trash as needed
3:00– 3:15	Clean mirror
3:15– 3:30	Change sanitary bags
3:30	Punch out

Position #3: Utility worker

11:30 A.M.	Punch in
11:30–noon	Wash trays, clean tray room
12:00–12:10	Prepare water to wash trays
12:10–12:20	Gather dirty trays in food court
12:20– 1:00	Deliver clean trays to food stands
1:00– 1:20	Gather dirty trays in food court
1:20– 2:00	Wash trays
2:00– 2:15	Break
2:15– 2:25	Deliver clean trays to food stands
2:25– 2:35	Gather dirty trays
2:35– 3:00	Wash trays
3:00– 3:15	Clean phones as needed
3:15– 3:30	Clean tray room
3:30	Punch out

Position #4: Maintenance assistant

11:30 A.M.	Punch in
11:30–11:40	Prepare trash cart
11:40–noon	Empty trash in food court
noon–12:10	Take full trash bags to truck
12:10–12:30	Empty trash cans in food court
12:30–12:40	Take full trash bags to truck
12:40– 1:00	Check hallways, take trash to truck
1:00– 2:00	Alternate emptying trash and taking full cart to truck
2:00– 2:15	Break
2:15– 3:30	Alternate emptying trash and taking full cart to truck
3:30	Punch out

(continued)

Table 3.3.   (continued)

Position #5: Maintenance assistant

Time	Task
11:30 A.M.	Punch in
11:30–11:40	Gather supplies
11:40–11:50	Clean toilets
11:50–11:55	Clean mirrors
11:55–noon	Clean sinks, hand dispensers
noon–12:05	Spot clean walls
12:05–12:10	Empty trash
12:10–12:20	Sweep, mop as needed
12:20–12:25	Clean door, radiators
12:25–12:45	Check hallway for trash, take trash to truck
12:45– 2:00	Alternate maintaining clean bathroom and checking hallway for trash
2:00– 2:15	Break
2:15– 2:45	Spot clean bathroom
2:45– 3:00	Check hallway for trash
3:00– 3:15	Clean, sweep around water fountain
3:15– 3:20	Mop floor
3:20– 3:30	Put supplies away
3:30	Punch out

She had attended a segregated school for 15 years, and her work history consisted of an individual placement at a local hospital cafeteria. Unfortunately, she had numerous seizures during the 3 months of employment, as well as three incidents of falling backwards on the job. Due to these difficulties, the hospital asked her to resign. Based on this history of seizures and poor mobility, it was decided that the cluster placement would be

Table 3.4.   Sample task analysis used by the restroom attendant

Clean the toilets

1.	Get two bottles from caddy.	20.	Dip brush in toilet.
2.	Take to first stall.	21.	Circle in bowl 3 times.
3.	Push up lid with bottle.	22.	Circle on rim 3 times.
4.	Pour in both cleaners. (Squeeze lids are open.)	23.	Tap brush.
		24.	Wipe outside of toilet with cloth.
5.	Go to second stall.	25.	Wipe bottom of seat.
6.	Push up lid with bottle.	26.	Put seat down.
7.	Pour in both cleaners.	27.	Wipe top of seat.
8.	Go to third stall.	28.	Wipe stainless steel.
9.	Push up lid with bottle.	29.	Flush toilet.
10.	Pour in both cleaners.	30.	Pick up Sanicare.
11.	Go to fourth stall.	31.	Go to second stall.
12.	Push up lid with bottle.	32.	Repeat steps 18–30.
13.	Pour in both cleaners.	33.	Go to third stall.
14.	Put bottles in caddy.	34.	Repeat steps 18–30.
15.	Put on gloves.	35.	Go to fourth stall.
16.	Get Sanicare, cloth, and toilet brush.	36.	Repeat steps 18–30.
17.	Go to first stall.	37.	Put supplies in caddy.
18.	Spray Sanicare under rim of toilet.	38.	Take off gloves.
19.	Set bottle on floor.	39.	Put gloves in caddy.

appropriate for this young woman. The employment specialist could provide the needed intervention during any seizures and assist if she had a fall at the site.

The fourth cluster placement was added 1 month later, which was 3 months from the cluster start-up date. At this time, the two workers in the afternoon had reached skill acquisition on all of their tasks but continued to require prompts to sequence job duties and to stay on task. The employer requested another worker in the afternoon time period to empty the trash in the entire food court area.

This new position also was part time for 20 hours per week in the afternoon and was titled maintenance assistant. At this time the employment specialist asked for an additional morning position since only one individual was working during this time slot. However, the morning was a slow work shift, and the employer was not in need of additional workers during this period.

The primary job duty of the maintenance assistant was emptying the trash cans in the food court and taking them out to a truck located in the parking lot. Table 3.3 shows the sequence of these job duties. The two other workers in the afternoon had reached skill acquisition on all of their tasks but required prompts to sequence job duties and to stay on task.

The young man selected for the new maintenance position was 21 years old, with a reported IQ of 27 and a history of autistic-like behavior. This behavior consisted of biting his fingers when frustrated and being unable to initiate social interactions. When observed in his segregated classroom environment, it was noted that he did not perform tasks independently. The teacher and parents were only interested in a placement in which the young man would receive continued supervision. In fact, the mother was hesitant to place him in a community position and had always expected only sheltered employment for her son.

Intensive training was needed by this worker. Initially, he was unable to find his way around the food court, locate the trash cans in the work area, or find his way around the parking lot to empty the trash. The employment specialist developed a schedule for providing the needed supervision to the two workers who had reached skill acquisition while providing initial training to the new worker. A least prompt strategy was also used in training for the maintenance assistant job duties. A sequence of these duties is shown under Position #4 in Table 3.3.

Additional workers were not added until 7 months from the start-up date of the cluster placement. The food court supervisor requested two additional workers, a male to maintain the men's restroom in the afternoon and evening and a woman to maintain the women's restroom in the evening. He reported that the mall had received extensive feedback from the patrons regarding the excellent condition of the restrooms. Therefore, management wanted to provide restroom maintenance on a full-time basis. The cluster supervisor negotiated with the employer to establish the female evening position as an independent placement. An employment specialist who was responsible for individual placements on the project would train this individual to independence, fade from the site, and provide follow-along support as needed. She also negotiated with the supervisor for the male afternoon and evening position to be semi-independent. The person selected for this time period would work hours overlapping those of the cluster placement employees for 4 hours but would also work independently for 4 hours per day.

A young man who had an IQ of 43, in the moderate range of mental retardation, was selected for the afternoon and evening position of maintenance assistant. This worker was considered ideal for the position requirements based on his work history. He had been placed by the project sweeping and picking up trash in an office building during his last year of school and had maintained the position for approximately 10 months. He was fired for taking excessive breaks and requiring too much supervision. At the time of consideration for the new position, he had not been working for 1 month, and his mother was anxious for him to return to work. He was known to be a good worker when given intermittent supervision; he was also known as quick to learn new skills. His mother was very supportive of the new job possibility since it was close to home and would provide some supervision for job maintenance.

Since there was limited time to train an additional individual in the afternoon time slot due to other employee needs, the cluster supervisor arranged to begin training the new worker in the morning when her responsibilities were not as intense. By this time, the morning worker was independent in task performance except for assistance in sequencing of tasks and maintenance of work standards and production. The mall supervisor agreed to this training schedule with the assurance that the worker would move to the afternoon and evening slot as soon as possible. Since some of the job duties were already familiar tasks, the change of shifts was completed within 2 weeks of placement. These duties are listed under Position #5 in Table 3.3.

After working for 1 month at 40 hours per week, the young man and his family requested that he no longer work evenings. They felt that the hours were too demanding, and they preferred the afternoon time slot in the cluster placement. The change was made with the agreement of the food court supervisor.

The individual selected for the evening restroom female attendant also had a history of independent supported employment placement. She was 20 years old, with an IQ of 29, in the severe range of mental retardation. In addition, she had a secondary diagnosis of cerebral palsy which was noted in a slow awkward gait and limited motor functioning in her hands. She was able to make a fist bilaterally and oppose all of her fingertips to her thumb; however, she was unable to execute a fine pincer grasp on either hand.

This young woman had been working for 11 months in an independent placement through this project, folding towels in a hotel laundry until the hotel was sold and the workers laid off. The restroom position appeared to be a good job match for her skills since it required only light cleaning. The list of job duties for Position #2 in Table 3.3 shows her job responsibilities. As prearranged with the mall supervisor, another staff employment specialist responsible for the individual placement model was assigned to provide training in this position during the evening hours; this training was not considered part of the cluster placement responsibilities. After 1 month of training, however, it was determined that the female employee selected for the evening restroom attendant was displaying only 33% skill acquisition for all tasks. She was requiring model prompts as well as physical prompts to complete the steps in the task analyses. Primarily she was having difficulty learning some of the fine motor manipulations of the materials. Project staff determined that she needed more intensive supervision than had been anticipated. A decision was made to consider placement within the cluster rather than continuing the individual position.

In reviewing the supervisory needs of the cluster placement employees, it was determined that the young woman who had the job of restroom attendant in the afternoon and who had seizures and cerebral palsy was independent in her job duties. The cluster supervisor had primarily been providing assistance during any seizure incidents and when the young woman fell at the site. However, it was also noted that the coworkers had gradually taken over these responsibilities since the afternoon maintenance assistant was hired. After discussing with project staff and parents the possibility of switching the afternoon worker and the evening worker, the cluster supervisor approached the mall supervisor and requested a transfer of positions. The mall supervisor agreed to provide the necessary supervision for the employee with the medical concerns in order to place her in the independent evening position. The food court supervisor agreed that the present evening worker needed the support of the cluster placement.

The change was facilitated by assigning two employment specialists to assist with the transfer of workers. One employment specialist spent approximately 3 weeks implementing intensive training and fading strategies to assist in transferring the employee from the cluster to the independent evening position. The other employment specialist assisted the cluster supervisor for 1 week in the development of a schedule for supervision and training of the four workers that would comprise the afternoon cluster.

After 8 months, six individuals were employed by the mall's food court. One person received full-time supervision for 4 hours in the morning, four workers received 4 hours of full-time supervision in the afternoons, and one worker was in an individual placement in the evening, receiving only follow-along support. At this time some concern was raised regarding the supervisory needs of the individual working with intensive support in the mornings. It was felt that she no longer needed such close supervision. The mall management, however, was still unwilling to group any more workers during this time period since work responsibilities were minimal.

Finally, after 10 months of work at the mall, the food court supervisor said that a position was available during the afternoons, Sunday through Wednesday for 20 hours per week. The job duties would include maintaining the restrooms on Sunday and Monday afternoons when the cluster was not working. The duties Tuesday and Wednesday would focus on busing the tables in the food court, as well as helping with cleaning and delivering trays to the food stands. The cluster supervisor suggested to the food court supervisor that the morning cluster worker could easily be transferred to the afternoon period and assume the new job position. She could work independently on Sunday and Monday completing tasks for which skill acquisition was already complete. On Tuesday and Wednesday when new job duties were being initiated, the cluster supervisor would be available for assistance. The food court supervisor was assured that an employment specialist who was responsible for individual placement would be at the job site on Sunday and Monday, when the cluster was not in the mall, until the employee performed independently. In addition, she would assist the cluster supervisor in developing a training and supervisory schedule for the other two days of work. Approximately 3 weeks of additional employment specialist support were required to shift the worker to her new job duties on Tuesday and Wednesday with the supervision of the cluster supervisor. Eight weeks of training and fading were required to help the worker become independent working Sunday and Monday when the cluster was not at the mall. This change provided an ideal shift in responsibilities for this worker since she was given the opportunity to become independent on job tasks that were routine and was also provided with supervision for those tasks that were new and unknown.

When the morning worker was transferred to the afternoon semi-independent position, a space became available for an additional worker during the cluster placement hours. Since the training and supervision were high during this time period, it was decided that an individual with intensive training needs should be selected for this time slot. The young woman targeted to become the new restroom attendant and assume the job duties outlined in Position #1 in Table 3.3 had severe mental retardation, with an IQ of 15. She was 23 at the time of placement and had recently graduated from school. She was not receiving day program services and had essentially been sitting at home since the time of graduation. Her teachers reported that she was slow to reach skill acquisition, did not initiate tasks, and was not able to sequence tasks without directions. Her parents had been approached prior to graduation concerning a job and had been resistant. However, when they learned that their daughter would be receiving intensive support, they agreed to the placement. At the time of this writing, the young woman has been working for 8 weeks and can complete approximately 30% of her job duties independently. The cluster supervisor provides intensive instruction, using a least prompt strategy to assist her in the remainder of the tasks. Table 3.5 shows a summary of the timeline for placement into all the cluster positions described above.

As indicated in Table 3.5, the cluster placement gradually evolved over the course of a 10-month period to provide 7 positions for workers with severe disabilities. The gradual addition of employees over this time allowed for intensive job-site training on all job duties from the first day of work for each individual. A new worker was not added until the previous individual had reached skill acquisition on all tasks and could perform the job duties without assistance for approximately 10–15 minutes. Workers were at the site from 8:00 A.M. to 8:00 P.M., with a maximum of 5 workers at the site during any one time period. Figure 3.5 shows the weekly schedule of workers at the site.

Cluster workers received instruction not only in specific job duties, but also in job-related community functioning skills, including purchasing snacks, leisure materials (e.g., magazines), using the mall's banking facilities, and appropriate social skills. The acquisition of these skills has been crucial in maintaining three of the workers at the site. One worker was removing other employee's money from the locker area. The cluster supervisor taught her to cash her paycheck at the mall's bank and to retain some of her earnings to purchase snacks. This eliminated the stealing and also improved relationships with the coworkers. A second cluster employee was walking around the food court during her breaks and requesting free food from the merchants. Instruction was provided to assist her in purchasing these items, and there were discussions with the merchants

Table 3.5.   Timeline of cluster placements for food court positions

Month	Number of workers hired	Hours and days worked
Month 1	First worker hired in cluster placement	Tuesday–Saturday mornings
	Second worker hired in cluster placement	Tuesday–Saturday afternoons
Month 3	Third worker hired in cluster placement	Tuesday–Saturday afternoons
Month 4	Fourth worker hired in cluster placement	Tuesday–Saturday afternoons
Month 7	Fifth worker hired in semi-independent placement	Tuesday–Saturday afternoons/ evenings
	Sixth worker hired in indepedent placement	Tuesday–Saturday evenings
Month 8	Sixth worker moves to cluster placement	Tuesday–Saturday afternoons
	Third worker moves from cluster to independent placement	Tuesday–Saturday evenings
	Fifth worker shifts to afternoon-only cluster placement	Tuesday–Saturday afternoons
Month 10	First worker moves from cluster to semi-independent placement	Sunday–Wednesday afternoons
	Seventh worker hired in cluster placement	Tuesday–Saturday mornings
Totals:	5 workers in cluster placement 1 worker in semi-independent position 1 worker in independent position	

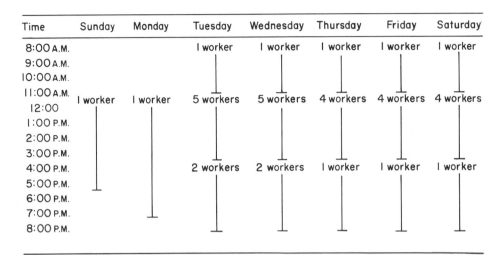

Time	Sunday	Monday	Tuesday	Wednesday	Thursday	Friday	Saturday
8:00 A.M.			I worker	I worker	I worker	I worker	I worker
9:00 A.M.							
10:00 A.M.							
11:00 A.M.	I worker	I worker	5 workers	5 workers	4 workers	4 workers	4 workers
12:00							
1:00 P.M.							
2:00 P.M.							
3:00 P.M.							
4:00 P.M.			2 workers	2 workers	I worker	I worker	I worker
5:00 P.M.							
6:00 P.M.							
7:00 P.M.							
8:00 P.M.							

Figure 3.5.   Weekly schedule for cluster workers.

about the inappropriateness of providing free food. An additional worker had difficulty with silly, inappropriate chatter. The food court supervisor requested that this problem be eliminated since it was offensive to mall patrons. The cluster supervisor initiated a behavior management program to decrease the inappropriate chatter, while increasing appropriate verbalizations.

CLUSTER PLACEMENT OUTCOMES

Currently the average hourly wage for the cluster workers is $4.38, with all of the individuals receiving an 8.4% raise upon the completion of 90 days of employment. To date, cluster workers have collectively earned $22,337 during 57 weeks of employment. Individual earnings range from $664 (8 weeks) to $4,857 (57 weeks) for a 20-hour work week. Table 3.6 shows a summary of the wages earned by this group of workers.

The characteristics of the cluster arrangement have facilitated integration with nonhandicapped peers. As stated previously, the cluster workers were dispersed throughout the work area of 5,700 square feet, with access to at least 45 nondisabled workers and as many as 484 mall customers. The cluster employees have developed meaningful social relationships and social skills, which is evident in daily social interactions and friendships for each worker. This includes sharing hobbies and interests during break periods, as well as exchanging snack items and vacation photos. One of the cluster employees has developed a friendship with a regular mall patron, and the two discuss their common interest in planes and trains. The patron has made arrangements to take the worker on a ride in his private plane, with the approval of the worker's parents.

This same worker also benefited from an ongoing relationship with a nondisabled coworker. When he first began employment, he would not converse with the supervisor or mall personnel and rarely made eye contact with the public. A fellow employee, who performed the same job duties as the cluster worker, began to accompany him to the trash disposal area and to request assistance in removing trash from the back of each store. The two employees often take breaks together and the coworker has begun assisting other workers in understanding the cluster worker's conversation since he is often difficult to understand.

Table 3.6. Employee wage history

Employee	Number of weeks employed	Beginning wage	First increase	Second increase	Total wages to date
Position #1	57	$4.15	$4.25	$4.50	$ 4,857
Position #2	57	$4.15	$4.25	$4.50	$ 4,857
Position #3	51	$4.15	$4.25	$4.50	$ 4,359
Position #4	44	$4.15	$4.25	$4.50	$ 3,778
Position #5	20	$4.10	$4.25	n/a	$ 1,988
Position #6	22	$4.15	$4.25	n/a	$ 1,834
Position #7	8	$4.15	n/a	n/a	$ 664
				Total	$22,337

Another cluster employee has demonstrated a marked increase in self-confidence since the beginning of her employment. Initially this worker spent most of the day with her head down, speaking infrequently and defensively to individuals who initiated conversation. When coworkers entered her work area, she would ignore their gestures of friendship and react inappropriately to conversation. This worker also rejected the supervisor's attempts to correct her mistakes and responded negatively to initial skill acquisition training. After 57 weeks on the job, she has developed a special relationship with the evening crew supervisor and spends time during breaks with her fellow employees laughing at jokes and stories.

Additional examples demonstrating the benefits of meaningful interactions can be presented for all of the remaining cluster workers. One worker has become friends with the personnel at the Italian restaurant. Another has befriended a nondisabled coworker, sitting with her during breaks. This same individual has experienced an increase in self-initiated contacts with the general public in her performance as a restroom attendant. Initially she ignored questions and did not acknowledge greetings expressed by shoppers using the restroom facilities. Now she is directing persons to available stalls and assisting shoppers as needed.

To date, the cluster site has maintained 100% retention rate for all its workers. This has been possible because of the cooperative attitude of the mall food court supervisor. He has been flexible in providing additional responsibilities to the workers as needed to provide job expansion. He has also facilitated movement to independent or to more supervised positions, based on the needs of the employees. This flexible attitude has been a criticial component for job maintenance. Workers are constantly challenged to perform at their maximal abilities with as little supervision as possible.

SUMMARY

This chapter has outlined an alternative strategy for placement of young persons with severe mental retardation into community employment opportunities. Specifically, we advocate the identification of jobs located very close to each other that will allow for integration at the work site, while providing continual supervision for job maintenance. This also allows the workers to receive the same wages and benefits as the other company employees and can provide opportunities for both full- and part-time employment. Readers are reminded that this kind of placement approach is *not* optimal for most workers and should only be sought for persons who are very young and can move easily from one job to another or for persons who have not been able to retain employment with less intrusive interventions.

REFERENCES

Bourbeau, P. (1985). Mobile work crews: An approach to achieve long-term supported employment. In P. McCarthy, J.M. Everson, M.S. Moon, & J.M. Barcus (Eds.), *School to work transition for youth with severe disabilities* (pp. 151–166). Richmond: Virginia Commonwealth University, Rehabilitation Research and Training Center.

Brown, L. (1989, April). Rehabilitation and Research Training Center (RRTC) Symposium on Supported Employment, Virginia Commonwealth University, Richmond.

Lattuca, F., Venne, R.W., & Campbell, J.F. (1989). Building and maintaining supported work and training alliances for persons with severe disabilities. In W.E. Kiernan & R.L. Schalock (Eds.), *Economics, industry, and disability: A look ahead* (pp. 67–76). Baltimore: Paul H. Brookes Publishing Co.

Moon, M.S., Goodall, P., Barcus, J.M., & Brooke, V. (1986). *The supported work model of competitive employment: A guide for job trainers* (2nd ed.). Richmond: Virginia Commonwealth University, Rehabilitation Research and Training Center.

Moon, M.S., & Griffin, S.L. (1988). Supported employment service delivery models. In P. Wehman & M.S. Moon (Eds.), *Vocational rehabilitation and supported employment* (pp. 17–30). Baltimore: Paul H. Brookes Publishing Co.

O'Bryan, A. (1985). The STP benchwork model. In P. McCarthy, J.M. Everson, & J.M. Barcus (Eds.), *School to work transition for youth with severe disabilities* (pp. 183–194). Richmond: Virginia Commonwealth University, Rehabilitation Research and Training Center.

Rhodes, L.E., & Valenta, L. (1985a). Enclaves in industry. In P. McCarthy, J.M. Everson, M.S. Moon, & J.M. Barcus (Eds.), *School to work transition for youth with severe disabilities* (pp. 127–150). Richmond: Virginia Commonwealth University, Rehabilitation Research and Training Center.

Rhodes, L.E., & Valenta, L. (1985b). Industry-based supported employment: An enclave approach. *Journal of The Association for Persons with Severe Handicaps, 10*(1), 12–20.

Wehman, P., Hill, M., Hill, J.W., Brooke, V., Pendleton, P., & Britt, C. (1986). Competitive employment for persons with mental retardation: A follow-up six years later. *Mental Retardation, 23*(6), 274–281.

Wehman, P., Kregel, J., & Shafer, M.S. (1989). *Emerging trends in the national supported employment initiative: A preliminary analysis of 27 states.* Richmond: Virginia Commonwealth University, Rehabilitation Research and Training Center.

PERSONS WITH SEVERE MENTAL RETARDATION WORKING IN COMPETITIVE EMPLOYMENT

TWO CASE STUDIES

4

Supported employment was designed to provide the opportunity for paid employment within integrated work settings for all adult individuals with handicaps, regardless of the severity of the handicapping condition. Unfortunately, however, individuals with truly severe disabilities continue to be excluded from these services (Davis, Bates, & Cuvo, 1983; Wehman, Parent, Wood, Kregel, & Inge, 1989). A very limited number of demonstration projects across the country have attempted to find employment for individuals with more severe disabilities. Wehman, Kregel, and Shafer (1989) report that only 11% of the individuals placed into supported employment jobs in the 27 states funded by federal initiatives have a severe disability. Why are programs excluding the very individuals for which supported employment was designed?

Wehman et al. (in press) believe that there are two primary reasons why persons with severe mental retardation are being excluded from supported employment programs. First, the majority of service providers for adults do not believe that these individuals are able to participate in meaningful work and earn minimum wages. Those professionals who do believe employment is a viable option simply do not have the skills to work with more severely disabled individuals. In addition, the professional literature available on skill acquisition using errorless learning strategies is very limited (Schuster, Gast, Wolery, & Guiltiman, 1988; Test, Grossi, & Keul, 1988). This limited availability of information has a negative impact on the placement of individuals with severe disabilities into supported, competitive jobs.

The majority of the literature available focuses on the use of least prompts as the teaching strategy of choice (Barcus, Brooke, Inge, Moon, & Goodall, 1987; Cuvo, Leaf, & Borakove, 1978; Test et al., 1988). This technology has also been referred to as a response prompt hierarchy since the trainer progresses from the least prompt (usually verbal instruction) to the most intrusive (usually physical) until one prompt stimulates the correct employee response. Clearly, the use of least prompts is a viable option for training in new job tasks. However, there is a need for additional acquisition strategies for use at competitive job sites.

One such strategy is the application of time-delay procedures. To date, the literature on time delay has focused on training in skills such as manual sign production (Browder, Morris, & Snell, 1981), sight word reading (Gast, Ault, Wolery, Doyle, & Belanger, 1988), language use (Halle, Marshall, & Spradlin, 1979), cooking skills (Schuster et al., 1988), and bedmaking (Snell, 1982). However, it is suggested that the strategy is also very appropriate for job-site training.

TRAINING COMPONENTS OF TIME DELAY

The time-delay procedure is an errorless learning strategy that initially pairs a controlling stimulus (prompt) with a second stimulus (task request and materials). Two types of time-delay strategies have been described in the literature and are referred to as progressive and constant time delay. When using a progressive time-delay strategy, the trainer initially gives a prompt simultaneously with the presentation of task materials and the request to perform the skill. This simultaneous delivery of the prompt, materials, and request is referred to as 0-second delay. Gradually increasing amounts of time, usually seconds, are allowed to elapse between delivery of the request to perform a task and provision of the prompt to assist the individual to complete the task correctly. For example, training for the initial set of trials is done at 0 seconds, the next set at 2 seconds, the next at 4 seconds, and so forth, until the individual performs without prompts, and stimulus control is shifted to task request and materials (Snell & Gast 1981). The changes in delay level and number of trials at each level are determined prior to training by the employment specialist and are based on the needs of each individual learner. Constant time delay (Gast, Ault, Wolery, Doyle, & Belanger, 1988) also begins the training with a predetermined number of trials at 0-second delay. However, after the initial trials are conducted, a constant delay interval (e.g., 3 seconds) is selected for all remaining trials.

Unlike the system of least prompts, the time-delay strategy designates one prompt to use for instruction based on employee characteristics. Verbal, model, gesture, or physical prompts are all possible choices for the procedure. The trainer should select the prompt that the individual will respond to consistently without making errors. For example, if an employee is proficient in following model prompts, the employment specialist should use these on time delay. The employment specialist should carefully monitor the training data to make sure that the worker is not making errors during the prompting procedure. If the employee is consistently making errors in the task after the selected prompt is delivered, the trainer may need to consider changing to another prompt. It is imperative that the worker correctly respond to the selected prompt in order for the procedure to be errorless learning.

Several studies have suggested that time delay may be a more effective strategy than the system of least prompts in the instruction of individuals with moderate and severe handicaps. Gast et al. (1988) found in their study comparing the two strategies that constant time delay resulted in fewer than half the errors, required fewer prompts per minute, and required fewer in-session decisions by the trainer than did the system of least prompts. Progressive time delay has also been found to be more efficient in number of sessions, trials, errors, and direct instructional time than least prompts (Bennett, Gast, Wolery, & Schuster, 1986; Godby, Gast, & Wolery, 1987). These findings may have some interesting implications for instruction at a community supported employment job site. For example, it is important to make sure that the new employee with a disability looks competent from the first day of employment. If time-delay produces fewer errors in performance than other strategies, the worker may be viewed as more competent from the very beginning of instruction. In addition, the time-delay procedure may look less intrusive to the coworkers since fewer prompts per minute are required. The following two case studies illustrate the use of a constant time-delay strategy at a supported employment job site.

CASE STUDY ILLUSTRATIONS

Participants

Two young women who were assessed as having mental retardation in the severe range were referred to the Supported Employment Project for Youth with Severe Disabilities by the vocational coordinator of a local segregated school for individuals with moderate to profound mental retardation. This project was funded by a federal grant and operated out of the Rehabilitation Research and Training Center at Virginia Commonwealth University.

The first young woman, Mary, was 21 years old, with an IQ of 37 as measured by the Stanford-Binet Intelligence Scale. She had cerebral palsy as indicated by an unsteady awkward gait pattern; a visual impairment, which was corrected with glasses; scoliosis; and seizures controlled by medication. She also had immature social skills, that is, crying when corrected by adults and inappropriate laughter. Mary's strong skill was her ability to communicate verbally. However, she often repeated stories and comments unnecessarily. Her teacher described her as dependent on teacher prompts and supervision, with an inability to initiate work tasks.

The second young woman, Joan, was 19 years old, with a measured IQ of 29 according to scores from the Stanford-Binet Intelligence Scale. She also had cerebral palsy, which was evident in decreased fine motor functioning and a slow unsteady gait pattern. Her major physical limitation was an inability to use a fine pincer grasp bilaterally and low muscle tone. This low muscle tone made her appear very weak and resulted in decreased endurance. Joan's social skills were good, and she could speak, though in unclear sentences. Her teachers often described her verbalizations as inappropriate, nonsensical, and excessive.

Both individuals had attended a self-contained school for all of their education. Mary had received some community-based instruction on laundry skills at a local adult home. Joan had received training on stocking food at a community grocery store. Neither of the students had had any paid employment experiences nor had they been targeted for supported employment transition services within the school system due to severe mental retardation and immature social behaviors.

Setting

A full-time position as a laundry aide at a newly-built hotel was identified by an employment specialist who was assigned to complete job development for Mary and Joan. The job duties included sorting clothes, operating the washers and dryers, folding towels and sheets, pressing napkins and pillowcases, bagging supplies for housekeeping, and delivering items throughout the hotel. Three people performed these job duties during each of three consecutive 8-hour shifts, 7 days a week. Production requirements were average to fast paced depending on the time of day and season of the year. Communication was minimal and not required for job completion. Coworkers socialized infrequently with either of these young women but interacted frequently with the housekeeping and maintenance staff when entering their area.

The laundry room was large, crowded, and noisy. Temperature conditions were average and were controlled with heating and air conditioning. Supervisors usually were present and greeted employees frequently throughout the day. Instruction, reinforcement, and assistance were provided infrequently on an intermittent schedule. The department head reported a major problem with high employee turnover and absenteeism.

Job Placement

Prior to job placement Mary's and Joan's skills and interests were assessed by an employment specialist through interviews with teachers and parents, observations, formal record reviews, and situational assessment experiences as outlined in Chapter 5. Based on these situational assessments and the job/consumer matching process (Moon, Goodall, Barcus, & Brooke, 1986), it was determined that Mary and Joan both would be appropriate for the laundry aide position. One priority for these young women was a relatively stationary work station since they had difficulty with ambulation. The laundry aides would be in the main work area and would only be required to take several steps from the presser to the work table. In addition, the break area where all hotel employees ate lunch was located in the next room, as was an employee restroom. The physical navigation required within this work space would be ideal for these two young women's limitations.

A major issue, however, was that neither of these women could meet the endurance criteria of working the full-time position. Also, their parents wanted them to work only part time and continue in their school programs for the other portion of the day. The employment specialist, therefore, met with the employer and suggested that the full-time position be split into two part-time jobs, with Joan working the first shift and Mary the second. The employer agreed to the job modification, and the job duties were identified as pressing napkins and pillow cases and folding towels. After an initial interview with the supervisor, Mary and Joan were hired by the employer at a starting salary of $4.25 per hour.

Measurement and Recording Procedures

A task analysis was developed for training purposes as well as to measure skill acquisition on all tasks for both employees. Examples of the task analyses for folding the towels and pressing the napkins are shown in Table 4.1. Probe data were collected daily until skill acquisition was reached. A (+) was recorded for an independent correct response and a (−) for an incorrect response or no response. The probe was discontinued at the first (−) and training was then begun.

Training data were collected daily throughout skill acquisition training. A (+) was recorded for independent correct responses on the step in the task analysis the employee was working on in the backward-chaining procedure. A (+) with a circle indicated that the step was performed correctly but after the prompt was delivered. A (−) indicated that the step was performed incorrectly either before or after the prompt was delivered.

Time-Delay Procedure

A constant time-delay procedure was selected for training in all job duties. In the first week of trials both employees were trained at 0-second delay for all steps in the task analyses. Mary received a model prompt on time-delay and Joan a physical prompt. These prompts were selected based on the individual worker characteristics. Mary had a history of responding appropriately to model prompts, so this prompt was selected for her training. A physical prompt, however, was selected for Joan due to the physical lim-

Table 4.1.   Task analyses for laundry aide job duties

Task: Folding towels
Employee: Mary
Environment: Laundry room
Instructional cue: "Fold the towels."

1.   Go to cart.
2.   Pick up towel (right hand, right corner/left hand, left corner).
3.   Lay on table (lengthwise).
4.   Fold bottom up to middle.
5.   Rub edge (with both hands, center to edge).
6.   Fold top down (to bottom edges).
7.   Rub edge (with both hands, center to edge).
8.   Fold in half (right hand, right corner/left hand, left corner).
9.   Put towel on pile.
10. Pick up another towel.

Task: Pressing napkins
Employee: Joan
Environment: Laundry room
Instructional cue: "Press the napkins."

1.   Go to counter.
2.   Pick up napkins.
3.   Put on shelf (of presser).
4.   Pick up napkin.
5.   Put on shelf (in front of you).
6.   Pick up 2 napkins.
7.   Put on shelf (in front of you).
8.   Pick up 1 napkin.
9.   Put on presser.
10. Pick up 2 napkins.
11. Put on presser.
12. Push to side.
13. Pick up 1 napkin.
14. Put on shelf.
15. Pick up 2 napkins.
16. Put on shelf.
17. Pick up 1 napkin.
18. Put on presser.
19. Pick up 2 napkins.
20. Put on presser.
21. Go to pressed napkins.
22. Pick up 1 napkin.
23. Put on table.
24. Rub.
25. Pick up 2 napkins.
26. Put on table.
27. Rub.
28. Repeat, beginning with step 13.

itations in her hands. It was determined that she was unable to view a model prompt and then physically copy the movement. The selection of the physical prompt was therefore necessary in order to ensure that she did not make any errors when learning the task.

One week of training was completed at 0-second delay. In other words, the employment specialist gave Mary a model prompt or Joan a physical prompt simultaneously with the presentation of task materials and the request to perform the job duty. This was necessary based on the workers' histories of slow skill acquisition and patterns of error responding.

Beginning at week 2, a backward-chaining procedure was implemented for training in conjunction with the constant time delay. The employment specialist assisted Mary and Joan in completing all steps in the task analysis using the constant delay level of 0 seconds until they had gone through all but the last step of the task. At this point a 3-second delay was instituted, and Mary and Joan were given time to complete the step independently. If the step was not completed within the 3-second time period, a model prompt was provided for Mary and a physical prompt was provided for Joan. All criteria were met when the step was performed with 100% accuracy without prompting for all trials in 1 work day. As soon as the criteria were met on the last step, the constant delay level of 3-seconds was applied to the next step backwards in the chain. All other steps in the chain remained at 0-second delay. Training progressed in this manner until the employees were performing all steps in the task analyses without prompting.

An error correction procedure was designed in case errors were to occur during the training. The trainer interrupted all errors that occurred during the 3-second time delay by immediately stopping the incorrect response and providing the prompt. If Mary or Joan made 3 consecutive errors on any step in the task analysis, the trainer delivered 10 trials at 0-second delay. After the error correction procedure was completed, the trainer returned to the 3-second time delay.

Reinforcement

The trainer praised the trainees on a variable ratio schedule of every 2 correct responses during the 0-second time-delay level and on a fixed schedule of every correct response during the 3-second time delay level if the worker responded independently without the prompt. The praise consisted of verbal statements specific to completing the steps in the task, working quickly, working quietly, and staying on task (e.g., "Nice working quickly, Joan;" "Good stacking the towels, Mary"). A calender with fast food restaurant symbols glued on each payday was used for marking off the end of each work day with an "X." The trainer took Mary and Joan to lunch at a fast food restaurant every payday for the first month of skill acquisition training and intermittently thereafter. Table 4.2 shows a summary of the time-delay program components for these two workers.

GENERALIZATION AND MAINTENANCE PROCEDURES

The fading of trainer intervention was initiated when the program criterion was met; program criterion was defined as 3 consecutive days of 100% correct responses at a 3-second constant delay level for all steps in the task analyses. When criterion was met, the delay level was increased to 5 seconds, and the trainer stayed within 3 feet of the employee. Reinforcement was provided in the form of praise at the completion of each task (e.g., folding a towel, pressing two napkins). Errors were interrupted by reduction of trainer distance and provision of a model prompt for Mary and a physical prompt for Joan. The time-delay level and trainer distance continued to be increased as the reinforcement was decreased during each phase of the fading program. Table 4.3 shows the components of each phase of the fading schedule, and Figures 4.1 and 4.2 show the data on skill acquisition.

Table 4.2. Components of the constant time-delay procedure

Steps	Components of Mary's and Joan's programs
1. Select a prompt that the worker responds to consistently.	Mary responded consistently to model prompts so this was selected for her training.
	Joan did not respond to model or verbal prompts without making errors. Therefore, a physical prompt was selected for her training.
2. Determine a pre-set number of trials and delay seconds.	One week of 0-second delay was used for training in all trials of pressing the napkins, pressing the pillowcases, and folding the towels.
	A constant delay level of 3 seconds was selected for all remaining training trials to skill acquisition.
3. Identify a reinforcer.	Praise on a variable ratio schedule of every 2 correct responses during the 0-second time delay level was used.
	Social praise on a fixed ratio schedule of every independent correct response during the 3-second constant time delay was used.
	There were trips to a fast food restaurant on paydays for the first month of skill acquisition.

INTERFERING BEHAVIORAL ISSUES DURING JOB-SITE TRAINING

Data collected during the implementation of the maintenance and generalization strategies for job-site training for both Mary and Joan indicated that interfering behaviors that interrupted work completion were occurring. Joan made inappropriate vocalizations, and Mary had difficulty staying on task unless the employment specialist was providing direct instruction. After talking with the supervisor, the employment specialist determined that it was imperative to initiate a behavior program for each of these young women before she could fade from the job site. A description of each of the programs designed follows.

Joan's Behavior Intervention Program

Joan's inappropriate vocalizations were defined as talk-outs that were not required to complete the job as a laundry aide. These included such vocalizations as, "I'm going to talk with Ms. Smith," "Yabadabadoo," and "Look at me." Vocalizations that were not considered inappropriate included asking questions about work completion, responding to a comment or question initiated by another person, or greeting another employee. The employment specialist took a baseline of the behavior using a frequency recording procedure (Kazdin, 1980) by randomly observing Joan for ten 5-minute periods of time throughout her entire workday. This frequency count showed that she was vocalizing inappropriately on an average of 11 times in a 5-minute period.

A differential reinforcement of low rates (DRL) procedure was selected to help Joan control her excessive vocalizations. This strategy was selected because the employment specialist wished to decrease, but not eliminate vocalizations (Deitz & Repp, 1973; Sulzer-Azaroff & Mayer, 1977). A DRL procedure specified that a reinforcer is delivered at the end of a predetermined interval as long as the targeted behavior does not exceed a certain limit. If the behavior exceeds the established criterion, reinforcement is withheld and a new interval is established. As the reduction in behavior begins, fewer and fewer occurances of the behavior are allowed for the individual to obtain reinforcement (Sulzer-Azaroff & Mayer, 1977). Joan's baseline performance of 11 talk-outs was used to set the first criterion for her DRL program. Her entire workday was divided into 5-minute intervals, with eight allowed vocalizations during this period of time. The employment special-

Table 4.3.　Fading of trainer intervention schedule

Phase	Time-delay level	Trainer distance	Reinforcement schedule	Program criterion
1-Acquisition	3 seconds	<3 feet	FR:1	100% accuracy for three consecutive probes
2-Fading	5 seconds	<3 feet	FR:1	100% accuracy for three consecutive probes
3-Fading	6 seconds	3 feet	FR:1	100% accuracy for three consecutive probes
4-Fading	6 seconds	5 feet	VR:2	100% accuracy for three consecutive probes
5-Fading	6 seconds	10 feet	VR:3	100% accuracy for three consecutive probes
6-Fading	6 seconds	15 feet	VR:3	100% accuracy for three consecutive probes
7-Fading		Outside laundry room	FI:15 (time)	100% accuracy for three consecutive probes
8-Fading		Outside laundry room	FI:30 (time)	100% accuracy for two consecutive probes
9-Fading		Outside laundry room, off job site	FI:45 (time)	100% accuracy for two consecutive probes
10-Fading		Outside laundry room, off job site	FI:75 (time)	100% accuracy for two consecutive probes
11-Fading		Off job site	FI:120 (time) (1 visit) (at end of day)	100% accuracy for two consecutive probes
12-Fading		Off job site	FI:120 (time) (1 visit) (every other day)	100% accuracy for two consecutive probes
13-Fading		Off job site	FI:120 (time) (1 visit) (every 3rd day)	100% accuracy for two consecutive probes
14-Fading		Off job site	FI:120 (time) (1 visit) (every 4th day)	100% accuracy for two consecutive probes
15-Fading		Off job site	VI:120 (time) (1 visit) (once a week)	100% accuracy for two consecutive probes

FR = fixed ratio, VR = variable ratio, FI = fixed interval, VI = variable interval.

ist used a yellow Post-it Note to represent a 5-minute interval for Joan. She divided each Note into eight sections and explained that she would mark an "X" in each box whenever Joan talked inappropriately during work. At the end of a 5-minute interval, Joan was given the yellow Note if she had not exceeded the criterion. She collected these Notes in a

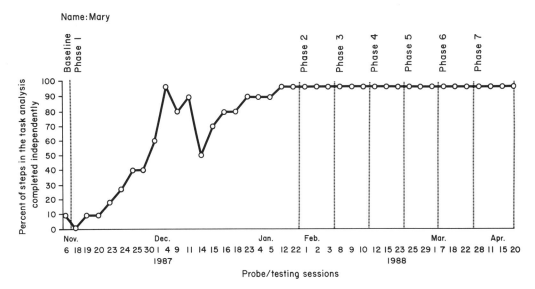

Figure 4.1. Skill acquisition data for Mary folding the bath towel.

folder until she had eight, at which time she was allowed to exchange them for money to use in the vending machine. If Joan's vocalizations exceeded eight in a 5-minute interval, she was told that she did not earn the Note and would need to try again. Table 4.4 shows an overview of the DRL procedure.

When Joan's inappropriate vocalizations did not exceed eight occurrences during all 5-minute intervals over the entire workday, the number of allowed talk-outs was changed to four in 5 minutes. Gradually the number of vocalizations was systematically reduced until Joan's talk-outs occurred no more than one time in 15 minutes. Table 4.5 shows a summary of her program objectives. Figure 4.3 displays the program objectives for this program.

Mary's Behavior Intervention Program

Probe data collected 1 month after Mary's placement indicated that her independent work performance had decreased on many steps in the task analysis that she previously had performed correctly. A partial interval recording procedure indicated that Mary was off task during 60% to 75% of her work day. Off-task behavior was defined as hands not in

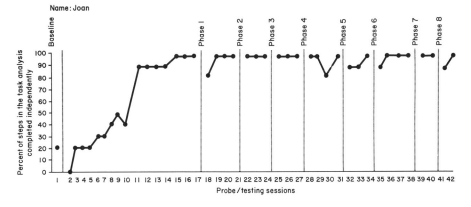

Figure 4.2. Skill acquisition data for Joan folding the bath mat.

Table 4.4.   Reducing the frequency of talk-outs using a differential reinforcement of low rates of behavior (DRL) procedure

Components of DRL	Components of Joan's program
1. Determine the problem.	1. Joan made inappropriate vocalizations such as "Yabadabadoo!" and "Look at me!" at a very high frequency.
2. Take a baseline of how many times the inappropriate behavior occurs within a specified time.	2. Joan's talk-outs occurred on an average of 11 times in a 5-minute interval.
3. Identify a reinforcer.	3. Joan responded well to checks ("X" mark) since these had been used with her in the school program. She also like candy and soda.
4. Set an initial goal of performance slightly lower than the number of oc-currences seen in the baseline period.	4. Joan's workday was divided into 5-minute intervals. Eight talk-outs were acceptable during this time period. Joan was shown a Post-it Note with eight sections and told that she could not talk more times than the number of spaces on the Note. When she talked inappropriately, she received an "X" on the Note.
5. Determine the reinforcement schedule.	5. Joan received a check on the Note if she did not exceed the number of allowed talk-outs. When she had earned eight Notes with checks, she received money that could be used to buy an edible reinforcer.
6. Gradually allow fewer and fewer inappropriate responses to be exhibited in order to obtain the reinforcement.	6. When Joan met the reduced criterion for no more than eight talk-outs in a 5-minute period for 1 workday, the number of acceptable talk-outs was further decreased. Criterion was changed to four in 5 minutes, two in 5 minutes, two in 8 minutes, one in 10 minutes, and so forth.

motion or eyes looking away from work for more than 3 seconds. On-task behavior was defined as looking at work, moving on to the next step in the task analysis, and hands in motion. The employment specialist collected data by dividing Mary's work day into 1-minute intervals. If at any time during the 1-minute interval Mary was off task, she recorded a ($-$) on the data sheet, indicating that the behavior was observed.

A differential reinforcement of incompatible behaviors/alternate response behavior (ALT-R) procedure was selected for behavior intervention (Evans & Meyer, 1985; Kazdin, 1980; Sulzer-Azaroff & Mayer, 1977). Mary's workday was divided into 1-minute intervals, which were marked on index cards. A partial interval recording procedure was used to monitor the program. If Mary was on task during the entire 1-minute interval, a check was marked beside the interval time period on the index card and verbal praise was given. If Mary was off task anytime during the interval, the space beside the time period remained blank, and Mary was told the reason that she did not earn a check. After Mary earned 15 checks, she was given a yellow Post-it Note to place in a folder. When she had earned four Notes, she could trade them for money to purchase a drink or candy from the vending machine. (Note: Post-it Notes, index cards, and folders were used since these items were used at the job site as office supplies.)

The program criterion was changed as Mary began to show progress in staying on task. The length of the intervals was gradually increased and the number of checks required to earn a Note was decreased. Table 4.6 shows the gradual changes in the program criterion. The data for Mary's program are represented in Figure 4.4.

Table 4.5. Program objectives for Joan's DRL procedure

Behavioral Objective Phase 1:
Joan will work an entire workday with no more than eight talk-outs during each 5-minute interval.

Behavioral Objective Phase 2:
Joan will work an entire workday with no more than four talk-outs during each 5-minute interval.

Behavioral Objective Phase 3:
Joan will work an entire workday with no more than two talk-outs in each 5-minute interval.

Behavioral Objective Phase 4:
Joan will work an entire workday with no more than two talk-outs in each 8-minute interval.

Behavioral Objective Phase 5:
Joan will work an entire workday with no more than one talk-out in each 8-minute interval.

Behavioral Objective Phase 6:
Joan will work an entire workday with no more than one talk-out in each 10-minute interval.

Behavioral Objective Phase 7:
Joan will work an entire workday with no more than one talk-out in each 12-minute interval.

Behavioral Objective Phase 8:
Joan will work an entire workday with no more than one talk-out in each 15-minute interval.

Behavioral Objective Phase 9:
Joan will work an entire workday with no more than one talk-out in a 30-minute interval.
When Joan reached the objective in Phase 9, program criterion was considered met.

DISCUSSION

A total of 148 intervention hours were required for Joan and 140 hours for Mary to the point of job stabilization and the end of initial skill acquisition. These were the lengths of time necessary before the employment specialist could begin to fade from the immediate work area for predetermined periods. Both young women required intensive instruction on all skills from the first day of work, as well as intensive programming to remediate inappropriate work behaviors.

Mary and Joan represent typical individuals with severe disabilities who are

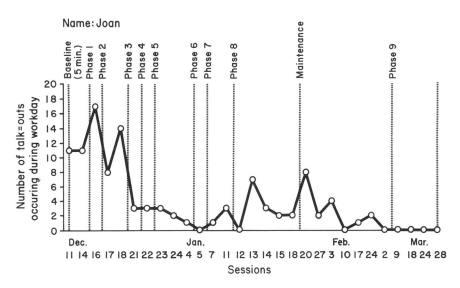

Figure 4.3. Joan's DRL program data.

Table 4.6. Mary's program objectives for the Differential Reinforcement of Incompatible Be-
haviors/Alternate Response Behavior (ALT-R) program

Behavioral Objective Phase 1:
  Mary will remain on task for at least 95% of all 1-minute intervals for 2 consecutive workdays.

Behavioral Objective Phase 2:
  Mary will remain on task for at least 95% of all 3-minute intervals for 2 consecutive workdays.

Behavioral Objective Phase 3:
  Mary will remain on task for at least 95% of all 5-minute intervals for 2 consecutive workdays.

Behavioral Objective Phase 4:
  Mary will remain on task for at least 95% of all 8-minute intervals for 2 consecutive workdays.

Behavioral Objective Phase 5:
  Mary will remain on task for at least 95% of all 10-minute intervals for 2 consecutive workdays.

Behavioral Objective Phase 6:
  Mary will remain on task for at least 95% of all 15-minute intervals for 2 consecutive workdays.
  *When Mary reached the objective in Phase 6, the employment specialist began to fade from the
  work site gradually. The off-task behavior no longer seemed to be a problem, and the job-site
  supervisor was satisfied with Mary's performance.*

placed into supported employment positions for the first time. These individuals will usually require systematic instruction across all job duties from the first day of employment
in order to promote errorless learning. In addition, most new supported employment
employees with severe mental retardation will require assistance in developing appropriate social behaviors and interactions, as well as work behaviors. The case studies presented in this chapter demonstrate the use of time delay, differential reinforcement of low
rates of behavior, and differential reinforcement of incompatible behaviors at a job site.
Although no formal research designs were used to validate the success of these programs, employment specialists should find the information useful in designing strategies
for working with individuals with severe disabilities at community job sites.

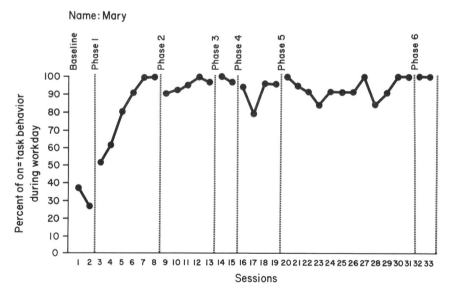

Figure 4.4. Mary's ALT-R program data.

REFERENCES

Barcus, M., Brooke, V., Inge, K.J., Moon, M.S., & Goodall, P. (1987). *An instructional guide for training on a job site: A supported employment resource.* Richmond, VA: Virginia Commonwealth University, Rehabilitation Research and Training Center.

Bennett, D.L., Gast, D.L., Wolery, M., & Schuster, J. (1986). Time delay and system of least prompts: A comparison in teaching manual sign production. *Education and Training of the Mentally Retarded, 21,* 117–129.

Browder, D.M., Morris, W.W., & Snell, M.E. (1981). Using time delay to teach manual signs to a severely retarded student. *Education and Training of the Mentally Retarded, 16,* 252–258.

Cuvo, A.J., Leaf, R.B., & Borakove, L.S. (1978). Teaching janitorial skills to the mentally retarded: Acquisition, generalization, and maintenance. *Journal of Applied Behavior Analysis, 11,* 345–355.

Davis, P.J., Bates, P., & Cuvo, A.J. (1983). Training a mentally retarded woman to work competitively: Effect of graphic feedback and a changing criterion design. *Education and Training of the Mentally Retarded, 18,* 158–163.

Deitz, S.M., & Repp, A.C. (1973). Decreasing classroom misbehavior through the use of DRL schedules of reinforcement. *Journal of Applied Behavior Analysis, 6,* 457–463.

Evans, I.M., & Meyer, L.H. (1985). *An educative approach to behavior problems: A practical decision model for interventions with severely handicapped learners.* Baltimore: Paul H. Brookes Publishing Co.

Gast, D.L., Ault, M.J., Wolery, M., Doyle, P.M., & Belanger, J. (1988). Comparison of constant time delay and the system of least prompts in teaching sight word reading to students with moderate retardation. *Education and Training in Mental Retardation, 23,* 117–128.

Godby, S., Gast, D.L., & Wolery, M. (1987). A comparison of time delay and system of least prompts in teaching object identification. *Research in Developmental Disabilities, 8,* 283–305.

Halle, J.W., Marshall, A.M., & Spradlin, J.E. (1979). Time delay: A technique to increase language use and facilitate generalization in retarded children. *Journal of Applied Behavior Analysis, 12,* 431–439.

Kazdin, A.E. (1980). *Behavior modification in applied settings.* Homewood, IL: Dorsey Press.

Moon, M.S., Goodall, P., Barcus, J.M., & Brooke, V. (1986). *The supported work model of competitive employment: A guide for job trainers* (2nd ed.). Richmond: Virginia Commonwealth University, Rehabilitation Research and Training Center.

Schuster, J.W., Gast, D.L., Wolery, M., & Guiltiman, S. (1988). The effectiveness of constant time delay procedure to teach chained responses to adolescents with mental retardation. *Journal of Applied Behavior Analysis, 21*(2), 169–178.

Snell, M. (1982). Analysis of time delay procedures in teaching daily living skills to retarded adults. *Analysis and Intervention in Developmental Disabilities, 2,* 139–155.

Snell, M., & Gast, D.L. (1981). Applying delay procedures to the instruction of the severely handicapped. *Journal of The Association of the Severely Handicapped, 5*(4), 3–14.

Sulzer-Azaroff, B., & Mayer, G.R. (1977). *Applying behavior analysis procedures with children and youth.* New York: Holt, Rinehart, & Winston.

Test, D.W., Grossi, T., & Keul, P. (1988). A functional analysis of the acquisition and maintenance of janitorial skills in a competitive work setting. *Journal of The Association for Persons with Severe Handicaps, 13*(1), 1–7.

Wehman, P., Kregel, J., & Shafer, M.S. (1989). *Emerging trends in the national supported employment initiative: A preliminary analysis of twenty-seven states.* Richmond, VA: Virginia Commonwealth University, Rehabilitation Research and Training Center.

Wehman, P., Parent, W., Wood, W., Kregel, J., & Inge, K. (1989). Supported employment for persons with severe and profound retardation. In P. Wehman & J. Kregel (Eds.), *Supported employment for persons with disabilities* (pp. 19–52). New York: Plenum Press.

USING A SITUATIONAL
ASSESSMENT STRATEGY TO
APPROACH COMMUNITY-BASED
EMPLOYMENT

5

Assessment of individuals with severe handicaps has often posed a problem for supported employment programs. Typically, the more traditional methods of vocational assessment have focused on identifying those skills that an individual needs to improve or acquire before employment (Peterson, 1986). This approach to vocational assessment, when used for individuals with severe handicaps, focuses on the person's deficits rather than strengths. The opinion that these individuals are not ready for employment is then very easily accepted. Ironically, the very individuals intended to be served by supported employment may be excluded when typical vocational assessment is done (Menchetti & Rusch, 1988).

Intelligence testing has also been used to determine an individual's readiness for employment. This criterion in not valid for individuals with severe disabilities since IQ tests rely on reading skills, receptive language skills, intact neurological functioning, and the absence of sensory deficits (Berkell, 1987). An IQ score obviously would not be reflective of *abilities* since the person would have severe deficits in all these areas. In fact, many professionals point out that the use of standardized tests with individuals who have severe handicaps has not been adequately validated (Cronbach, 1960; Gold, 1973; Menchetti & Rusch, 1988; Menchetti, Rusch, & Owens, 1983; Schalock & Karan, 1979) to predict future successful employment.

If the more traditional approaches are not useful in predicting success in supported employment, what assessments should be employed? Moon, Goodall, Barcus, and Brooke (1986) describe a consumer assessment process that provides information to the supported employment personnel (employment specialist) for effectively matching the individual with severe handicaps to a job in the community. This process includes

---

This chapter was co-authored by Wendy Parent, a research associate at the Rehabilitation Research and Training Center at Virginia Commonwealth University.

identifying and analyzing jobs in the community, assessing individual (consumer) characteristics for people in the supported employment referral pool, and finally, comparing the requirements of the job to the available consumers until a best match is made between the job and consumers. Interviews with the primary caregivers, current and/or past work or school supervisors, review of formal records, and behavioral assessments in real work settings provide information for completion of the assessment.

Gaylord-Ross (1986) also advocates an environmental and behavioral approach to assessment of consumers. Environmental assessment entails identifying potential environments in which the individual may ultimately function and observing him or her in the actual setting performing work demanded by that environment. This is not the same as simulated work samples, in which the person is assessed while performing tasks that are similar to those found in the real environment but are performed in a simulated setting (Berkell, 1987). In fact, simulated work samples are not advisable with individuals with severe mental retardation since they fail to take into consideration such things as social interactions with coworkers and supervisors, mobility in the community and at the work site, environmental conditions such as temperature and noise, endurance, and production. Only in real work environments can the employment specialist begin to assess the individual's skill level in order to match him or her to a specific job.

Environmental assessment has also been referred to as on-the-job evaluation. Wright (1980) states that this type of evaluation is the most direct method of assessing work behavior. If the most accurate test of vocational skill is the one that closely approximates actual work, then on-the-job evaluation is the best measurement for individuals with severe handicaps. For the purpose of this chapter, on-the-job evaluation, environmental assessment, and behavioral assessment are considered the same and will be referred to as situational assessment.

VALUE OF SITUATIONAL ASSESSMENT

Situational assessment can be manipulated in order to provide the evaluator/employment specialist with valuable information. Most often individuals (consumers) with severe handicaps do not have any work history on which to base work preferences. In addition, the more traditional preference inventories using reading skills or picture cues do not accurately reflect valid occupational choices (Berkell, 1987). Instead, a variety of situational assessments across settings, and time may provide insight into consumer preference and skills. For instance, during a situational assessment, the employment specialist may be able to identify nonverbal signs of occupational choice such as refusal to do certain types of work, performing specific tasks to production standards, and completing some work tasks to quality standards but not others even when all tasks have been learned.

Scheduling situational assessments during various times of the day may indicate specific times of optimal performance. For instance, the employment specialist may determine that a consumer's attention is more focused and quality of work more accurate during the morning than in the afternoon. The employment specialist then could concentrate on locating a job in which the majority of the work load demands occur in the morning rather than in the afternoon.

Situational assessment can also provide information on how the individual will respond to factors in the real environment, such as noise, movement, objects, people, and amount of space. For instance, individuals with severe handicaps often have physical limitations or medical needs that affect how they respond to an environment. A person who has difficulty walking may not do well in a cluttered work environment. He or she may also have difficulty if a job requires that work be done while walking but have no problem if the job allows for being stationary. Another person who is easily startled may find excessive movement and noise problematic.

A situational assessment may also reveal how an individual responds to specific persons, supervisors, or coworkers of the opposite sex. For instance, a consumer may take directions very well from a female employment specialist but very poorly from a male supervisor. Varying the employment specialist may help indicate this.

The remainder of this chapter focuses on the development of a situational assessment process. The steps outlined here are steps that have proven useful in assessing consumers with severe and profound mental retardation who were placed by the Supported Employment Project for Youth with Severe Disabilities at the Rehabilitation Research and Training Center (RRTC) in Richmond, Virginia. This project placed students from the surrounding school systems into competitive jobs. The mean IQ score of the individuals placed was 33 and the age range was 19–22. All employment was part time, averaging 20 hours per week.

STEPS IN DEVELOPING A SITUATIONAL ASSESSMENT

The first step in the situational assessment procedure is to identify jobs that are representative of those in the local community. Sources for determining the types of jobs frequently available include the classified section of the newspaper, the yellow pages of the telephone book, and direct communication with employers. Those businesses that have the targeted job positions need to be identified and contacted to determine if they would be appropriate locations for conducting situational assessments. It is important to develop sites that are separate from paid supported employment sites since the presence of unpaid consumers may confuse the supervisors and coworkers.

In addition, it is recommended that businesses that include several of the targeted positions be considered for situational assessment sites, in order to allow for ease in organizing, scheduling, and transporting those consumers to be assessed. For example, in Richmond, Virginia a large number of jobs are available in food service and janitorial positions. Instead of contacting a number of individual businesses, the Rehabilitation Research and Training Center established its situational assessment sites in a local hospital, using the laundry, dietary, and supply departments. If a hospital is not available, other suggestions include a nursing home, business complex, or community college or university.

The steps in developing a situational assessment site include: 1) contacting the personnel director, 2) identifying and analyzing appropriate jobs, 3) scheduling the situational assessments, and 4) recording assessment observations. When setting up the situational assessment site in the local hospital, the RRTC identified one person as the liaison (coordinator) between the center and hospital. This person was responsible for all communications with the personnel department and with the individual department supervisors. She was also responsible for developing all procedures and schedules. A detailed listing of the steps and activities involved in developing a situational assessment site are provided in Table 5.1.

CONTACTING THE PERSONNEL DIRECTOR

Initial employer contact should be made by telephone or letter to the personnel director or manager of the company. It is suggested that the supported employment liaison pro-

Table 5.1. Steps and activities for developing a situational assessment site

Steps	Activities
I. Identify available jobs in the local community appropriate for individuals with severe disabilities.	1. Survey the telephone book yellow pages. 2. Read the classified advertisements of the newspaper. 3. Review jobs already held by individuals with disabilities in the community.
II. Identify businesses with the targeted jobs.	

III. Contact the personnel director.	1. By letter and/or telephone:
	  a. Briefly describe the program and the reason for contact.
	  b. Identify potential job types that may be appropriate for assessment.
	  c. Schedule an appointment to visit.
	2. Visit in person:
	  a. Describe supported employment and the purpose of a situational assessment.
	  b. Discuss employer, trainer, and trainee responsibilities.
	  c. Develop a situational assessment contract.
	  d. Meet with the department supervisor(s).
	  e. Schedule an appointment to observe in the identified department(s) to develop task analyses and job duty schedules.
	  f. Send a thank you letter.

IV. Identify and analyze appropriate jobs.	1. Discuss possibilities with the personnel director. 2. Visit the identified departments. 3. Determine the jobs best suited for situational assessments. 4. Observe coworkers performing the jobs. 5. Develop a job duty schedule and write task analyses.
V. Schedule the situational assessments.	1. Identify available times with the department supervisor(s). 2. Request at least 4 consecutive hours for each assessment. 3. Contact appropriate persons (i.e., parents, teachers, facility staff, consumers). 4. Identify staff to perform the assessments. 5. Send a copy of the schedule to the personnel director, department supervisor(s), parents, teachers, facility staff, and so forth. 6. Provide trainers with information about the job: names, addresses, directors, and telephone numbers, task analyses, and responsibilities.
IV. Record assessment observations.	1. Complete the Situational Assessment Screening Form. 2. Send a thank you letter to the personnel director and supervisor(s). 3. Provide feedback to the consumer, parent/guardians, teachers, facility staff, and so forth.

vide a brief description of the program, the situational assessment process, and the types of jobs sought. In addition, the liaison should clearly state that the reason for contact is to establish an assessment site and not to place people into paid or volunteer positions. After addressing the employer's questions, the supported employment staff should schedule a meeting with the personnel director or manager and further discuss the development of a situational assessment site. A sample letter from the RRTC requesting the use of the local hospital as an assessment site is shown in Figure 5.1.

The meeting should begin with a review of the information presented on the telephone or in the letter. Often a comprehensive explanation of supported employment and situational assessments is required by some personnel directors. Others will request that key logistical issues be highlighted and the specifics discussed with direct department supervisors.

A key area of concern for most personnel directors is the issue of liability and insurance responsibilities. Usually students are covered by school insurance when community-based training is included as a goal in the individualized education program. Parent/guardian permission forms should also be obtained prior to assessment. Figure 5.2 shows a sample parent/guardian permission form. Similarly, adult consumers would be insured under their own personal insurance policies for medical expenses. Supported employment training personnel are covered under the workers' compensation insurance that is provided by their employer since community placement and training is part of their job description. However, injury due to negligence by the employer would be the responsibility of the business's workers' compensation insurance. Often, employers will have other prerequisites that are specific to the business, such as a medical examination report or employer release form. It is recommended that the liaison write a contractual agreement, with the responsibilities of the employer and supported employment provider clearly stated, to avoid problems or misunderstandings at a later date. Both parties should review and sign the agreement. It should be kept in the supported employment agency's files.

IDENTIFYING AND ANALYZING APPROPRIATE JOBS

The identification of jobs within the business can begin with information provided by the personnel director or business representative. These jobs must be representative of jobs found frequently in other businesses in the community. Frequently, the personnel director will be able to provide written job descriptions that can be useful for identifying job types. However, the most accurate determination of potential jobs is made by direct observation of different departments and analysis of the potential jobs. Be sure to request a meeting with each department supervisor to observe the jobs at the time of the initial visit. If this is not possible, then before leaving make arrangements to visit at a later date. Remember to send a thank you letter to the personnel director after the meeting and to maintain frequent, ongoing communication throughout the assessment process. Figure 5.3 shows a sample thank you letter.

Information about general job duties, department regulations, and employer standards can be obtained most accurately during the meeting with the department supervisor. The liaison can best determine the most appropriate jobs and a specific job duty schedule by actually observing the workers performing their jobs. Many times the positions will involve multiple job tasks that are too lengthy or complicated for a 4-hour assessment period. In addition, the total job duty may be too difficult for an individual with a

Mr. _____
Employee Development Specialist
Hunter Holmes McGuire Veterans Administration Medical Center
1201 Broad Rock Boulevard
Richmond, VA 23149

Date

Dear Mr. _____ :

The Rehabilitation Research and Training Center (RRTC) at Virginia Commonwealth University has been awarded a federal grant to assist individuals with severe disabilities in finding competitive employment. The project works in cooperation with Richmond and Henrico Public Schools and serves students who are enrolled in public school programs. Students selected to participate receive assistance in finding a job, intensive training at the job site, and ongoing assistance in the work as needed in order to maintain employment. This process is called supported competitive employment.

We have found that it is very important to observe an individual in a "real" job prior to selecting a work site for him or her. This situational assessment gives us valuable information about the person's skills and interests so that the best job match can be made. These assessments take approximately 4 hours to complete, and we prefer to observe one individual in at least 3 different jobs.

Currently, we are seeking a company that would be willing to allow us to complete these assessments at its job site. Specifically, we are interested in working in your housekeeping, laundry, dietary, and supply departments. A staff member from the project would be with the individual being assessed at all times and would ensure that any work assigned to us was completed before leaving. There is *no cost* to you for the work done.

We would like to schedule our first assessments between August 31 and September 10. The exact times and dates for each shift would be scheduled with the individual department supervisors. Please consider participating with us in facilitating employment for individuals with severe disabilities. I will be calling you within the week to set up an appointment to discuss this further. Should you wish to speak to me, please feel free to call 367-1851. Thank you in advance for your time and consideration.

Sincerely,

The Supported Employment Project
for Youth with Severe Disabilities

Figure 5.1.   Sample letter to personnel director at potential situational assessment site.

Please fill in the child's name and sign and return this form to school as soon as possible:

_____ has permission to travel with an employment specialist from the Rehabilitation Research and Training Center to and from Hunter Holmes McGuire Veterans Administration Medical Center for vocational assessments.

I understand he/she will be working at the hospital in the housekeeping, laundry, dietary, and/or supply departments. Three assessments will be conducted for 4 hours each on 3 separate days. I will be informed of the dates and times when these are arranged.

Parent/Guardian signature: _____

Figure 5.2. Sample parent/guardian permission form.

severe handicap to perform. For example, the responsibilities of a laundry aide may be to press sheets; fold pajamas, underpads, and blankets; and operate the washer and dryer during an 8-hour work period. It may be unrealistic to expect someone with severe mental retardation to be able to complete all of these duties. The trainer/employment specialist should carefully select portions of the job for the 4-hour assessment that would realistically reflect a position in the environment. For example, the employment specialist could ask the supervisor what duties need to be done on a consistent basis, but may not be done because the workers avoid the task or never have the time to complete it. Remember, whatever tasks are selected need to be completed to the employer's requirements and should be maintained during the assessment period to prevent interruptions in the natural work flow. Changes in the work routine or production standards should never be implemented without the permission of the supervisor.

At this point, the employment specialist who will be involved with the situational assessments should be included in the development of the task analyses. A detailed analysis should be completed for each selected job duty prior to the time when the consumers are brought to the job site (Moon et al., 1986). The employment specialist should observe the coworkers performing the job duties and identify each step that is completed. If it is not possible to watch the coworkers, the employment specialist should ask how the task should be performed. After an initial task analysis has been developed, the employment specialist should perform the job duty and revise the task analysis as necessary. It may be advisable to check with the supervisor to ensure that the task is being completed to his or her standards. An example of a task analysis used in the situational assessment for RRTC consumers is shown in Table 5.2.

SCHEDULING THE SITUATIONAL ASSESSMENTS

Available times and days for conducting a situational assessment need to be obtained from each department supervisor. It is recommended that the situational assessment

Mr. _____
Employee Development Specialist
Hunter Holmes McGuire Veterans Administration Medical Center
1201 Broad Rock Boulevard
Richmond, VA 23149

Date

Dear Mr. _____ :

Thank you for meeting with me on August 6 to discuss setting up an assessment program at McGuire Veterans Administration Medical Center in the housekeeping, laundry, dietary, and supply departments. After we have visited these departments and
learned the job duties we will be performing, we can schedule the students for assessment times. An employment specialist will accompany each student during the 4-hour
work shifts and guarantee that the work is completed to the supervisor's standards.
The week of August 31–September 10 is the first targeted assessment period.

I am grateful to you for allowing us to provide our students the opportunity to work in a
real job setting. The assessment process will assist us in identifying student interests
and skills for placement into a competitive job in the community. I appreciate your continued interest and support to improve employment opportunities for individuals with
severe disabilities. Please contact me at 367-1851 if you have any questions or would
like additional information.

We are looking forward to working together with you and the staff at McGuire Veterans
Administration Medical Center.

Sincerely,

The Supported Employment Project
for Youth with Severe Disabilities

Figure 5.3.   Sample thank you letter to the personnel director.

time match the projected hours of employment for the supported employment consumers. Since the targeted length of employment for the consumers at RRTC is 20 hours
per week, each situational assessment was scheduled for 4 hours in length.

Typically, four to six consumers can participate during a week-long schedule of
situational assessments, which will require at least two trainers. A schedule should be
determined that will allow each individual the opportunity to perform the targeted jobs
and to work with the different trainers. Copies of the situational assessment schedule
should be given to all the trainers, personnel director, department supervisors, consumers, parents/guardians, teachers, and day program staff. An example of a scheduling
arrangement is shown in Table 5.3.

The students who participated in the RRTC situational assessments were from

Table 5.2.   Task analyses for a laundry aide position

Trainer:
Trainee:
Environment: Laundry room
Instructional cue: "Fold the pajama top."

1. Pick up pajama top.
2. Hold at collar (sleeves facing you).
3. Fold in half (sleeves inside).
4. Hold at collar.
5. Fold in half (toward you).
6. Put left hand on opposite side.
7. Hang pajama top over left hand.
8. Grab folded side with right hand.
9. Stack (folded side out).
10. Repeat steps 1–9.

Trainer:
Trainee:
Environment: Laundry room
Instructional cue: "Fold the pajama pants."

1. Pick up pajama pants.
2. Hold at waist band.
3. Fold in half (toward you).
4. Put left hand on opposite side.
5. Hang pajama pants over left hand.
6. Grab folded side with other hand.
7. Put left hand on opposite side.
8. Hang pajama pants over left hand.
9. Grab folded side with right hand.
10. Stack (folded side out).
11. Repeat steps 1–10.

Trainer:
Trainee:
Environment: Laundry room
Instructional cue: "Fold the underpads."

1. Pick up the underpad.
2. Lay flat (white side up).
3. Grab bottom corner (one hand).
4. Grab bottom corner (other hand).
5. Fold to top corners.
6. Put left hand on left side.
7. Put right hand on right side.
8. Fold to left (1/3).
9. Fold to left (all).
10. Pick up underpad.
11. Stack (folded side towards you).
12. Repeat steps 1–11.

the local city and county school system. The teachers identified those students in special needs classes between the ages of 18 and 22 who had an IQ of less than 39. The teachers were responsible for contacting the parents or guardians to determine if they were interested in supported employment for their sons or daughters. After the teacher received a release of information form, an employment specialist visited and explained the supported employment program, the purpose of a situational assessment, and the potential for employment. Figure 5.4 shows a sample preassessment letter to the parents.

The liaison between the business and the supported employment program should coordinate the dates, times, and persons repsonsible for the situational assessments. There should be a clearly stated procedure so that each trainer/employment specialist

Table 5.3.   Situational assessment scheduling arrangement

Trainees   **Trainers**
Angela Jones   Linda Austin
David Smith   Steve White
John Moore
Mary Johnson
Susan Myers

	Monday Sept. 12	Tuesday Sept. 13	Wednesday Sept. 14	Thursday Sept. 15	Friday Sept. 16
9:00–1:00 Dietary Services	Angela Steve	Susan Steve	John Linda	Mary Linda	—
9:00–1:00 Supply Services	—	—	Mary Steve	John Steve	—
11:30–3:30 Laundry Services	David Linda	Angela Linda	—	—	—

	Monday Sept. 19	Tuesday Sept. 20	Wednesday Sept. 21	Thursday Sept. 22	Friday Sept. 23
9:00–1:00 Dietary Services	—	—	David Steve	—	—
9:00–1:00 Supply Services	Susan Linda	David Linda	Angela Linda	—	—
11:30–3:30 Laundry Services	John Steve	Susan Steve	—	Mary Linda	—

can perform his or her responsibilities with a minimal amount of disruption to the job site. All trainers should have readily available a description of relevant job information, including the site contact person, supervisor names, telephone numbers, uniform requirements, and a general job description. Figure 5.5 shows a sample copy of the job information fact sheet. In addition, each employment specialist should have a copy of the task analyses, the schedule, directions to the consumers' homes and job site, and names and addresses of all parents and the school.

Since multiple trainers interact with the consumers during the assessment, it may be advisable to have a standard procedure for communicating with the parents and consumers. Each person involved should have a list of all of the consumers, telephone numbers for the parents and school, and directions to all of the consumers' homes. It is suggested that each parent be contacted the day before the assessment to confirm the date, time, home address, and to remind the parent to send money with his or her son or daughter for lunch or break time. The employment specialist can also answer any questions and address any concerns that may have developed. In addition, contact should be made with the person(s) at the location where the consumer will be picked up and dropped off to ensure that all information about the schedule and appearance requirements are known. It is advisable to pick up the consumer early so that there will be ample time to assess the individual's orientation skills. Table 5.4 outlines some of the trainer responsibilities for conducting the situational assessment.

DEVELOPING A SITUATIONAL
ASSESSMENT EVALUATION FORM AND RECORDING DATA

The Supported Employment Project for Youth with Severe Disabilities used the RRTC Consumer Employment Screening Form (Moon et al., 1986) as the foundation for de-

Date: _____

Dear _____ :

Thank you for giving your permission for _____ (*son/daughter*) to participate in the Supported Employment Project for Youth with Severe Disabilities. As you remember, he/she will be on our referral list to be placed in a community-based competitive job. This job will be part time and will be approved by us with you prior to the first day of work.

At this time, we would like to assess _____ (*son's/daughter's*) skills through a situational assessment process. He/She will be accompanied by an employment specialist to a job in the community and will be assigned real work to complete. _____ will be supervised at all times and will be at the work site for approximately 4 hours.

The first assessment will take place on Monday, August 31 and will be at Hunter Holmes McGuire Veterans Administration Medical Center in the laundry department. The employment specialist will pick up your son/daughter from school at 8:30 A.M. and return him/her after 1:30 P.M. *Please make sure that he/she has approximately $2.00 for a lunch break.* If at all possible, _____ should be wearing white pants, a green shirt, and tennis shoes.

I will be calling you the day before the assessment to remind you where your son/daughter will be working on Monday. Again, I thank you for your interest and cooperation. Without your support, we would be unable to make employment possible for _____ .

Sincerely,

Employment Specialist
Supported Employment Project for
Youth with Severe Disabilities

Figure 5.4. Sample preassessment letter to parent/guardian.

veloping a Situational Assessment Screening Form. The intent was to develop a tool that could be used to gather information from parents, teachers/service providers, and each employment specialist who worked with an individual at an assessment site. The information gathered could be compiled on the Situational Assessment Screening Form, analyzed, and then transferred to the Consumer Employment Screening Form for matching individuals to jobs in the community.

One employment specialist was assigned to collect information from the parents and teacher prior to assessment. Their input was recorded on the Situational Assessment Screening Form under the specified columns. After this was completed, the form was passed to the employment specialist who was responsible for the first situational assessment. Each successive employment specialist obtained the form prior to his/her

JOB SITE: McGuire Veterans Administration Medical Center

ADDRESS: 1201 Broad Rock Boulevard

TELEPHONE NUMBER:

CONTACT PERSON: Employee Development Specialist,
                        Personnel Department, 2nd Floor
                        Telephone Extension:

DEPARTMENT: Laundry

LOCATION: Basement

SUPERVISOR:

ASSISTANT:

TELEPHONE/EXT.:

POSITION: Laundry aide

HOURS: Indicated on schedule

UNIFORM: White pants, green shirt, tennis shoes

JOB DUTIES: Fold underpads
                        Fold pajamas
                        Fold blankets

DESCRIPTION: The underpads involve three folds; it should take approxi-
                        mately 15 seconds to fold one. The individual works at a table
                        with another coworker. The pajamas require folding the tops
                        and bottoms separately and placing them on the shelves ac-
                        cording to the colors. It should take approximately 20 sec-
                        onds to fold each piece. The pajamas are on a large table and
                        several people work together. The blankets require two per-
                        sons to fold. This is a task to be completed only if there is
                        down time.

Figure 5.5.   Job information fact sheet for situational assessment.

involvement with the consumer at an assessment site until all three assessments were
completed. A staff team meeting was held at the end of all situational assessments to
include all staff involved with the consumers. (Figure 5.6 shows a completed Situational
Assessment Screening Form for one individual, Mary.) At that time, joint input was obtained to complete the RRTC Consumer Employment Screening Form.

USING SITUATIONAL ASSESSMENT
DATA FOR JOB DEVELOPMENT: A CASE STUDY

Information gathered during the situational assessment for Mary was utilized by the employment specialist to identify the best possible job match for her. It was determined that
Mary would need special considerations for job development since she had severe mental
retardation, mild cerebral palsy, a history of emotional immaturity problems, and no work

Table 5.4.   Trainer responsibilities for conducting the situational assessments at a hospital

1. Each trainer is responsible for calling each parent the day before to confirm the date, time, and home address. Also, verify that money is available for lunch/break.

2. Each trainer will transport the trainee to the hospital at the beginning of the work shift and back to his or her home, school, or day program at the end.

3. The trainer will accompany the trainee to lunch/break at the hospital after the work shift.

4. All trainers and trainees will meet at the Information Desk located at the main entrance of the hospital.

5. The trainer will bring the Situational Assessment Screening Form. Bring the one used for another situational assessment, if possible. If not, bring a blank one to be completed at the work site.

6. The trainer will contact the personnel director in Room 202 after the work shift.

7. The trainer may want to bring snacks, candy, or soda to use as a reinforcer, if needed.

8. The trainer will communicate any significant events, problems, or changes to the next trainers before they are scheduled to arrive at the hospital.

experience. Initially, nursing homes and hospitals were contacted because of Mary's interest in a laundry position and the parents' desire for a job with frequent socialization and supervision. As indicated by the situational assessment data, job positions targeted were stationary and repetitive, with frequent supervision, low production standards, minimal fine motor requirements, and coworker contact.

A dietary aide position at a nursing home was identified in the classified advertisements. The job requirements included using a cart to assist the dietary supervisor with serving meals to the persons living in the nursing home, and cleaning the kitchen area when finished. However, a detailed job analysis revealed that the dietary aide would be expected to make coffee, take out trash, inventory food, and serve individual meals. The poor mobility skills Mary displayed when using the supply cart during the situational assessment indicated the inappropriateness of this job match for her. Not only was the job considered unsafe for her, but her unsteady gait presented a safety hazard for the individuals being served as well.

Mary's parents located a second job in the laundry room of another nursing home. The initial employer interview showed that the job requirements included sorting and folding the clothes of the persons living in the nursing home. This job was not pursued further by the employment specialist due to the fine motor and discrimination skills necessary to complete the tasks. Although Mary performed best during this situational assessment, a major concern with this position was her ability to meet the production and quality standards while performing multiple sorting and detailed folding tasks.

A cold call to a new hotel identified several openings in the laundry department. The requirements of these full-time positions included operating the machines, folding towels, pressing napkins, and preparing orders for the housekeepers. Unfortunately, due to Mary's limitations, she could not operate the machines or prepare orders for the housekeepers. However, after a talk with the supervisor, it was determined that she would be interested in creating a part-time position involving pressing napkins and folding towels. These two job duties were critical, yet often left unfinished during the course of the day. A thorough job analysis conducted by the employment specialist indicated that the characteristics of the job matched Mary's skills and interests. The information obtained during the job analysis was summarized on the Job Screening Form (Moon et al., 1986). Mary was hired by the hotel as a laundry attendant earning $4.15 per hour. Her part-time hours were arranged for the morning shift since her work performance and alertness were better during the morning situational assessments than during the afternoon assessments.

Directions: *Indicate the response for each item in the appropriate category based on information gathered from the consumer's parents, teacher, and observations during the situational assessments. For each item, describe the behavior, characteristic, or activity. When applicable, include the frequency of its occurrence and the environment where it occurs (antecedent, consequences, location, people).*

	Parent: mother	Teacher: Mrs. B.	Dietary—Situational Assessment I	Supply—Situational Assessment II	Laundry—Situational Assessment III
Strength: lifting and carrying · Poor (< 10 lbs.) · Fair (10–20 lbs.) · Average (30–40 lbs.) · Strong (> 50 lbs.)	10–15 lbs., not very strong	Poor, has a hard time carrying items over 10 lbs.	10 lbs. only, had a hard time pushing supply cart	Poor, needed assistance over 10 lbs.	No problems since items in laundry not over 10 lbs.
Endurance · Works < 2 hours · Works < 2–3 hours · Works 3–4 hours · Works > 4 hours	< 2 hours	< 2 hours in school	Worked 1 hour and said she was tired	Worked 2 hours before asking for break	Worked 3 hours before asking for break
Orienting · Small area only · One room · Several rooms · Building wide · Building and grounds	Several rooms	School wide	Small room only, could not find way from dish area to carts	One room only, could not find way from trash area to supply	Not observed
Physical mobility · Sit/stand in one area · Fair ambulation · Stairs/minor obstacles · Physical abilities	Fair ambulation, falls often over own feet	Same as parent comment.	Poor mobility that affected ability to use hands when walking	Unsteady gait, tripped over curb leaving building	Not a problem in the laundry area

Independent work rate (No prompts)
- Slow pace
- Steady/average pace/ sometimes fast
- Above average/ sometimes fast
- Continual fast pace

Appearance
- Unkempt/poor hygiene
- Unkempt/clean
- Neat/clean but clothing unmatched
- Neat/clean and clothing matched

Communication
- Uses sounds/ gestures
- Uses key words/signs
- Speaks unclearly
- Communicates clearly, intelligible to strangers

Social interactions
- Rarely interacts appropriately
- Polite, responses appropriate
- Initiates social interactions infrequently

Category	Obs 1	Obs 2	Obs 3	Obs 4	Obs 5
Independent work rate	Slow pace	Slow pace	Slow! Asked for verbal praise (e.g., "Am I doing a good job?")	Slow	Steady/average pace, had some trouble starring around room
Appearance	Always likes to look nice	Neat/clean clothing matched	Very neat!	Same	Same
Communication	Communicates clearly	No problem	Intelligible to strangers	Same	Same
Social interactions	Very polite, sometimes shy with strangers	Sometimes interacts inappropriately (e.g., tickles, hugs)	Polite, responses were appropriate	Initiated too frequently, yelling to coworkers across room	Polite, initiated interactions

(continued)

Figure 5.6.   Completed Situational Assessment Screening Form.

81

Figure 5.6. (continued)

	Parent: mother	Teacher: Mrs. B.	Dietary—Situational Assessment I	Supply—Situational Assessment II	Laundry—Situational Assessment III
Social interactions *(continued)* • Initiates social interactions frequently					
Attention to task/ perseverance • Frequent prompts required • Intermittent prompts/ high supervision • Intermittent prompts/ low supervision • Infrequent prompts/ low supervision	Needs a lot of supervision to continue working	Frequent prompts are always needed to keep Mary on task	Frequent prompts required	Frequent prompts required	Responded to gesture prompts to keep working
Independent sequencing of job duties • Cannot perform tasks in sequence • Performs two to three tasks in sequence • Performs four to six tasks in sequence • Performs seven or more tasks in sequence	Cannot do at home	Can sequence two to three tasks after skill training	Needed prompt to sequence tasks	Waited for instructions to move to next task	Sequenced two to three tasks (e.g., stacking folded laundry and moving on to next item to fold)

Category / Item					
Initiative/motivation · Always seeks work · Sometimes volunteers · Waits for directions · Avoids next task	Sometimes volunteers to do work at home	Sometimes volunteers for work in the class	Usually waited for directions	Waited for directions	Sometimes volunteers (i.e., "What do I do now?")
Adapting to change · Adapts to change · Adapts to change with some difficulty · Adapts to change with great difficulty · Rigid routine required	Adapts with great difficulty, she will cry easily if things are not consistent	Same as parent comment	Not observed	Seemed to need a rigid schedule	Not observed
Reinforcement needs · Frequently required · Daily · Weekly · Paycheck sufficient	Frequent	Frequent! Asks often for praise of work completed	Frequent verbal praise to encourage through difficult tasks	Seemed dependent on verbal praise and prompts	Seemed to need verbal praise after each item folded
Level of support · Very supportive of work · Supportive of work with reservations · Indifferent about work · Negative about work	Very supportive	Parents very supportive but overprotective	Not applicable	Not applicable	Not applicable
Discrimination skills · Cannot distinguish between work supplies	Fair, Mary can distinguish between simple items (e.g., Comet vs. Windex)	Can be trained to easily distinguish between work supplies	Made gross discriminations of work supplies (i.e., mop, bucket, rags)	Could not distinguish size of trash bags	No problem in this area

(continued)

Figure 5.6. (continued)

	Parent: mother	Teacher: Mrs. B.	Dietary—Situational Assessment I	Supply—Situational Assessment II	Laundry—Situational Assessment III
Discrimination skills *(continued)*					
· Distinguishes between work supplies with an external cue					
· Distinguishes between work supplies					
Time awareness					
· Unaware of time and clock function					
· Identifies breaks/lunch					
· Can tell time to the hour	Tells time to the hour	Same	Same	Same	Same
· Can tell time in hours and minutes					
Functional reading					
· None					
· Sight words/symbols	Some words by sight (e.g., men, women, exit, Coke)	Same	Found women's restroom by the sign	Not observed	Not observed
· Simple reading					
· Fluent reading					
Functional math					
· None					
· Simple counting	Simple counting to 10	Same	Observed counting to 4 when putting shelves on cart	Not observed	Not observed

	Column 1	Column 2	Column 3	Column 4	Column 5
• Simple addition/subtraction					
• Computational skills					
Independent street crossing					
• None					
• Two lane street (with or without light)	2 lane street only	Same	Would only cross in outlined pedestrian crosswalk	Not observed	Looked both ways when crossing 2 lane street
• Four lane street (with or without light)					
Handling criticism/stress					
• Resistive/argumentative	Cries when frustrated	Does not accept criticism readily, cries under stress	No problems	Withdrew into silence when corrected	Responded by saying, "I was going to do that!"
• Withdraws into silence					
• Accepts criticism/does not change					
Acts/speaks aggressively					
• Hourly	Never	Never	Not observed during 4-hour assessment	Not observed	Not observed
• Daily					
• Weekly					
• Monthly					
• Never					
Travel skills					
• Requires bus training	None . . . willing to learn	None	None	None	None
• Uses bus independently (with or without transfers)					
• Able to make own travel arrangements					

(continued)

Figure 5.6. (continued)

	Parent: mother	Teacher: Mrs. B.	Dietary—Situational Assessment I	Supply—Situational Assessment II	Laundry—Situational Assessment III
Work experiences · Employment site · Job tasks performed · Dates, hours, wages	Situational job sites through school	Food bank, clothing rack. nursing home laundry			
Physical limitations · Impairment · Medications · Medical restrictions	Seizure medication, cerebral palsy, and scoliosis. The seizures are under control. Mary also has severe visual limitations and must wear glasses. Perceptual problems are also evident when she attempts to perform tasks.				
Responding to survival words · Street signs · Restrooms · Danger, stop	Yes, she recognizes all of these	Same	Recognized signs for the restroom	Same	Recognized the exit sign
Hurtful to self/others · Banging head, pulling hair · Biting, scratching · Hitting, pinching	Never!	No	Not observed	Not observed	Not observed
Destructive to property · Breaks, burns, tears things	Never!	No	Not observed	Not observed	Not observed
Disruptive behavior that interferes with activities of others · Yelling, screaming · Clinging	Sometimes cries for no ap-	Same as parent comment	Some inappropriate laughter, but this did	Cried several times when corrected	Not observed

86

Behavior					
• Laughing/crying for no reason • Interrupting		parent reason	not interfere		
Unusual or repetitive behaviors/habits • Pacing • Rocking • Twirling fingers • Twitching	None	None	Not observed	Not observed	Not observed
Behavior that is socially offensive to others • Talking too loudly • Burping, picking nose, • Touching, hugging	Sometimes talks too loudly and will hug and touch inappropriately	Same as parent comment	Not observed	Talked too loudly to get coworker's attention five times in 4-hour period	Not observed
Withdrawal or inattentive behavior • Keeping away from people • Expressing unusual fears • Showing little interest in activities	She will hide when she is angry	She will get very quiet and withdraw after she has cried and been angry	Not observed	Pulled away from the trainer for 5 minutes after corrected, would not talk	Not observed
Uncooperative or non-compliant behavior • Refusing to attend school/work • Refusing to follow rules/requests	Will pout and act defiant if corrected	Same as parent comment	Not observed	Pouted when criticized and told to return to work, did return immediately on verbal prompt	Not observed

(continued)

Figure 5.6. (continued)

	Parent: mother	Teacher: Mrs. B.	Dietary—Situational Assessment I	Supply—Situational Assessment II	Laundry—Situational Assessment III
Uncooperative or non-compliant behavior *(continued)* • Acting defiant/pouting					
Leisure skills/interests	Card games, TV, teen magazines, social clubs with mom	Loves to talk! Likes to dress-up and use make-up; this has been used as reinforcer	Not observed	Not observed	Not observed
Chores or responsibilities	Cleans up room (i.e., hangs up clothes, makes bed)	Delivers notes to the office on a regular basis for the teacher	Not applicable	Not applicable	Not applicable
Activities, foods, and items that are reinforcing	Bowling, going out for pizza, candy, popcorn, make-up, audiotapes	Same comments as parent	Used break as a reinforcer for working, soda given	Coke	Coke
Money skills • Discriminates between coins • Makes minor purchases	Makes minor purchases (i.e., soda, candy, make-up) by herself	Makes minor purchases using <2 dollars	Used the vending machine independently	Did not show any skills during lunch	Same as I

- Makes major purchases
- Amount of spending money given to consumer
- Willingness of family to give consumer money from paycheck

Asking for assistance
- Peers
- Coworkers
- Acquaintances
- Persons in authority

Will ask for help if she needs it	Often asks for help even if she does not need it	Asked for help even when it was not needed	Same as I	No problems observed

Other:

Mary had a lot of difficulty moving and doing fine motor skills at the same time. For example, in the dietary department she could not bend over and put the shelves on the cart at the same time. When she tried she often would lose her balance and fall forward. It seems that a stationary position would be most appropriate for her.

SUMMARY

Information obtained from a situational assessment is only part of the entire set of data that will be used in determining job placement for individuals with severe handicapping conditions. However, the situational assessment data can be used in a number of ways. Most important, when a person has been assessed over a brief period of time, such as 2 weeks, in several different jobs, employment specialists should have a good idea of job preferences, endurance, communication skills, general mobility, and orientation capacity. Along with data on family support and transportation availability, this type of information will help determine the specific kind of job to be sought for an individual. It is believed that a situational assessment most benefits the consumer when it is completed before job placement is sought. When used in this way, a particular job can be found that more closely matches the consumer's strengths and weaknesses. If an employment team has a specific job in mind and is trying to choose a person for that job, assessment data often will become the rationale for *not* placing people with severe handicaps.

Situational assessment data can also be used to formulate the pre-employment curricula for students in schools or adult vocational training programs. It is mandatory that the persons conducting the assessments communicate results to teachers, parents, and others providing instruction or assistance to the consumers involved. It is suggested that assessments be conducted on a regular basis to determine progress in skill development. When this is done concurrently with teaching of skills identified from the assessment, there is typically an improvement in skill level and an increased preference for particular types of work.

REFERENCES

Berkell, D.E. (1987). Vocational assessment of students with severe handicaps: A review of the literature. *Career Development for Exceptional Individuals, 10*(2), 61–75.
Cronbach, L.J. (1960). *Essentials of psychological testing.* New York: Harper & Row.
Gaylord-Ross, R. (1986). The role of assessment in transitional, supported employment. *Career Development for Exceptional Individuals, 9*(2), 129–134.
Gold, M. (1973). Research on the vocational rehabilitation of the retarded: The present, the future. In N. Ellis (Ed.), *International review of research in mental retardation* (Vol. 6, pp. 97–147). New York: Academic Press.
Menchetti, B.M., & Rusch, F.R. (1988). Vocational evaluation and eligibility for rehabilitation services. In P. Wehman & M.S. Moon (Eds.), *Vocational rehabilitation and supported employment* (pp. 79–90). Baltimore: Paul H. Brookes Publishing Co.
Menchetti, B.M., Rusch, F.R., & Owens, D.M. (1983). Vocational training. In J.L. Matson & S.E. Breuning (Eds.), *Assessing the mentally retarded* (pp. 247–284). New York: Grune & Stratton.
Moon, M.S., Goodall, P., Barcus, J.M., & Brooke, V. (1986). *The supported work model of competitive employment: A guide for job trainers* (2nd ed.). Richmond: Virginia Commonwealth University, Rehabilitation Research and Training Center.
Peterson, M. (1986). Work and performance samples for vocational assessment of special students: A critical review. *Career Development for Exceptional Individuals, 9*(2), 67–76.
Schalock, R.L., & Karan, O.C. (1979). Relevant assessment: The interaction between evaluation and training. In G.T. Bellamy, G. O'Connor, & O.C. Karan (Eds.), *Vocational rehabilitation of severely handicapped persons* (pp. 33–54). Baltimore: University Park Press.
Wright, G.N. (1980). *Total rehabilitation.* Boston: Little, Brown.

FINDING APPROPRIATE JOBS FOR PERSONS WITH SEVERE MENTAL RETARDATION

6

Most people with severe mental retardation are being passed over for placement consideration in supported employment (Wehman, Kregel, Shafer, & West, 1989). This trend of excluding persons with severe mental retardation has continued despite the demonstrations and existing evidence that competitive employment can be of significant benefit to persons with severe mental retardation and to the community (Bellamy, O'Connor & Karan, 1979; Gold, 1976; Wehman, Hill, Wood, & Parent, 1987). In order to reverse the trend we must begin to analyze our own service delivery implementation strategies to assist this population of individuals in gaining equal access to the marketplace (Hill & Morton, 1988). This chapter looks at some practical job development practices and strategies that have assisted supported employment personnel in successfully securing jobs for persons with severe mental retardation.

ESTABLISHING A SERVICE MIX

The major supported employment approaches presently being implemented across the United States include: the individual placement model (Wehman & Kregel, 1985), the enclave model (Rhodes & Valenta, 1985), the mobile work crew (Bourbeau, 1985), and the small business option (Mank, Rhodes, & Bellamy, 1986). Each of these approaches has been utilized successfully for persons with severe mental retardation. Understanding and developing these models, separately or in combination (e.g., a cluster placement approach as described in Chapter 3), at the local service level will assist supported employment programs in establishing a service mix or a range of service options.

Supported employment service providers who are truly interested in serving large numbers of high school-age youth and adults with severe mental retardation must be in a position to offer a variety of supported employment options. Currently, very few supported employment service providers have developed a full range of employment options within their local communities (Moon & Griffin, 1988). There are many factors that may explain this phenomenon, including relative newness of supported employment, limited number of direct service staff, prohibitive start-up cost of particular models, and lack of service providers with strong business management skills. Yet, as supported employment programs obtain new sources of revenue and begin to expand their current services, they will need to establish a supported employment service mix that will allow the employment specialist, along with the potential supported employment employee and his or her family, to choose the most appropriate employment option.

The individual placement model is considered by many professionals to be the least restrictive and, therefore the most normalizing, of all supported employment options (Rehab Brief, 1986). This particular employment model, with its one-to-one training, will be an effective service delivery option for many individuals with severe mental retardation. However, greater diversity of employment models must be developed for the following reasons. First, persons with severe mental retardation present a vast range of differences in intellectual functioning, motor skills, mobility, daily living skills, communication and social skills, and emotional development. Finding the appropriate job match in some communities may cause many of these individuals to remain on waiting lists for extended periods of time. Second, while much has been written on appropriate educational programs for persons with severe mental retardation, many of these individuals continue to be served in segregated center-based schools with little or no community-based instruction (Bates, 1989; Sailor & Guess, 1983; Sternberg, 1988). We know that the supported employment employees who have been most successful have been those individuals with previous employment experiences or who have received community-based instruction (Hill, Hill, Wehman, Banks, Pendleton, & Britt, 1985). Assisting an individual to gain important work skills while being employed in a cluster or a dispersed worker placement or a small business option, for example, may be an appropriate alternative for these individuals. Third, family members who have been led to believe that their son's or their daughter's only vocational alternative will be an adult activity center may choose a group model with its continuous support. As families experience the success of supported employment, they may be more open to considering a less restrictive employment option in the future.

JOB DEVELOPMENT

A major concern among new providers of supported employment services are the issues surrounding job development (Barcus, Wehman, Moon, Brooke, Goodall, & Everson, 1988). Individuals responsible for providing this new employment service to a community generally ask such questions as: "How do you market supported employment?" "Is there a process for doing job development?" "What do you say when you talk to an employer?" A great deal of information is available on this subject, including material on: responsive marketing (Shafer, Parent, & Everson, 1988); marketing management (Kiernan, Carter, & Eugene, 1989); job development strategies in supported competitive employment (Moon, Goodall, Barcus, & Brooke, 1986); and job development training (Mcloughlin, Garner, & Callahan, 1987). These resources, along with the many other commercially available products, will provide supported employment service providers with a wealth of information as they attempt to secure employment opportunities for persons with severe disabilities.

While general information gained from currently available job development resources will be applicable to the majority of supported employment programs, there are additional strategies to consider for local service providers interested in facilitating community job placement for persons with severe mental retardation. Approaches described in this chapter will be useful for both the newly hired service provider and the seasoned veteran. Specific topics include believing in the competency of the people you serve, knowing the local labor markets, finding the employment niche, and selling the service.

BELIEVING IN THE COMPETENCY OF THE PEOPLE YOU SERVE

We think that persons with severe mental retardation remain unemployed largely because service providers simply do not believe that persons with severe mental retardation can be employed (Ferguson & Ferguson, 1986; Hansen, 1980). If service providers are not personally acquainted with a person with severe mental retardation or if their only experiences with people who have severe mental retardation have been limited to a segregated facility, then they probably will be skeptical about forecasting community supported employment for any individual with severe mental retardation. However, it is important to realize that when this happens, the service provider is forming his or her opinions without taking the opportunity to get to know an individual on a personal level and without consistently applying the existing technology in integrated community environments. Therefore, the service provider denies persons with severe mental retardation the opportunity to demonstrate their competencies.

Before a supported employment service provider embarks on specific job development activities, he or she must first believe in the competency of persons with severe mental retardation. To assist service providers in developing positive attitudes, several combinations of the following ideas could be implemented:

- Talk with other providers of supported employment services for persons with severe mental retardation.
- Observe a person with severe mental retardation working competitively (at a community access job site).
- Talk with family members of persons with severe mental retardation who are receiving supported employment.
- Talk with employers who have hired persons with severe mental retardation.
- Watch videotapes of persons with severe mental retardation demonstrating vocational competence.
- Visit a community-based training site.
- Attend in-service training events.

Using the ideas listed above will provide an avenue for supported employment service providers to address their underlying fears and to gain the confidence to begin specific job development activities for persons with severe mental retardation.

It was not until we actually worked alongside persons with severe mental retardation in competitive employment sites and shared in their success that the authors became believers in the truest sense of the word. While reading books and journals, visiting employment sites, and listening to success stories will be helpful to change the negative vocational image of persons with severe mental retardation, it is only through direct experience that a real change will occur.

KNOWING THE LOCAL LABOR MARKETS

Prior to contacting employers, supported employment service providers should spend some time analyzing the local labor market (Martin, 1986; Moon et al., 1986). Time spent doing so will lead to the development of jobs with reputable companies that are economically stable. Generally, service providers should do this analysis while also engaging in consumer assessment tasks. Conducting a local labor market analysis while completing situational assessments (see Chapter 5) will allow the supported employment service provider to gain general knowledge about the community, while gaining specific information about the individual desires and strengths of potential supported employment employees.

Developing a comprehensive picture of a community's labor market could require a considerable amount of time. Size of the service area, diversity of the labor market, and the service provider's familiarity with a community all will be factors in determining the amount of time and research required. Compiling lists of questions, such as those in Table 6.1, will assist supported employment services in analyzing their local labor markets.

Responses to the questions in Table 6.1 will assist the supported employment service provider in gathering general information about a local community labor market. These data will form the groundwork for finding employment in stable jobs where persons with severe mental retardation can become integrated into the work force.

FINDING THE EMPLOYMENT NICHE

Finding a job opening or assisting a company in creating a job that is well suited to both the individual strengths and desires of a person with severe mental retardation and to the particular needs and work demands of a company, is finding an employment niche. Typically, a supported employment program manager or employment specialist reviews the job duties and the production demands of one or several positions within a particular work environment to locate a position or create a new position. These new jobs involve real work and may begin as 20-hour-a-week positions that can grow into full-time positions.

Table 6.1. Questions related to analysis of the local labor market

1. **Who are the major employers in your community?**
   a. Number of employees:
   b. Type of work performed:
   c. Entry level requirements:
   d. Community reputation:
2. **What types of employment are most commonly found in your community?**
3. **Which companies or types of employment have the largest turnover rate in your community?**
4. **Which companies or types of employment are anticipating growth (new job openings) in the next year?**
   a. Market trend:
   b. Potential date for job vacancies:
5. **What companies are known to have hired persons with disabilities?**
   a. Type of employment:
   b. Name of employer:
   c. Types of disabilities:
6. **Does your community have seasonal employment?**
   a. Name of employer:
   b. Type of work performed:

An employment niche can be found in either a small or large business, although specific considerations must be analyzed prior to contacting a small business.

Small businesses, those sometimes referred to as "Mom and Pop" businesses, historically have been a good source of jobs for supported employment services (Goodall, Verstegen, & Nietupski, 1988). These work environments have fewer than 500 employees and generally create a warm and intimate work place where social relations are satisfying and conflict free (Schumacher, 1973). However, as economic conditions tighten, owners of small businesses often are forced to consolidate their work force and require employees to be cross-trained on additional duties in the work environment. When this happens, the employee with severe mental retardation may be the first to be separated from his or her job or face a reduction in work hours due to the increased complexity of the work scope. While small businesses should not be ruled out as potential sites for supported employment, the service provider looking for long-term, stable employment for persons with severe mental retardation will have to ask many more specific questions about the overall economic health of the business.

When performing job development activities for persons with severe mental retardation, service providers will be most interested in jobs that have a limited number of tasks, moderate to low production rate, proximity to coworkers, and movement within a medium to small work area. Within the climate of many large businesses there exist multiple employment possibilities matching the above criteria. Some of these employment opportunities will be listed as standard job vacancies; however, many of the best situations will be created as a result of a specific need that the business is facing.

For example, a large hotel chain advertised openings for five chambermaid positions. The supported employment specialist knew that typical chambermaid positions had too many job changes for his consumers, but he was still curious about the position and other potential employment opportunities at this particular hotel. Upon further investigation, the employment specialist learned that each of the 15 chambermaids was responsible for polishing silver for 1 hour a day. The service provider immediately saw an employment niche—the job of polishing silver. Despite the fact that the employer had never considered hiring a person just to polish silver, she was very open to designing a 20-hour-a-week position, with a starting salary of $4.50 per hour, involving only polishing silver. While the employment specialist was not sure which consumer would be best suited for the job, he did know that he represented many consumers who liked to sit and use their hands while working.

Another example of an employment niche was discovered in a community with a tourist economy. This particular labor market had a large number of food establishments, many of which were fast food businesses. One particular fast food chain had 12 restaurants in the surrounding community. Every Sunday the employment specialist would read numerous advertisements for job openings within the company. From past experience, the supported employment specialist knew that fast food establishments need employees with high production output. However, she was curious as to who prepared the small containers of cole slaw, jello, and mashed potatoes. After talking with a manager of the local fast food chain, the employment specialist learned that the district manager was becoming concerned about customer complaints about the cole slaw. The manager and the service provider discussed the possibility of having a supported employment consumer make the cole slaw for all of the restaurants in one location, thereby solving the quality control problem. Unlike the first example, this employment niche was discovered through a problem-solving process. What started as an unlikely prospect led to a placement, with supported employment addressing a local community business concern.

In both examples, the supported employment service provider did not go into the meeting with the employer presenting a slick, well laid out plan. Rather, the employment specialist: 1) believed in the competency of the consumers; 2) knew the desires and strengths of the consumers; and 3) remained open and listened to the employers to determine where and how a person with severe mental retardation would best fit into the overall business operation. Once the supported employment service provider discovers an employment niche, it is necessary for him or her to work the position for a couple of days. This will give the service provider an opportunity to ensure that the new employee can actually perform the job tasks and to develop a detailed analysis of the individual or group positions to present to the management of the business.

SELLING THE SERVICE

The thought of having to walk into a corporate office to explain supported employment services to a business manager is enough to intimidate many employment specialists. Supported employment service providers often are uneasy moving around the business community because they have not been trained in the customs and protocol of this foreign environment. Yet, after most supported employment program managers and employment specialists talk with a few employers, they find that their fears are unfounded, especially if they keep the following points in mind:

- Know the type of service or product that the business provides.
- Practice your supported employment presentation.
- Avoid using human service lingo.
- Know exactly how to describe the strengths of the persons you serve.
- Present a business image.
- Be respectful of the employer's time.
- Allow the employer many opportunities to ask questions.
- Raise routine questions and/or concerns that other employers ask.

At the end of the initial meeting with an employer the supported employment service provider will want to arrange for a follow-up meeting (Moon et al., 1986). This provides the job developer with an opportunity to assess the employer's interest in the supported employment service. For those employers who do not appear to want another meeting, leaving a packet of information on supported employment provides an opportunity to reconsider the decision.

Some supported employment service providers will be more comfortable and probably more successful than others at performing specific job development activities. However, all service providers can overcome their fears and work on their job development skills. The following sample scripts from the two previous job examples are provided to assist.

Individual Placement Example

Employment specialist	Good morning, my name is Jeffrey Fry from Employment, Inc. Thank you for taking the time to meet with me.
Employer	Hello, please be seated. I'm Susan Jones and I'm the supervisor for housekeeping here at the hotel. How can I help you?
Employment specialist	As I briefly explained to you on the telephone, I'm an employment specialist with Employment, Inc. We provide job placement and training services

for persons with disabilities. Have you ever hired a person with a disability?

Employer   Well, we did hire this gentleman about a year ago who had all kinds of problems, but he just didn't work out.

Employment specialist   Our program is designed to work closely with employers to ensure that the new employee learns the job and works according to the manager's expectations. Our service is unique from that of other programs in that we provide a professional, such as myself, to work alongside the new employee until he or she learns the job. Even after the employee is successfully completing the job we would continue to stay in touch with the employee and the supervisor to ensure ongoing job satisfaction.

Employer   What exactly do you mean by disabled? What kind of problems do these people have?

Employment specialist   The workers we place have a disability called mental retardation. Of course, all workers are different, but generally the individuals we work with have difficulty talking, reading, writing, or learning new skills. This is not to say that an individual could not learn, it is just that the learning process might take a longer period of time. That's why we carefully assess each job opening and each worker that we serve to assist in making a good job match. Then from the first day of employment I would accompany the individual you hire and assist with things like transportation, work quality, work completion, and getting to know coworkers and the job site.

Employer   I wouldn't mind hiring a disabled person if, of course, they could do the job. But you can see from the chambermaid's job description that the job is very difficult.

Employment specialist   You're right, your chambermaids do have very complex job descriptions. However, I feel confident that I could train one of the people that I represent to shine the silver that you currently have all the chambermaids doing at the end of their shift. That would give each maid an additional 2 hours each day to clean hotel rooms.

Employer   You know, that's not a bad idea. If your person started off working 30 hours a week until we see about the volume . . . I wouldn't have to hire another chambermaid. But I can't afford to pay both of you to do one job.

Employment specialist   Oh no, my agency pays for my services. I would only stay at the job site until both you and the new employee were satisfied with the placement. Then, after the employee learned the job, I would gradually reduce my time here, but I would be available to return to the job site.

Employer   Well, we have our own ways of doing things around here. Do you already know how to polish silver?

Employment specialist   A really nice feature of the service is that I can come on the job and learn how to polish silver from the chambermaids. In fact, if you have some free time now perhaps we could look at the area where your staff polishes silver. If not, I would be interested in setting up a time when we can assess the position and see if we have someone who could work for you.

Employer	Actually, I have another meeting in about 15 minutes. How about next Thursday morning at 9:30?
Employment specialist	Great! In the meantime I'd like to leave this brochure with you that describes our service in more detail. When you're reading it, if you have any questions please don't hesitate to call.
Employer	Okay, thank you . . . and I'll see you on Thursday.
Employment specialist	Thank you again for your time. I'll look forward to seeing you next week.

Dispersed Group or Cluster Placement Example

Employment specialist	Hello, my name is Alice Smith from Supported Employment, Inc. I spoke with you by phone, last week.
Employer	Yes, how do you do. I'm Mike Carrol. Please come in and sit down. I took your suggestion and I called my buddy John Avery about your program—he gave your program a great recommendation!
Employment specialist	That's really nice to hear. John hired Martha, one of the people we represent, and she has been working very successfully for over a year now assembling hospital supply kits. I don't know how much John told you about our company but you know we are a job placement and training service for persons with disabilities. Initially what I do is go out and analyze different community job opportunities to determine if the positions are appropriate for the people I represent. I noticed in the Sunday paper that the Food Court, here at the mall, has a number of positions open. Could you tell me a little more about your job openings?
Employer	As I'm sure you know, the mall has just opened a Food Court, and business is really picking up. Presently we need additional employees to bus tables, to keep the four restrooms in this area clean and to wash the food trays. But I don't think that a handicapped person could really do this type of work.
Employment specialist	The unique aspect to our service and the reason why we have been so successful is that we provide a trained professional to work with new employees here at the job site assisting the individuals in learning the work routine, becoming familiar with the job site, and getting to know the co-workers. In fact, many of the people we represent have been very successful in the type of service positions that you have just mentioned.
Employer	My friend John did tell me how you worked at his company for four full months helping that woman learn her job, and a year later you are still continuing to check to make sure that everything is going OK. Your company can't possibly afford to provide that same type of service for every person you place.
Employment specialist	That's exactly the type of service that we provide to every person we represent.

Actually because this is such a large job site and you have so many job openings in such disperse areas, I would be interested in looking at a couple of different jobs.

If you would be interested in hiring four or five individuals doing a variety of different jobs, my company could assign a full-time person to train and supervise your new employees. This is something we call an enclave.

Employer	But eventually your supervisor would have to leave. Right?
Employment specialist	No, as long as the people we represent remain your employees our supervisor would remain here with them.
Employer	No kidding? Well, how much does this cost me?
Employment specialist	Nothing, this service is provided at no additional expense to the employer. You would just put the employees on your payroll as you would any new employee.
Employer	Sounds great. What particular positions were you interested in?
Employment specialist	I would like to look at the tray washer, table busing, and janitorial positions. Perhaps one day later this week I could come back and really analyze each of these positions.
Employer	OK, if you do that on Monday then we could meet and talk about this enclave idea on Wednesday at 9 A.M.
Employment specialist	Great. It will probably take me at least 8 hours on Monday to analyze each of these job duties. Would you like me to wear one of your uniforms?
Employer	No, that won't be necessary. What I will do to make sure that you get all the information you need is tell my assistant manager Susan to answer any of the questions you might have.
Employment specialist	OK. Well, I'll be here at 8 A.M. on Monday and I'll look for Susan the assistant manager.
	Thank you again for your time, and if I don't see you on Monday, we will meet on Wednesday at 9 A.M.
Employer	That's correct, but I'll probably talk with you on Monday when you are out here. Good-bye.
Employment specialist	Thank you and good-bye.

SUMMARY

If the supported employment service provider is committed to assisting persons with severe mental retardation in gaining equal access to the marketplace, then a logical first step in doing so is to acquire good job development practices. This chapter has reviewed believing in the competency of the people you serve, and covered strategies for knowing the local labor markets, finding the employment niche, and selling the service. Implementing some or all of these strategies and evaluating service outcomes should go a long way in reversing current service delivery practices by including persons with severe mental retardation in community job placement.

REFERENCES

Barcus, M., Wehman, P., Moon, S., Brooke, V., Goodall, P., & Everson, J. (1988). Design and implementation of a short-term inservice training program for supported employment service providers. *Rehabilitation Education, 2*, 17–33.

Bates, P. (1989). Vocational training for persons with profound disabilities (pp. 265–294). In F. Brown & D.H. Lehr (Eds.). *Persons with profound disabilities: Issues and practices.* Baltimore: Paul H. Brookes Publishing Co.

Bellamy, T., O'Connor, G., & Karan, O.C. (1979). *Vocational rehabilitation of severely handicapped persons.* Baltimore: University Park Press.

Bourbeau, P.E. (1985). Mobile work crews: An approach to achieve long-term supported employment. In P. McCarthy, J. Everson, S. Moon, & M. Barcus (Eds.), *School to work transition for youth with severe disabilities* (pp. 151–166). Richmond: Virginia Commonwealth University, Project Transition into Employment.

Ferguson, D.L., & Ferguson, P.M. (1986). The new victories: A progressive policy analysis for work reform for people with very severe handicaps. *Mental Retardation, 24*, 331–338.

Gold, M. (1976). Task analysis of a complex assembly task by the retarded blind. *Exceptional Children, 42*, 78–84.

Goodall, P., Verstegen, D., & Nietupski, J. (1988). In-state economic development and marketing. In M. Barcus, S. Griffin, D. Mank, L. Rhodes, & M.S. Moon, (Eds.), *Supported employment implementation issues* (pp. 73–100). Richmond: Virginia Commonwealth University, Rehabilitation Research and Training Center.

Hansen, C.L. (1980). *History of vocational habilitation of the handicapped.* Washington, D.C.: United States Department of Education, Office of Special Education and Rehabilitative Services.

Hill, J., Hill, M., Wehman, P., Banks, D., Pendleton, P., & Britt, C. (1985). Demographic analysis related to successful job retention for competitive employment persons who are mentally retarded. In P. Wehman & J. W. Hill (Eds.), *Competitive employment for persons with mental retardation: From research to practice* (Vol. 1, pp. 65–93). Richmond: Virginia Commonwealth University, Rehabilitation Research and Training Center.

Hill, J., & Morton, M.V. (1988). *Transition programming: Improving vocational outcome.* Rockville, Maryland: Aspen Publishers, Inc.

Kiernan, W.E., Carter, A., & Eugene, B. (1989). Marketing and marketing management in rehabilitation. In W.E. Kiernan & R.L. Schalock (Eds.), *Economics, industry, and disability: A look ahead* (pp. 49–56). Baltimore: Paul H. Brookes Publishing Co.

Mank, D.M., Rhodes, L.E., & Bellamy, G.T. (1986). Four supported employment alternatives. In W.E. Kiernan & J.A. Stark (Eds.), *Pathways to employment for adults with developmental disabilities* (pp. 139–153). Baltimore: Paul H. Brookes Publishing Co.

Martin, J.E. (1986). Identifying potential jobs. In F.R. Rusch (Ed.), *Competitive employment issues and strategies* (pp. 165–185). Baltimore: Paul H. Brookes Publishing Co.

Mcloughlin, C.S., Garner, J.B., & Callahan, M. (1987). *Getting employed, staying employed: Job development and training for persons with severe handicaps.* Baltimore: Paul H. Brookes Publishing Co.

Moon, M.S., Goodall, P., Barcus, M., & Brooke, V. (Eds.). (1986). *The supported work model of competitive employment for citizens with severe handicaps: A guide for job trainers* (rev. ed.). Richmond: Virginia Commonwealth University, Rehabilitation Research and Training Center.

Moon, M.S., & Griffin, S.L. (1988). Supported employment service delivery models. In P. Wehman & M.S. Moon (Eds.), *Vocational rehabilitation and supported employment* (pp. 17–30). Baltimore: Paul H. Brookes Publishing Co.

Rehab Brief. (1986). *Supported Employment, 10* (1). Washington, D.C.: U.S. Department of Education, National Institution on Disability and Rehabilitation Research, Office of Special Education and Rehabilitative Services.

Rhodes, L.E., & Valenta, L. (1985). Enclaves in industry. In P. McCarty, J.M. Everson, M.S. Moon, & J.M. Barcus (Eds.), *School-to-work transition for youth with severe disabilities* (pp. 129–149). Richmond: Virginia Commonwealth University, Project Transition into Employment.

Sailor, W., & Guess, D. (1983). *Severely handicapped students: An introductional design.* Boston: Houghton Mifflin.

Schumacher, E.F. (1973). *Small is beautiful: A study of economics as if people mattered*. London: Blond and Briggs.

Shafer, M.S., Parent, W.S., & Everson, J.M. (1988). Responsive marketing by supported employment programs. In P. Wehman & M.S. Moon (Eds.), *Vocational rehabilitation and supported employment* (pp. 235–250). Baltimore: Paul H. Brookes Publishing Co.

Sternberg, L. (1988). An overview of vocational concerns for students with severe or profound handicaps. In L. Sternberg (Ed.), *Educating students with severe or profound handicaps* (pp. 3–13). Rockville, MD: Aspen Publishers.

Wehman, P., Hill, J.W., Wood, W., & Parent, W. (1987). A report on competitive employment histories of persons labeled severely mentally retarded. *Journal of The Association for Persons with Severe Handicaps, 12*(1), 11–17.

Wehman, P., & Kregel, J. (1985). A supported work approach to competitive employment of individuals with moderate and severe handicaps. *Journal of The Association for Persons with Severe Handicaps, 10*(1), 3–11.

Wehman, P., Kregel, J., Shafer, M., & West, M. (1989). Supported employment implementation I: Characteristics and outcomes of persons being served. In P. Wehman, J. Kregel, & M.S. Shafer (Eds.), *Emerging trends in the national supported employment initiative: A preliminary analysis of twenty-seven states* (pp. 46–73). Richmond: Virginia Commonwealth University, Rehabilitation Research and Training Center.

ORIENTATION TO THE JOB AND ASSESSMENT OF TRAINING NEEDS

7

One element of job-site training for persons with severe disabilities has been referred to as orientation and assessment (Barcus, Brooke, Inge, Moon, & Goodall, 1987; Moon, Goodall, Barcus, & Brooke, 1986). This component of training for workers with severe mental retardation begins prior to the first day of employment with the employment specialist completing a thorough job duty analysis of the specific duties that the targeted position involves (Belmore & Brown, 1978; Ford & Mirenda, 1984; Sweet, Shiraga, Ford, Nisbet, Graff, & Loomis, 1982). The employment specialist must also identify nonvocational job-related skills within the work environment and the worker's community that may have an impact on the worker's success. The identification of natural supports such as the employer, immediate supervisor(s), coworkers, and friends within the work and community environment are critical to development of training strategies (Nisbet & Callahan, 1987). By analyzing the job environment prior to placement, the employment specialist can determine the type of orienting skills that are required for the position (Mcloughlin, Garner, & Callahan, 1987; Moon et al., 1986; Moon & Griffin, 1988; Rusch, 1986). Based on this type of information, an instructional plan, which includes identification of initial training strategies, can be developed prior to the worker's first day of employment. The orientation and assessment phase to job-site training may be considered complete when the worker has become familiar with the general expectations of the job environment (Mcloughlin et al., 1987) and can orient herself or himself within the work environment without assistance from the employment specialist.

ASSESSMENT OF THE JOB SITE

Before a worker begins a new job, the employment specialist must concentrate on learning to perform the job and organizing the daily routine. The major work areas in which various job tasks are performed must be identified, along with critical vocational and nonvocational skills related to each duty (Moon et al., 1986). A task analytic approach is used for identifying and sequencing job duties, establishing a work routine, and designing appropriate training and support methods.

Sequencing Job Duties

The employment specialist should work the job a minimum of one day before introducing the worker to the position. While performing the job, the employment specialist should note the major duties and approximate time required to perform each task (Belmore & Brown, 1978; Moon et al., 1986). The sequence of the job duties is recorded so that a routine can be established and movement required between work areas can be determined (Mcloughlin et al., 1987). This information should be recorded on a Sequence of Job Duties Form such as in Figure 7.1. Amy, a supported employment specialist, used this form as a guide in determining what job duties needed to be completed and the specific time of day when the work had to be done.

Job Duty Analysis

Once the sequence of major job duties has been firmly established, the next step is to analyze the specific skills required to perform each major job duty successfully. The pro-

---

Position: _Kitchen attendant_

Job site: _The mall_

☐ Daily
   (Job duties remain the same from
   day to day)

☐ Varies day to day
   (If checked here, complete a separate
   form for each different sequence)

   If above box is checked, indicate day
   for which this form is completed:

   ☐   ☐   ☐   ☐   ☐   ☐   ☐
   Mon. Tues. Wed. Thurs. Fri.   Sat.   Sun.

Approximate Time	Job Duty
12:00–12:05 P.M.	Punch in
12:05–12:15	Set up work area
12:15– 1:15	Sanitize trays
1:15– 1:25	Pick up and deliver trays
1:25– 2:00	Sanitize trays
2:00– 2:15	Break
2:15– 3:00	Sanitize trays
3:00– 3:25	Pick up and deliver trays
3:25– 3:45	Sanitize trays
3:45– 4:00	Clean up work area

Comments:

Signature/title: _____ _Amy Jones_ _____ Date: _____ 2/4 _____

Figure 7.1.   Sequence of job duties.

cess of breaking a major job duty into its component skills is referred to as a job duty analysis (Barcus et al., 1987; Mcloughlin et al., 1987; Snell & Browder, 1986). Here the employment specialist must identify, isolate, and describe each job skill that the employee will be required to perform, including any special tools or machinery to be used (Buckley, 1988; Chadsey-Rusch & Rusch, 1988). The information should be recorded on a Job Duty Analysis Form (Barcus et al., 1987; Moon et al., 1986; Rusch & Mithaug, 1980). This enables the employment specialist to incorporate information from interviews with the employer, from analyzing the work environment, from sequencing the job duties, and from personally performing the job duties (Moon et al., 1986). Table 7.1 provides a set of guidelines that have proven to be useful in completing this analysis (Barcus et al., 1987; Mcloughlin et al., 1987; Moon et al., 1986).

In the example provided in Figure 7.2, the employment specialist expanded the sequence of job duties (see Table 7.1) using a task analytic approach to break each of the job duties down into the component parts. A review of the job duty analysis completed for the kitchen attendant position makes it apparent that this approach is both a precise and a lengthy process. However, a task analytic approach to job-site training will prove to be an important tool in ensuring that the worker learns all of the job tasks associated with a particular job. It is critical for this process to be completed before the new employee with severe mental retardation begins work.

Identifying Natural Supports

Natural supports are those formal and informal mechanisms existing in a work environment that can be drawn upon to increase and to sustain an employee's performance through the use of active assistance and/or through approval or sanctioning of worker achievements. These supports are not artificial and are not manufactured for an employee with a disability. Every employment setting is unique and provides some level or degree of natural support for workers (Henderson & Argyle, 1985; Hirszowicz, 1982; Nisbet & Hagner, 1988). Formal supports may include employee assistance programs, employee associations, and supervision (Googins, 1989). Informal supports may include help with work, job duty interdependence, directional cues, and coworker support (Barcus et al., 1987; Nisbet & Hagner, 1988; Shafer, 1986). Along with analyzing the job duties (Barcus et al., 1987; Moon et al., 1986) the employment specialist must examine

Table 7.1. Guidelines for job duty analysis

Identify only those job skills that can be observed and measured.

Include only those observable skills a worker must perform in order to master the job task.

Break each job task into the sequential steps required to successfully perform the task.

Include all necessary machinery and tools.

Concentrate on the job task that is being analyzed rather than the worker who will master it. (By focusing on the task, those skills that are essential to successful completion of the job task can be easily identified.)

Talk with coworkers to learn tricks of the trade.

Field test the job task analysis by observing a coworker completing the task.

Determine the most efficient procedure to complete a task.

Be concerned with reducing unnecessary worker movement when completing the task.

Have the final job task analysis approved by the employer/supervisor.

Give the employer a copy for his or her records.

Employee: _____Susan North_____   Job title: _____Kitchen Attendant_____
Trainer: _____Amy Jones_____   Job site: _____The Mall_____

Approximate times	Task performed	Task Analysis/Diagrams/Effective Training Techniques
1. 12:00 P.M.	1. Punch in	1. **Procedure for punching in:**
		1. 1. Locate card (with green dot) in rack.
		1. 2. Slide card into time clock.
		1. 3. Listen to clock punch.
		1. 4. Remove card.
		1. 5. Replace card in rack.
2. 12:00–12:15	2. Set up work area	2. **Procedure for setting up work area:**
		2. 1. Fill sink #1 with hot water and pink soap.
		2. 2. Fill sink #3 with hot water and 4 blue tablets.
		2. 3. Use sink #2 as rinse sink; test faucet sprayer.
		2. 4. Place utility cart by sink #1.
3. 12:15–1:15	3. Sanitize trays	3. **Procedure for sanitizing trays:**
		3. 1. Stand in front of sink #1.
		3. 2. Place green rack on utility cart.
		3. 3. Fill rack with dirty trays.
		3. 4. Place in sink #1.
		3. 5. Push "ON" button.
		3. 6. Flip over all trays in green rack.
		3. 7. Push "OFF" button.
		3. 8. Pick up rack of trays and place into sink #2.
		3. 9. Rinse trays.
		3.10. Pick up rack of trays and place in sink #3.
		3.11. As rack of trays is sanitized, repeat steps 3.1–3.9 with another rack.
		3.12. Place sanitized trays on counter.
		3.13. Slide trays onto drying cart.
		3.14. Continue until trays are clean.
4. 1:15–1:25	4. Pick up and deliver trays	4. **Procedure for picking up and delivering trays:**
		4. 1. Place sanitized trays on utility cart.
		4. 2. Move to the necessary areas following the pattern shown in the example (see box at end of figure).
		4. 3. Place stacks of dirty trays on utility cart
5. 1:25–2:00	5. Sanitize trays	5. **Procedure for sanitizing trays:** See 3.1–3.14
6. 2:00–2:15	6. Break	6. **Break is taken in the employee section of the food court:**
		6. 1. Martha and Bill take break at the same time.

(continued)

Figure 7.2.   Job duty analysis.

Figure 7.2. *(continued)*

Approximate times	Task performed	Task Analysis/Diagrams/Effective Training Techniques
		6. 2. Coworkers go to deli area for free soda.
7. 2:15–3:00	7. Sanitize trays	7. **Procedure for sanitizing trays:** See 3.1–3.14
8. 3:00–3:25	8. Pick up and deliver trays	8. **Procedure for picking up and delivering trays:** See 4.1–4.3
9. 3:25–3:45	9. Sanitize trays	9. **Procedure for sanitizing trays:** See 3.1–3.14
10. 3:45–4:00	10. Clean up	10. **Procedure for cleaning work area:**
		10. 1. Finish sanitizing procedure for racks of trays in sinks #1 and #3.
		10. 2. Drain water out of sinks.
		10. 3. Wipe water off counter.
		10. 4. As water drains get broom, dust pan, and mop from supply area.
		10. 5. Sweep work area.
		10. 6. Start at rear wall and work toward door.
		10. 7. Sweep dirt into dust pan.
		10. 8. Wipe water out of sinks.
		10. 9. Mop work area.
		10.10. Mop at rear wall and walk back to door area.
		10.11. Pick up supplies and return to supply area.
11. 4:00	11. Punch out	11. **Procedure for punching out** See 1.1–1.5

French fries	Ice cream	Taco	Chicken	Deli	KITCHEN work station
Deliver trays	Deliver trays	Deliver trays	Deliver trays	Deliver trays	Start here

Pick up trays

Pick up trays

Pick up trays

DINING AREA

Pick up trays

Pick up trays

Pick up trays

the physical and social characteristics of each employment setting to identify the variety and intensity of supports existing within the specific workplace.

Employee Assistance Programs   Benefit packages that include access to employee assistance programs have emerged in many corporations and are designed as a support for employees in resolving personal and family issues. These programs have emerged to support workers in balancing work and home life roles and responsibilities. Googins (1989) suggests that employee assistance programs have the potential to assist persons with disabilities in both reducing stigma attached to them and integrating them into the general employee population. The employment specialist should identify the services available through these programs and the limitations of the services they provide.

Employee Associations   In some companies there are employee associations to which many employees of the business belong. The employment specialist should identify the association representative, the membership process, and benefits and/or supports offered to the members of the association.

Supervision   Another form of support within the workplace is the supervision of workers by managers (Nisbet & Hagner, 1988). The type and amount of supervisory support varies widely from job site to job site. The employment specialist should identify the proximity of the supervisor to the worker's job environment and the frequency with which the supervisor interacts with workers in that specific work area (Brass, 1985; Kirmeyer & Lin, 1986; Sundstrom, 1986).

For example, when the employment specialist visited the work site at a local factory, he discovered that the supervisor's office was on the second floor, while the workers' primary work space was on the first floor. The supervisor visited the work area on an average of two times per day (one time in the morning; one time in the afternoon) and no designated supervisor was present in the workers' immediate work area the remainder of the day. This situation would provide minimal supervisory support to an individual with severe mental retardation, and might not be appropriate for job placement.

In other situations, the position may be such that the duties are performed in a variety of areas under the supervision of multiple managers. The employment specialist will need to identify the supervisor for each work environment and his or her proximity to the job area. In addition, the frequency of interactions with coworkers in the area during the time the worker is scheduled to perform a job duty should be determined.

Job Duty Interdependence   Job duties performed by one worker within a work place may require interdependency with other employees throughout the work site in order for the duties to be completed successfully (Shafer & Nisbet, 1988). The employment specialist must identify the level of interdependence of the new employee's assigned job tasks with other job duties within the work site. For instance, worker A is responsible for restocking the salad bar on an as-needed basis, and worker B is responsible for preparation of the items that are restocked. Worker A's completion of restocking duties is directly dependent on worker B's preparation of the salad bar items. In another situation, two employees are assigned the same work area and job duties. The work pace is extremely demanding and the two individuals are responsible for completing the work within the area by the end of their shift. In this case, the workers are mutually responsible for the work and must coordinate their performance in order to complete their duties successfully. This type of job sharing situation may be ideal for individuals with severe disabilities. The interdependence required could help facilitate integration at the job site with nondisabled coworkers.

Coworker Support   Another major source of support within a work environment can be found in the relationship that forms between coworkers (Nisbet & Hagner,

1988). Common interactions between employees include joking, teasing, helping with work, casually talking, discussing work, breaks or lunch, discussing personal life, giving or asking for advice, and teaching or demonstrating work tasks (Henderson & Argyle, 1985; Nisbet & Hagner, 1988). The employment specialist should identify the proximity of coworkers to the primary work area; whether coworkers assist each other during performance of various job duties; whether employees normally take breaks together at the same time or breaks are staggered; and whether employees socialize at break and lunch or after work hours? The employment specialist needs to get a feel for the social and cultural characteristics of the work site.

Directional Cues   A directional cue is any written or pictorial instruction and/or label that is posted within the work environment. These directional cues may instruct an employee on the step-by-step operation of a piece of equipment, outline a particular safety procedure, or identify the location of a work station and supplies or the location of other important work areas. The employment specialist should identify any directional cues within each of the environments in which the employee will work. Table 7.2 outlines the supports identified within a local business where an employee named Jack is to be hired.

Identifying Natural Reinforcers

The best reinforcers to utilize during job-site training are those that occur naturally in the work environment, such as paychecks and supervisor or coworker praise (Barcus et al., 1987; Moon et al., 1986). The employment specialist should take time for observation at the work site to identify reinforcers that naturally occur there. Following is a list of some naturally occuring reinforcers:

- Paycheck
- Coworker praise
- Supervisor praise
- Positive written supervisor evaluation
- Pay raises and/or bonuses
- Parental/guardian/spouse praise

Initially, these natural reinforcers may not be sufficient, and the employment specialist might need to consider utilization of other tangible reinforcers, such as magazines or a cup of coffee together after work. Tangible reinforcers should not be used during job-site training unless a procedure is built in for fading to naturally occurring reinforcers.

Identifying Potential Employee Reinforcers

It is up to the employment specialist to discern effective reinforcers for the worker before the first day of work or during the first few days on the job. In some cases, simply asking a new worker about likes and dislikes is sufficient. However, this method may not be valid for employees with severe or multiple handicaps who have limited language skills. In these cases the employment specialist should observe the consumer in a variety of settings prior to placement. Interviewing family members and professionals who know the individual is crucial in determining how likely the worker is to respond to naturally occurring reinforcement such as verbal praise and paychecks.

A reinforcement questionnaire may be used to identify reinforcers that may be appropriate for the new employee (Moon et al., 1986). This method also provides an opportunity to establish a rapport with the worker and relevant others. Below is a description of use of a reinforcement questionnaire to collect information for a worker named Chris.

Table 7.2.   Worker supports

Employee: Jack
Job site: May Day Hospital
Employee's position: Laundry attendant
Employment specialist: Mike

Employee assistance program
Richmond Employee Assistance Program (REAP)

Employee association(s)
Union
Hospital baseball team

Supervision
Jan, Director of Dietary/A.M. supervisor only
David, head laundry attendant/A.M. and P.M. hours

Job duty interdependence
Martha brings towels to folding area
Jack takes empty cart to David

Coworkers
David is the coworker advocate for Jack
Generally eats lunch with David, Jeff, and Martha

Directional cues
Arrow pointing to laundry area at entrance
No smoking sign is used to identify Jack's folding area and the placement of the cart

Prior to the first day of work, the employment specialist met with Chris at his home to determine his likes and dislikes. In addition, his parents and his brother Jack reviewed the reinforcement questionnaire. The employment specialist also contacted one of Chris's former teachers, who knew him well. The teacher provided the employment specialist with a unique perspective on the reinforcers that had proven to be especially motivating to Chris while in school. Figure 7.3 shows Chris's completed reinforcement questionnaire.

DEVISING A TRAINING SCHEDULE FOR INTENSIVE INSTRUCTION

Devising a training schedule will ensure that company standards are maintained and the employee receives consistent and individualized instruction. Frequently individuals with severe mental retardation are employed in jobs that have no more than two major duties. In many instances the employment specialist will choose to use a total task instructional format in which instruction occurs on all steps of a job each time they naturally occur (Mcloughlin et al., 1987; Snell, 1987). The new employee and the employment specialist work together to complete the employee's assigned duties, with the employment specialist providing instruction, prompting, cueing, and reinforcement throughout each task.

Even though systematic instruction is occurring on all job tasks, the employment specialist must identify times when intense instruction that includes data collection will occur. The employment specialist should choose times during the work day when production demands are low and when there is a minimum level of confusion in the employee's immediate work area. Figure 7.4 shows an example of a training schedule used in a retail business position for a new employee whose job requires him to prepare merchandise for the sales floor by hanging clothes on display racks.

Task Analyzing Job Duties

At this point, the employment specialist has identified the specific major job duties in which training will begin and the time of day when instruction will occur. Next, he or she

Consumer: _____Chris_____

Birthdate: _____October 23, 1962_____

Trainer: _____Elizabeth_____

Do you enjoy a handshake or a pat on the back for a job well done?

Yes __X__   No _____

Do you like people to tell you how well you have done something?

Yes __X__   No _____

What are some things you like to do in your leisure time when you are alone?

Listen to music   Take care of my dog

Watch TV

What group activities do you enjoy doing in your free time?

Bowling   Playing basketball

Chinese checkers

Please list hobbies or games you enjoy.

Listening to music   Collecting cassettes

Please list hobbies you would like to learn.

Playing cards

Do you like listening to music?

Yes __X__   No _____

List type of music you enjoy or two songs you enjoy.

Rock and roll

Jazz

Name two people you enjoy spending time with.

_____Jack_____   Relationship: Brother

_____Simon_____   Relationship: Friend

If you had $.50 what would you buy? Soda

$ 1.00 _____

$ 5.00 music cassette

$25.00 new sneakers

(continued)

Figure 7.3.   Reinforcement questionnaire for a new employee.

Figure 7.3.   *(continued)*

What are some gifts you have given to friends and relatives?

Hat for my brother
Card for my mother

Signature: *Elizabeth*

Date: *January*

The following questions/items may have to be asked of parents, teachers, or other people who know this individual. When the consumer is able to communicate verbally, it is a good idea to get this information from him or her as well as from significant others.

List activities that people familiar with this individual have observed him or her enjoying.

Listening to music   *Watching television*

List tangible items that people familiar with individual have observed him/her enjoy.

Combination portable
  radio and cassette player

List any privileges that could be utilized with this individual.

Going to the movies   *Bowling*
Shopping at the mall

Does this individual like verbal praise for good work?
Yes __X__ No _____
Does this individual like a handshake or pat on the back?
Yes __X__ No _____
Would this individual know the meaning of a paycheck?
Yes __X__ No _____

Signature: *Mabel Johnson*

Relationship: *Mother*

Length of time you have known this person: *24 years*

Employee: Jack

Job site: Marshall's

Position: Merchandise racker

Job duty	Approximate time of job duty	Training time
1. Sort clothes	9:00–10:00 1:00– 2:00	9:30–10:00 1:30– 2:00
2. Hang clothes	10:00–11:30 12:00– 1:00	10:30–11:30 12:30– 1:00

Figure 7.4. Training schedule for merchandise racker position.

must break the specific job duty into teachable components. The set of guidelines in Table 7.3 has been developed to assist in creating an effective job duty task analysis.

A written task analysis of a job duty begins with the first step performed and lists all subsequent steps in sequence through the last step performed. Steps are worded in the second person so they may be used as verbal prompts (e.g., Pick up the green rack), and references are made to things that are observable (e.g., Push the "on" button). Natural cues should be built into the steps of the task analysis whenever appropriate, and judgment decisions should also be addressed. For instance, the employee could be trained to use work supplies as a natural cue. One employee might not remember which chairs he had cleaned when busing a cafeteria table. By including spraying all chairs as one step in the task analysis, the employee could use the spray mist as a cue that he had or had not cleaned a chair as he moved around the table. Table 7.4 shows a sample job duty task analysis that was designed and implemented by an employment specialist. All of the training procedures used for training in a job task can also be used for nonvocational skills (see Figure 7.5 for an example of a nonvocational skill training program).

IDENTIFICATION OF NECESSARY COMMUNITY SUPPORTS

Community Transportation Options

The employment specialist must ensure that arrangements for the worker to get to and from the job have been handled prior to the first day on the job. This entails looking at all available travel possibilities with the worker and the family or guardians to select the one

Table 7.3. Guidelines for job duty task analysis

Observe coworkers performing the job duty. As they perform the job duty, identify each step completed. (If this is not possible, the employment specialist should perform the task.)

Record each step in sequence on a task analysis recording sheet.

Use this task analysis to perform the job yourself.

Determine if all required steps have been identified accurately for efficient performance of the duty.

Revise the job analysis by adding or deleting steps based on your performance of the job.

Observe a coworker performing the task while following the task analysis that has been developed.

Revise your job duty analysis as needed.

Table 7.4. Job duty task analysis

Job duty: Sanitizing trays

1. Stand in front of sink #1.	18. Pick up faucet sprayer.
2. Pick up green rack.	19. Spray all trays (working forward).
3. Place green rack on utility cart.	20. Release water level.
4. Pick up a large stack of trays.	21. Return sprayer to hook.
5. Place stack in front of rack.	22. Pick up rack of rinsed trays.
6. Pick up top tray.	23. Place in 3rd sink.
7. Place tray in rear of rack.	24. Repeat steps 1–13.
8. Fill rack with trays (working forward).	25. Go to 3rd sink.
9. Pick up full rack.	26. Pick up rack of sanitized trays.
10. Place in 1st sink.	27. Place rack on counter.
11. Push "ON" button.	28. Go to 1st sink.
12. Flip over tray in rear of rack.	29. Push "OFF" button.
13. Flip over all trays in rack (working forward).	30. Repeat steps 15–24.
	31. Go to rack on counter.
14. Push "OFF" button.	32. Pick up 3–4 trays.
15. Pick up rack of clean trays.	33. Slide trays onto drying cart.
16. Go to 2nd sink.	34. Repeat steps 27–34.
17. Place rack in 2nd sink.	35. Continue until green rack is empty.

most appropriate. Some of the most desirable options include walking, bike riding, car pooling, and public transportation. In most instances the employment specialist can expect to be involved in designing and implementing a travel training program, regardless of which transportation option is ultimately chosen. For the first few days to several weeks of training, the employment specialist may have to add 1–2 hours for travel training before and after actual job-site training time.

Figure 7.5 shows a sample instructional program for travel training, and Figure 7.6 shows an accompanying Task Analysis Record Sheet. Both were designed for an individual with severe mental retardation to learn to ride a city bus. Developing a detailed program such as this will not only assist in making training effective and efficient but, if shared with family members, may assist in alleviating their concerns about the complexity of learning to ride public transportation.

JOB-SITE ORIENTATION

Orientation training begins the first day of employment and may continue through the subsequent elements of job-site training (i.e., skill acquisition, stabilization) to ensure maximum independence of the employee. There are several things an employment specialist can do to ensure that the training proceeds smoothly and quickly. An orientation checklist, such as the one shown in Figure 7.7, may be helpful in identifying and providing training in skills that are essential at a particular job site (Barcus et al., 1987). This checklist should be based on the analysis of the work environment conducted prior to the employee's first day of work.

During the first few days of employment, this checklist should be used to assess the worker's orientation to the work environment. Areas where the worker is having difficulty should be targeted for training or for identification of natural or artificial support. This checklist may help the employment specialist to monitor the worker's progress and support her or his movement within the work environment.

Instructional Program

Employee: *Mary Ann*   Date:

Trainer: *Kim*   Environment:

Instructional cue: *"Ride the bus."*

Behavioral objective: *The employee will ride the city bus independently with 100% accuracy according to the attached task analysis (TA) for three consecutive probe trials.*

Instructional Procedure: *A system of least prompts and instructional prompts will be implemented to fade the response prompts needed during initial training. A three prompt hierarchy system will be used with this procedure to include verbal, gestural, and physical prompts. (Step numbers in task analysis refer to Figure 7.6.)*

Phase I: Initial skill acquisition

During this phase of training the trainer will be positioned *1 foot* from the new employee, initiating each training session with the instructional cue "Ride the bus."

1. Wait 3 seconds for self-initiation of step 1; see Figure 7.6 in the task analysis (TA).
2. If the employee completes the step independently, proceed to the next step in the TA.
3. If the employee begins to make an error or does not respond within 3 seconds, provide a verbal prompt specific to step 1 in the TA.
4. If the employee completes the step independently, verbally reinforce and move to the next step in the TA.
5. If the employee begins to make an error or does not respond within 3 seconds, simultaneously provide verbal and gestural prompt.
6. If the employee completes the step independently, verbally reinforce and move to the next step in the TA.
7. If the employee begins to make an error or does not respond within 3 seconds, repeat the verbal prompt and physically guide the employee through the response.
8. Verbally reinforce and move to the next step in the TA.
9. Repeat the procedure for each subsequent step in the TA until the task is completed.

(At no time will the trainer allow the employee to make an error.)

Reinforcement: Verbal reinforcement will be delivered immediately on each completed step of the TA during the first 3 days of training. For example, if the employee boards the correct bus, the trainer will immediately say, "Good boarding the bus."

Phase II

A. Fading proximity:

TA
Steps 1–13 @ 3 feet behind
Steps 14–16 @ 10 seats/rows
Steps 17–23 @ 3 feet behind
Steps 24–26 @ 10 seats/rows
Step 27 @ 3 feet behind

(continued)

Figure 7.5.   Instructional program for riding a city bus.

Figure 7.5   (*continued*)

B. Phase criterion:

During this phase of training Mary Ann will ride the city bus with the trainer positioned 3 feet away from her with 100% accuracy according to the attached TA for 2 consecutive probe trials.

C. Error correction:

If at any point the trainee does not make the correct response, this fading phase will be discontinued for the remainder of the training session. That is, the trainer will return to a 1 foot distance from the consumer. Verbal reinforcement will be provided at the end of the completed task. This distance will be maintained throughout the task on the succeeding day, after which time the trainer will return to the fading distance.

Phase III

A. Fading proximity:

TA   A
Steps 1–5 Trainer absent
Steps 6–13 Trainer @ 5 feet
Steps 14–16 Trainer @ rear of bus (maximum distance)
Steps 17–23 Trainer @ 5 feet
Steps 24–26 Maximum distance
Steps 27 Trainer @ 5 feet

B. Phase Criterion:

If an error occurs on any given step of the TA, the trainer will return to the procedures outlined in Phase II for the remainder of the training session. These procedures will also be implemented during the following training session.

Phase IV

A. Fading proximity:

TA
Steps 1–5   Trainer absent
                    Verification of bus stop
Steps 6–27 Trainer in automobile shadowing bus

B. Phase criterion:

Mary Ann will ride the city bus with the trainer absent for the first five steps and shadowing in automobile for the remainder of the activity with 100% accuracy according to the attached TA for 2 consecutive probe trials.

C. Error correction:

If an error occurs on any given step of the TA, the trainer will return to the procedure outlined in Phase III for the remainder of the training session. These procedures will also be implemented during the following training session.

(continued)

Figure 7.5   (*continued*)

Phase V

A. Fading proximity:

Steps 1– 17 Trainer absent
Steps 18– 27 Shadowing in automobile

B. Phase criterion:

Mary Ann will ride the city bus independently with trainer shadowing in automobile for the remainder of activity with 100% accuracy according to the attached TA for 2 consecutive probe trials.

C. Error correction:

If an error occurs on any given step of the TA, the trainer will return to the
procedures outlined in Phase IV for the remainder of the training session. These
procedures will also be implemented during the following training session.

Phase VI

A. Fading proximity:

TA   A
Steps 1– 27 = Trainer absent
                    Meet at work

B. Phase criterion:

Mary Ann will ride the city bus independently with trainer waiting at the job
site with 100% accuracy according to the TA for 2 consecutive probe trials.

C. Error correction:

If an error occurs on any given step of the TA, the trainer will return to the
procedures outlined in Phase V for the remainder of the training session. These
procedures will also be implemented during the subsequent training session.

Guidelines for Orientation to the Job Environment

There are some general guidelines that the employment specialist may find useful when
training an individual to orient herself or himself within the environment. Whatever approach is selected, it is important to remain consistent. Map out a plan and use it every
day. Do not try one approach one day and alter it the next. The list in Table 7.5 may be
helpful in planning consumer orientation to the environment (Barcus et al., 1987; Moon et
al., 1986).

INSTRUCTIONAL PLAN

Once the required skills, natural supports, natural reinforcers, and job-site orientation
requirements have been identified, the task of developing a plan for instructing the
worker in job skills and job-related skills should begin. The employment specialist should
develop a written individualized systematic instructional plan that details instructional
assistance for the employee to learn all identified job duties and identifies the natural
supports that will be utilized to assist the employee in achieving independent performance of the job. The plan includes a training schedule that clearly identifies when in-

Trainer: ___Kim_____

Employee: ___Mary Ann_____

Environment: ___Bus_____

Instructional cue: ___"Ride the bus to work"___

1. Get two tickets.				
2. Get appropriate transfer money.				
3. Get cue card(s).				
4. Put items in wallet/pocket.				
5. Walk to appropriate bus stop.				
6. Identify appropriate bus.				
7. Approach bus.				
8. Board bus.				
9. Secure ticket/money.				
10. Place ticket in slot.				
11. Place money in fare box.				
12. Get transfer ticket from driver.				
13. Locate seat in front.				
14. Identify transfer point.				
15. Signal for stop.				
16. Exit bus.				
17. Walk to transfer bus stop.				
18. Identify appropriate bus.				
19. Approach bus.				

Figure 7.6.   Task Analysis Record Sheet.

(continued)

Figure 7.6.   (continued)

20. Board bus.				
21. Hand transfer to driver.				
22. Locate seat in front.				
23. Identify destination.				
24. Signal for stop.				
25. Exit bus.				
26. Walk to destination.				

Total steps correct:
Percent correct:

Instructional code
+ = Correct
− = Incorrect
P = Physical prompt
V = Verbal
M = Model or gestural

Distance code
1 = within 3 feet
2 = 3–10 feet
3 = beyond 10 feet

tense systematic instruction will occur (Barcus et al., 1987). It also contains a detailed task analysis of each specific job duty or job-related skill (Moon et al., 1986). Instructional techniques such as prompting hierarchies and response cues should be detailed, along with an identification of the type and amount of reinforcement to be delivered during training (Barcus et al. 1987; Moon et al., 1986). The authors strongly feel that employment specialists working with persons who have severe mental retardation need to thoughtfully plan and map out the necessary procedures for ensuring acquisition, maintenance, and generalization of job skills and job-related skills (Wehman, Moon, Everson, Wood, & Barcus, 1988). All of the above critical elements that form an instructional plan are delineated and described in extensive detail in Chapter 8. The instructional plan for riding a city bus is an example of a program that incorporates all the critical elements of assisting a new employee to learn job skills.

FIRST DAY OF WORK

The first day of work can be overwhelming to the employment specialist as well to the new employee. It may be the employment specialist's introduction to a specific job (e.g., pot scrubbing, laundry) and the demands of performing this job to the employer's expectations. Additionally, it may be the first opportunity for the employment specialist to interact with the new employee in a community-based job setting. Frequently it is the new worker's first introduction to a competitive job in an integrated setting and to the employment specialist as an instructor.

Consumer: _____   Job site: _____

Employment specialist: _____   Date of hire: _____

		Check when independent or when support has been identified.	
		Identify the type of support when appropriate	Record date
1.	Locates job site from bus stop.	1.	1.
2.	Enters job site at employee entrance.	2.	2.
3.	Locates appropriate restroom.	3.	3.
4.	Locates employee telephone.	4.	4.
5.	Locates break area.	5.	5.
6.	Locates time clock.	6.	6.
7.	Locates work station.	7.	7.
8.	Locates work supply area.	8.	8.
9.	Identifies coworkers.	9.	9.
10.	Identifies supervisor.	10.	10.
11.	Locates supervisor's office.	11.	11.
12.	Knows where to obtain assistance.	12.	12.
13.	Exits job site at appropriate exit.	13.	13.
14.	Locates bus stop from job site.	14.	14.
Additional environments:			
15.	Locates locker in shop.	15.	15.
16.	Uses back passageway #1 (from pet store to shoe store).	16.	16.
17.	Uses back passageway #2 (from ice cream store to book store).	17.	17.
18.	Locates freight elevator to the north.	18.	18.

(Review environmental analysis to include all pertinent environments.)

Figure 7.7.   Orientation checklist based on analysis of the work environment conducted prior to the employee's first day of work.

It is not unusual for an employment specialist to experience some anxiety with each new placement. However, this tension can be alleviated by implementation of an organized plan to introduce the worker to his or her new job and help make the first day of work a positive experience for the employee and the employment specialist. Table 7.6 provides strategies that have been used by employment specialists to ensure a positive first day at work (Barcus et al., 1987; Mcloughlin et al., 1987; Moon et al., 1986).

First impressions are long lasting and difficult to change. While the employment specialist must be concerned with the employee's first impressions of the job, he or she must be equally aware of the perceptions of the supervisor and coworkers. If the strategies outlined in Table 7.6 are followed, they can help to create a relaxed work at-

Table 7.5.   Guidelines for becoming oriented to the job environment

Teach the worker to follow the same route from home to the job site each day.

Enter and exit the building using the same doors each day. (Use the employee entrance/exit when applicable.)

Follow the same path from the employee entrance to the time clock, employee locker, and/or supply room daily.

Teach the location of the employee's primary work station in relation to the time clock/supply room.

Teach the location of other work environments (i.e., restrooms, break area, lunch area, supervisor's office, emergency exits) in relationship to the primary work station (e.g., the pot sink or dishroom).

Teach the location of the employee's primary work station in relationship to the other work environments (i.e., restrooms, supply area, break area, lunch area, supervisor's office).

Teach a sequence of movements from environment to environment that will lead the worker through the performance of his or her job duties in the sequence in which they must be executed.

mosphere for the new employee. This type of organization and planning establishes the employment specialist and the employee as competent individuals from the first day of employment.

MONITORING PROGRESS

The employment specialist must continually assess the worker's strengths and newly developed skills in relationship to the demands of the job (Gold, 1980). During the orientation and assessment phase of job-site training, additional data about the worker and the job can be obtained. For example, the new employee who has never scrubbed pots may decide after working for a few days that she does not like pot scrubbing, or the employ-

Table 7.6.   Strategies for a successful first day of work

Prior to first day

   Determine transportation options.

   Discuss the pros and cons of each option with the worker (and family).

   Make a mutual decision on the most feasible option.

   Design a transportation training program (if necessary) prior to the first day of work.

   Tour the work place.

   Meet all supervisors and coworkers.

   Participate in company orientation for all new employees.

   Inform worker and family of worker's schedule.

First day of work

   Drive worker to job (postpone travel training until second day).

   Arrive at the work site 30 minutes early.

   Locate the restrooms, telephone, employee lounge, supervisor's office, and time clock.

   Clock in for work.

   Introduce worker to coworkers.

   Work alongside the new worker and assign the worker to a portion of a job task or a step of a job task that she or he can complete independently or without total supervision.

   Reinforce the worker frequently for performing the job duties, interacting appropriately with coworkers, and "hanging in there."

   Model appropriate work and social interaction habits.

ment specialist may discover that the worker has difficulty taking directions from a particular person. It is not unusual for an employer to remember after the trainer and worker have been on the job for a couple of days that the position has an additional duty that needs to be done during a particular time period. Therefore, the employment specialist must be open to adding, deleting, and modifying the original list of job duties. A task analytic approach should be used to identify and sequence job duties, establish a work routine, and design appropriate training methods whenever the original list of job duties is modified.

EMPLOYEE EVALUATIONS

Evaluation of a new employee's job performance begins on the first official day of work. The employment specialist relies on formal and informal evaluation techniques for determining the worker's progress. Informal feedback from daily observations, interactions, and discussions with the worker, his or her family, and coworkers let the employment specialist know whether the worker is adapting to the job demands.

In addition to daily informal feedback, it is imperative that the employment specialist obtain a formal evaluation from the department supervisor (Moon et al., 1986). Ultimately, how successfully the worker integrates into the work force hinges on the supervisor's perception of the worker as a company employee. The employment specialist should obtain the first employee evaluation from the supervisor 2 weeks from the first day of work (Sale, Wood, Barcus, & Moon, 1989). The second employee evaluation should be obtained at the end of the first month on the job (Sale et al., 1989). For the duration of the initial training/skill acquisition period, monthly employee evaluations are usually sufficient. Figure 7.8 shows a sample employee evaluation that a new employee received after the first 2 weeks of work.

PREPARING A PROGRESS REPORT

Information from each supervisor's evaluation is compiled by the employment specialist into a progress report, which is reviewed with the worker and his or her family or group home counselor (Moon et al., 1986). The progress report reflects the supervisor's evaluation of the worker's job performance and indicates to the family and the employee that the employment specialist is actively monitoring the worker's progress. Figure 7.9 is an example of a progress report that the employment specialist prepared after reviewing the supervisors' employee evaluations shown in Figure 7.8.

SOLVING MAJOR ORIENTATION AND ASSESSMENT PROBLEMS

Factors that influence the stability of a placement during the orientation and assessment phase include: employee's ability to get to the job, motivation to do the job, physical ability to meet the demands of the job, social behavior sufficient for the job, and parent/guardian support (Kiernan & Schalock, 1989; Wehman & Moon, 1988). Looking at these key factors will help identify potential job compatibility problems that may not have been apparent prior to placement.

If an employee appears to be having difficulty at the end of the orientation and assessment phase, the employment specialist should first consider simple adaptations to the job. For example, an employee must select his time card from among 60 employee time cards located beside the time clock. If the worker cannot recognize his name but can

VIRGINIA COMMONWEALTH UNIVERSITY
REHABILITATION RESEARCH AND TRAINING CENTER

SUPERVISOR'S EVALUATION FORM

Name: ___*Jane*_____

Job site: ___*Ashland Industries*_____

1. The employee arrives and leaves *on time.*

1	2	3	4	5
Much too seldom	Not often enough	Undecided	Usually	Always

2. The employee maintains good attendance.

1	2	3	4	5
Much too seldom	Not often enough	Undecided	Usually	Always

3. The employee takes meals and breaks appropriately.

1	2	3	4	5
Much too seldom	Not often enough	Undecided	Usually	Always

4. The employee maintains good appearance.

1	2	3	4	5
Much too seldom	Not often enough	Undecided	Usually	Always

5. The employee's performance compares favorably with the other workers' performance.

1	2	3	4	5
Much too seldom	Not often enough	Undecided	Usually	Always

6. Communication with the employee is not a problem.

1	2	3	4	5
Much too seldom	Not often enough	Undecided	Usually	Always

7. The employee attends to job tasks consistently.

1	2	3	4	5
Much too seldom	Not often enough	Undecided	Usually	Always

8. Your overall appraisal of the employee's proficiency at this time.

1	2	3	4	5
Needs immediate improvement	Somewhat below standard	Satisfactory	Somewhat better than required	Always better than required

9. Do you wish to meet with a representative from the RRTC staff?

_____ YES   _____ NO

Additional comments:

SIGNATURE: _____

Figure 7.8. Employee evaluation.

VIRGINIA COMMONWEALTH UNIVERSITY
REHABILITATION RESEARCH AND TRAINING CENTER

PROGRESS REPORT

Employee's name: _Jane_   Date: _1/26_

Job trainer: _Paul_   Date of hire: _12/20_

All items that pertain to your performance are circled below:

1. The employee   a. generally arrives and leaves on time
                    b. maintains good attendance
                    c. takes meals and breaks appropriately
                    d. maintains a good appearance

Comments on uncircled items: _Needs to carry a comb to work each day._

2. The employee has a. mastered all aspects of present job
                    b. mastered many, but not all aspects of job (specify):
                    c. not mastered essential aspects of job to date (spec-
                       ify): _is learning new aspects of job each day_

3. The employee is a. fast-paced worker
                    b. regular-paced worker
                    c. sometimes a slow worker
                    d. slow worker

Aspects of job that your family or guardian could help you with at home to improve your performance at work: _It would be very helpful for family members to remind Jane to comb her hair and reinforce Jane when her hair is neat._

Positive aspects of work performance:

Job trainer's signature: _Paul_

Figure 7.9. Progress report.

identify a specific color, attach a colored sticker to the worker's time card. The worker will not have to recognize a printed word but will be able to perform the task correctly and independently.

Other adaptations may involve modifying an employee's job duties. If one task out of an entire routine prevents the individual from meeting the job requirements, consider trading that duty with a coworker for a task that the worker is able to perform. For example, the worker could wipe down tables for a coworker while the coworker puts up stock. When job duties are traded, they should be of equal duration and responsibility. Modification of job duties is done only with the consent of the department supervisor. Table 7.7 lists common orientation problems and suggests strategies for remediation.

If the employment specialist does identify problems on the job, he may find it helpful to discuss them with knowledgeable individuals who are not as close to the situation. Someone with a fresh perspective often can offer a simple, yet effective solution. In some instances, the employment specialist may determine that the job duties cannot be modified or the skills systematically trained, and resignation from the job may be an appropriate last resort.

Table 7.7. Common orientation and assessment issues

Issue	Situation	Possible solution
Motivation	Motivation to work decreases after working for 2 hours	Divide one 15-minute break into two 7-minute breaks (with approval of supervisor only!).
	Money is not motivating to the individual.	Show how paychecks (money) can buy items of choice.
	Low motivation to get to work on time.	Set up reinforcement program with reward contingent upon getting to work on time.
Transportation	Family does not want son or daughter to ride a bus.	Explain bus training procedures.
	Employee misses bus to work.	Reasses transportation skills of individual; re-establish transportation training program if necessary.
	Employee is unable to count change for bus.	Buy tickets if appropriate or carry a card to match appropriate coins for fare.
Family/ guardian	Group home counselors do not ensure that resident is up in time for work.	Set up and demonstrate an alarm clock program for the individual.
	Family is afraid that employee will be fired.	Maintain close contact with family through telephone calls, home visits, and progress reports.
	Family fears that a coworker will ridicule and tease son/ daughter.	If possible, introduce parent to a coworker and explain advocacy program.
Social behavior	Worker is uncomfortable greeting coworker.	Role play shaking hands and smiling when greeted. Practice this new skill when coworker approaches.
	Individual has inappropriate topics of conversation.	Model appropriate conversation.
	Worker carries age inappropriate lunch box to work.	Assist employee in selection of appropriate lunch box.
Physical ability	Worker is unable to lift a heavy object	Ask coworker in immediate area to assist.
	Worker is unable to reach the glass rack over dishwasher.	Redesign work area or buy a stool for employee that can be stored under the counter when not being used.
	Worker is afraid to climb a ladder.	Practice climbing a ladder at break time or during off hours. If fear is profound or it is risky for individual to climb a ladder, see if job could be modified.

In situations where the employment specialist feels that counseling the worker to resign is the only answer, it is necessary that the employment specialist know that everything possible has been done to save the placement. Seeking a second opinion from another employment specialist or from the supported work program supervisor reassures the employment specialist that resignation is the most appropriate course of action for a worker. Although the loss of a job may be traumatic for the worker and his or her family, the employment specialist can emphasize the benefits the worker derived from a competitive job. For example, during the period of employment, no matter how brief, the individual earned decent wages for performing valued work in an integrated setting. If resignation or termination does occur, explain to the worker and the family or group home counselor that another, more appropriate job will be sought for the individual. In addition, accentuating the worker's general abilities, while downplaying inability to complete specific portions of a job, eases the feelings of failure and disappointment that often arise.

Realize that job loss is difficult for all concerned (including the employment specialist), but remain upbeat about the individual's future job prospects. Job placement mistakes will be made; the employment specialist can deal with them gracefully and use them to enrich his or her experience as an employment specialist. If the job is appropriate for another individual in the referral pool, the employment specialist can negotiate with the employer for another worker to fill it. Employers generally are willing to do this since it means that they will not have to undertake a lengthy recruiting/interviewing/hiring process of their own. In addition, the supported work model ensures that the job is completed to standard from day 1; therefore, the change in workers will not create a significant interruption in work production. Production should remain stable from one worker to the next. Table 7.8 provides a list of some reasons for the resignation or termination of a worker during the orientation and assessment phase of job-site training.

SUMMARY

The initial component of job-site training is referred to as orientation and assessment and begins prior to the worker's first day of employment. Orientation and assessment can last a few days to several weeks, with the length of time depending on the complexity of the job, skill level of the employment specialist, and the skill level of the worker. It requires the employment specialist to analyze the skills necessary to perform the job, identify the natural supports and reinforcement available, and identify the orientation requirements. An instructional plan is developed before the employee's first day of employment, and the employment specialist is expected to work alongside the new employee for the entire workday. He or she may also need to work before and after the scheduled job hours providing transportation training for the worker. Solving orientation and assessment problems can involve seeking sources of second opinion. Orientation and assessment training may be considered complete when the worker has become familiar with the general expectations of the job and can move about within his or her job site without assistance from the employment specialist. Monitoring the worker's progress on the job may identify a need for modification of the original list of job duties. Formal and informal

Table 7.8. Reasons for termination or resignation of employment during orientation and assessment

Action initiated by	Reason
Employee	Dislikes particular job or job duties. Low motivation to work (refuses to work even after a formal reinforcement program is initiated).
Parent	Job too physically demanding. Fear of loss of benefits.
Employer	Economic recession. Insubordinate employee behavior toward employer. Employee stealing. Chronic tardiness/absenteeism. Grossly inappropriate social behavior.
Employment specialist	Poor employee/job match. Insufficient information obtained during consumer assessment. Inadequate job analysis. Change in job duties.

techniques for performance evaluation should be used. A progress report should be reviewed with the worker and his or her family. Job-site adaptations may be needed. If resignation or termination cannot be avoided, the positive aspects of the consumer's job experience should be highlighted for both the consumer and the employment specialist.

REFERENCES

Barcus, M., Brooke, V., Inge, K., Moon, S., & Goodall, P. (1987). *An instructional guide for training on a job site: A supported employment resource.* Richmond, VA: Virginia Commonwealth University, Rehabilitation Research and Training Center.

Belmore, K., & Brown, L. (1978). A job skill inventory strategy for severely handicapped potential workers. In N. Haring & D. Bricker (Eds.), *Teaching the severely handicapped* (pp. 223–262). Seattle, WA: American Association for the Education of the Severely and Profoundly Handicapped.

Brass, D. (1985). Men's and women's networks: A study of interaction patterns and influence in an organization. *Academy of Management Journal, 28,* 327–343.

Buckley, J. (1988). *Employment training specialists: Job description, training, and evaluation.* Eugene, OR: University of Oregon, Specialized Training Program.

Chadsey-Rusch, J., & Rusch, F.R. (1988). Ecology of the workplace. In R. Gaylord-Ross (Ed.), *Vocational education for persons with handicaps* (pp. 234–256). Mountain View, CA: Mayfield.

Ford, A., & Mirenda, P. (1984). Community instruction: A natural cues and corrections decision model. *Journal of The Association for Persons with Severe Handicaps, 9* (2), 79–87.

Gold, M.W. (1980). *Did I say that? Articles and commentary on the try another way system.* Champaign, IL: Research Press.

Googins, B. (1989). Support in integrated work settings: The role played by industry through employee assistance programs. In W.E. Kiernan & R.L. Schalock (Eds.), *Economics, industry, and disability: A look ahead* (pp. 223–235). Baltimore: Paul H. Brookes Publishing Co.

Henderson, M., & Argyle, M. (1985). Social support by four categories of work colleague: Relationships between activities, stress, and satisfaction. *Journal of Occupational Behavior, 6,* 229–239.

Hirszowicz, M. (1982). *Industrial sociology.* New York: St. Martins.

Kiernan, W.E., & Schalock, R.L. (Eds.). (1989). *Economics, industry, and disability: A look ahead.* Baltimore: Paul H. Brookes Publishing Co.

Kirmeyer, S., & Lin, T. (1986). Social supports: Its relationship to observed communication with peers and superiors. *Academy of Management Journal, 28,* 110–132.

Mcloughlin, C.S., Garner, J.B., & Callahan, M. (1987). *Getting employed, staying employed: Job development and training for persons with severe handicaps.* Baltimore: Paul H. Brookes Publishing Co.

Moon, M.S., Goodall, P., Barcus, M., & Brooke, V. (Eds.). (1986). *The supported work model of competitive employment for citizens with severe handicaps: A guide for job trainers.* Richmond, VA: Virginia Commonwealth University, Rehabilitation Research and Training Center.

Moon, M.S., & Griffin, S.L. (1988). *Supported employment service delivery models.* In P. Wehman & M.S. Moon (Eds.), Vocational Rehabilitation and Supported Employment (pp. 17–30). Baltimore: Paul H. Brookes Publishing Co.

Nisbet, J., & Callahan, M. (1987). Achieving success in integrated work places: Critical elements in assisting persons with severe disabilities. In S.J. Taylor, D. Biklen, & J. Knoll (Eds.), Community integration for people with severe disabilities (pp. 184–201). New York: Teachers College Press.

Nisbet, J., & Hagner, D. (1988). Natural supports in the work place: A reexamination of supported employment. *Journal of The Association for Persons with Severe Handicaps, 13*(4), 260–267.

Rusch, F.R. (Ed.). (1986). *Competitive employment issues and strategies.* Baltimore: Paul H. Brookes Publishing Co.

Rusch, F.R., & Mithaug, D.M. (1980). *Vocational training for mentally retarded adults: A behavior analytic approach.* Champaign, IL: Research Press.

Sale, P., Wood, W., Barcus, J.M., & Moon, M.S. (1989). *The role of the employment specialist.* In W.E. Kiernan & R.L. Schalock (Eds.), *Economic, industry, and disability: A look ahead* (pp. 187–205). Baltimore: Paul H. Brookes Publishing Co.

Shafer, M.S. (1986). Utilizing co-workers as change agents. In F.R. Rusch (Ed.), *Competitive employment issues and strategies* (pp. 215–224). Baltimore: Paul H. Brookes Publishing Co.

Shafer, M., & Nisbet, J. (1988). Integration and empowerment in the work place. In M. Barcus, S. Griffin, D. Mank, L. Rhodes, & M.S. Moon (Eds.), *Supported employment implementation issues: A summary of discussions from the VCU RRTC employment network issues forum* (45–72). Richmond, VA: Virginia Commonwealth University, Rehabilitation Research and Training Center.

Snell, M.E. (Ed.). (1987). *Systematic instruction of persons with severe handicaps* (3rd ed.). Columbus, OH: Charles E. Merrill.

Snell, M.E., & Browder, D.M. (1986). Community-referenced instruction: Research and issues. *Journal of The Association for Persons with Severe Handicaps, 11*(1), 1–11.

Sundstrom, E. (1986). *Work places.* Cambridge: Cambridge University Press.

Sweet, M., Shiraga, B., Ford, A., Nisbet, J., Graff, S., & Loomis, R. (1982). Vocational training: Archeological strategies applicable for severely multihandicapped students? In L. Brown, J. Nisbet, A. Ford, M. Sweet, B. Shiraga, & L. Gruenewald (Eds.), *Educational programs for severely handicapped students* (Vol. XII, pp. 99–131). Madison, WI: Madison Metropolitan School District.

Wehman, P., & Moon, M.S. (Eds.). (1988). *Vocational rehabilitation and supported employment.* Baltimore: Paul H. Brookes Publishing Co.

Wehman, P., Moon, M.S., Everson, J.M., Wood, W., & Barcus, J.M. (1988). *Transition from school to work: New challenges for youth with severe disabilities.* Baltimore: Paul H. Brookes Publishing Co.

INITIAL TRAINING AND SKILL
ACQUISITION ON THE JOB

8

The initial training and skill acquisition element of job-site training involves the direct instruction of job duties and related nonvocational skills (Moon, Goodall, Barcus, & Brooke, 1986). An employment specialist begins systematic instruction during the first day of a worker's employment, and he or she is available to be at the job site on a full-time basis for as long as necessary (Kiernan & Stark, 1986; Moon et al., 1986; Rusch, 1986; Wehman & Moon, 1988).

The major objective of initial training and skill acquisition is instruction and the utilization of natural supports, which enable the employee to perform the required job duties accurately, with decreasing amounts of assistance from the employment specialist (Barcus, Brooke, Inge, Moon, & Goodall, 1987; Mcloughlin, Garner, & Callahan, 1987). This component of job-site instruction may vary in length from several weeks to several months, depending on the complexity of the work environment (Moon et al., 1986). Factors such as the complexity of the job, the employment specialist's instructional skill level, and the worker's experience will have an impact on the effectiveness of the instruction and ultimately the success of the employee. This chapter describes strategies and techniques critical for the employment specialist to understand and consider when implementing systematic instructional programs in integrated employment settings.

SYSTEMATIC INSTRUCTION

Systematic instructional strategies are what most trainers use to instruct employees with severe mental retardation to perform job tasks such as folding laundry, polishing silverware, washing windows, or dry mopping floors, and related skills such as use of public transportation, communication with coworkers, and appropriate use of meal and break time (Nisbet & Callahan, 1987). When selecting and utilizing instructional strategies, the trainer should always consider and respect the dignity of the worker. The employment specialist must identify the employee's initial performance level on all job skills prior to implementing the instructional plan. Instruction should be modified as determined by ongoing assessment of the employee's progress in learning to perform the job tasks. Effective response prompts and cues, along with response chains, must be identified through careful analysis of instructional data records. Finally, all instructional procedures should include the systematic fading of intervention by the employment specialist.

Determining Initial Job Performance Level

It is imperative for the employment specialist to determine the inital job performance level of the worker. One of the best ways to do this is through task analytic assessment (Barcus et al., 1987; Bellamy, Horner, & Inman, 1981; Snell, 1987). The critical element of this assessment is providing the worker with the opportunity to perform the job-task steps independently, without providing the worker with feedback, prompting, or reinforcement. This type of data is referred to as probe data or continuing assessment data (Moon et al., 1986; Wehman, Moon, Everson, Wood & Barcus, 1988). It should be collected at least once a week and always prior to beginning a training period. Probe data are recorded simply with (+) for a step done correctly and (−) for a step done incorrectly (Barcus et al., 1987; Moon et al., 1986; Snell, 1987; Wehman et al., 1988). This lets the employment specialist know when the new employee is performing a specific task correctly and independently. The employment specialist should consider a job task learned when all steps in the task analysis are performed independently by the worker for three or four consecutive probe trails (Wehman et al., 1988). One way to ensure correct performance is to continue to collect probe data at least once a week after training has begun. This type of assessment can be completed as the employment specialist visits the job site long after he or she is no longer present on a daily basis.

There are two different ways that probe data can be collected using a task analysis (Snell, 1987). One method is referred to as multiple opportunity (Snell, 1987). Through this method, the employee is assessed on his or her ability to perform every step of the task analysis independently. The second procedure is known as the single opportunity method (Snell, 1987) and calls for discontinuing the probe as soon as the individual makes an error. The obvious advantage to the first method of probe data collection is that a more accurate description of employee performance is obtained. However, most employment specialists will find the second procedure to be more efficient (Barus et al., 1987; Moon et al., 1986). Data collection on the job site needs to be accurate but not time consuming (Barcus et al., 1987; Moon et al., 1986; Wehman et al., 1988). Sometimes probing every step in a task will interrupt the natural flow of work at the job site. Therefore, discontinuing the probe as soon as an error occurs, the single opportunity method, may be the data collection procedure of choice. Specific guidelines for each type of probe are described in Table 8.1. (Barcus et al., 1987; Moon et al., 1986; Snell, 1987; Wehman et al., 1988).

The task analysis recording sheet shown in Figure 8.1 shows probe data collected for washing trays at a cafeteria. The employment specialist collected probe data on tray washing three times during the first day at work for an employee named Charlie. The probe checks were scattered throughout the workday for an accurate picture of Charlie's performance during the entire workday. The employment specialist began the assessment by asking Charlie to wash the trays without any assistance. She discontinued the probe as soon as he made an error. The probe data for this task indicate that Charlie is initially performing 3 steps out of a total of 14 necessary to complete the task of washing trays independently.

Response Prompts

Prompts used during acquisition training to facilitate correct responses include verbal instructions, gestures, modeling, and physical assists. Anyone of these techniques can be used during job-site training. However, the most important factor to consider when

Table 8.1.   Guidelines for collecting probe data

Multiple opportunity

1. Have the worker move to the appropriate work area unless movement is part of the task analysis.
2. Stand beside or behind the worker so that data collection does not interrupt the work flow.
3. Tell the worker that he or she is going to work without assistance to see how much he or she can do independently.
4. Provide the work cue (i.e., "Scrub the pots").
5. Do not provide any prompts or reinforcement.
6. Wait 3–5 seconds for the employee to initiate a response.
7. Record (+) for correct performance or (−) for incorrect performance in the left side of each box on the task analysis record sheet.
8. If response is incorrect, set the worker up to perform the next step in the task analysis. Repeat until the entire task has been tested.

Single opportunity

1. Have the worker move to the appropriate work area unless movement is part of the task analysis.
2. Stand beside or behind the worker so that data collection does not interrupt the work flow.
3. Tell the worker that he or she is going to work without assistance to see how much he or she can do independently.
4. Provide the work cue (i.e., "Scrub the pots").
5. Do not provide any prompts or reinforcement.
6. Wait 3–5 seconds for the employee to make a response.
7. If he or she does not begin to work, discontinue the probe and score (−) for incorrect performance in the left side of each box on the task analysis record sheet.
8. If he or she begins to work, allow him or her to continue working as long as correct responses are being made. Score (+) for correct performance in the left side of each box on the task analysis record sheet.
9. As soon as an error is made, discontinue the probe and score (−) for the remaining steps in the task analysis.

choosing prompts is selecting those prompts that most naturally occurr within a specific work environment. For example, if an employee is working in an industrial laundry facility, model prompts may be most natural, since the worker can usually watch others use the machines, fold laundry, or put clean items away. Before any prompts can be used effectively, the job duty must be task analyzed as described in Chapter 7. After this has been completed, the trainer may try various types of prompts on each step to determine which is the most effective. Generally, the least amount of prompting necessary should be used. A description of each type of prompt follows.

Verbal Instructions   Verbally instructing the worker is usually the most natural form of assistance provided in the work setting, since verbal directions from a supervisor or coworker often serve as cues for employees (Bellamy et al., 1981; Mank & Horner, 1988; Mcloughlin et al., 1987; Snell, 1987; Snell & Browder, 1986). Instruction for individuals with severe mental retardation should be short, direct, and related to each step in the task analysis (Gold, 1980). In fact, each step in a task analysis should be written in the form of a short verbal prompt (Buckley, 1988; Chadsey-Rusch & Rusch, 1988; Mank & Horner, 1988).

Gestures   Pairing a verbal prompt with a gesture, such as pointing in a desired direction, is another form of assistance given to an employee in the work place (Moon et al., 1986; Snell, 1987; Snell & Browder, 1986). Gesturing is a form of communication that allows employees to participate in work and social interactions with supervisors and co-

Trainer: Wendy Parent Employee: Charlie Environment: Snack bar Instructional cue: "Wash the trays."	Probe	Probe	Probe	Prompt	Prompt	Prompt	Prompt	Prompt
1. Go to counter.	+/	+/	+/	+/1	+/1	+/1	+/1	+/1
2. Put spray bottle on counter.	+/	+/	+/	+/1	+/1	+/1	+/1	+/1
3. Put cloth on tray.	+/	+/	+/	+/1	+/1	+/1	+/1	+/1
4. Pick up trays.	−/	+/	−/	p/1	p/1	p/1	m/1	m/1
5. Go to other counter.	−/	−/	−/	m/1	m/1	m/1	m/1	m/1
6. Pick up trays.	−/	−/	−/	p/1	p/1	p/1	m/1	m/1
7. Go to other counter.	−/	−/	−/	m/1	m/1	m/1	v/1	v/1
8. Pick up trays.	−/	−/	−/	m/1	m/1	m/1	m/1	m/1
9. Go to kitchen.	−/1	−/1	−/1	m/1	m/1	m/1	m/1	m/1
10. Wash trays.	−/	−/	−/	p/1	p/1	p/1	p/1	p/1
11. Put trays away.	−/	−/	−/	p/1	p/1	p/1	p/1	p/1
12. Wash cloth.	−/	−/	−/	p/1	p/1	p/1	p/1	p/1
13. Wash hands.	−/	−/	−/	p/1	p/1	m/1	m/1	m/1
14. Go to dining area.	−/	−/	−/	m/1	m/1	m/1	m/1	m/1
Total steps correct	3	4	3	3	3	3	3	3
Percent correct	21%	28%	21%	21%	21%	21%	21%	21%

Instructional Code

+ = Correct   V = Verbal
− = Incorrect M = Model or gestural prompt
P = Physical prompt

Distance Code

1 = within 3 feet
2 = 3–10 feet
3 = beyond 10 feet

Figure 8.1. Task analysis record sheet for initial performance data.

workers. Gestures can involve pointing, tapping, or touching the correct choice (e.g., touching the appropriate sanitizing agent for rinse water).

Models Modeling a step of the task analysis involves demonstrating that step and then waiting for the employee to copy that behavior (Mank & Horner, 1988; Mcloughlin et al., 1987; Snell, 1987). Modeling should always be performed alongside the employee rather than across from or in front of an individual. This allows the employee to view the job skill as it is to be performed and does not require him of her to reverse the direction of the modeled step.

Physical Assists   Physical assists (i.e., hands-on assistance) may be required for some employees to complete portions of a task (Barcus et al. 1987; Mcloughlin et al. 1987; Snell, 1987). For example, when instructing an employee to sweep the floor, physical prompting may require that the employment specialist stand behind the employee, place his or her hand with the employee's on the broom, and move it in the appropriate sweeping pattern. Fast paced or crowded work environments are not the best place for this type of assistance.

Table 8.2 shows examples of response prompts used by employment specialists with Virginia Commonwealth University's Rehabilitation Research and Training Center. These prompts (verbal instructions, gestures, modeling, physical assists) were used in various employment settings to facilitate worker performance of job tasks.

Least Intrusive Prompts

One way to systematically fade the response prompts needed during initial training is to use a system of least intrusive prompts (Barcus et al., 1987; Moon et al; 1986; Snell, 1987). This allows the employment specialist to progress from verbal to model or gestural to physical prompts on each step of a task not performed correctly until one type of prompt stimulates the correct response. Most important, the employee is not given the opportunity to make an error. The employment specialist should always be ready to interrupt the beginning of an error or, in the case of no response, be ready to give the next prompt in the system of least intrusive prompts. Guidelines for training using a response prompt hierarchy are included in Table 8.3 (Barcus et al., 1987; Moon et al., 1986).

Table 8.4 gives a brief description of how a least intrusive prompt program was designed. There are several key components to a least intrusive prompt program. The trainer must select prompts that assist the worker to perform the task. A reinforcer must

---

Table 8.2.   Examples of response prompts used in employment settings

Verbal Instructions
  "Clean the tables."
  "Mop the floor."
  "Clean the windows."

Gestures
  Touching a stack of aprons to prompt the employee to put on an apron.
  Pointing to the time clock to remind an individual to punch in before work.
  Tapping a wrist watch to prompt the employee to take a lunch break.

Models
  Employment specialist gives cue "Fold the towels," and simultaneously demonstrates folding a towel.
  Give cue "Clean the window," and simultaneously squirt window with cleaning solution.
  Give cue "Turn on the water," and simultaneously turn the faucet handle.

Physical Assists
  Employment specialist uses his or her own hands over the employee's hands to guide the worker in sweeping a floor mat.
  Employment specialist touches the employee's elbow to guide her or him to pick up a cleaning rag.
  Employment specialist grasps the worker's hand and places it on a plate simultaneously with the cue "Pick up the plate."

Table 8.3.   Guidelines for using a response prompt hierarchy

1. Have the employee move to the appropriate work area unless movement is part of the task analysis (TA).
2. Stand behind or beside the worker so that you can provide prompts quickly when necessary.
3. Provide cue to begin task (e.g., "Wash the mirror").
4. Wait 3–5 seconds for self-initiation of Step 1 in the TA.
5. If the worker completes the step independently, proceed to Step 2 of the TA.
6. If the worker is incorrect or does not respond within 3–5 seconds, provide a verbal prompt specific to Step 1 in the TA (e.g., "Pick up the cleaner")
7. If the worker completes the step independently, reinforce and move to Step 2.
8. If the worker is incorrect or does not respond within 3–5 seconds, repeat the verbal prompt (e.g., "Pick up the cleaner") and simultaneously model the response (employment specialist picks up cleaner).
9. If the worker completes the step independently, reinforce and move to Step 2.
10. If the worker is incorrect or does not respond within 3–5 seconds, repeat the verbal prompt ("Pick up the cleaner") and physically guide the worker through the response (employment specialist guides the worker's hand to the cleaner).
11. Reinforce and move to Step 2.
12. Repeat the procedure for each step in the TA until the job duty is completed.
13. Always immediately interrrupt an error with the next prompt in the least prompt system.

be determined along with a schedule for delivery of the reinforcement, and error correction procedures should be clearly established.

Time Delay

Another way to systematically fade instructional prompts is known as time delay (Snell, 1987; Touchette, 1971). This procedure is also an errorless learning strategy that initially

Table 8.4.   Least intrusive prompts program

Component of least intrusive prompts	Patty's program components
1. Select a prompting hierarchy that the worker responds to consistently.	Patty responds to verbal instructions and both modeling and physical prompts have been effective.
2. Identify a reinforcer.	Patty is not currently motivated by the natural reinforcer (paycheck) for the job. She does respond to verbal praise.
3. Determine a schedule of reinforcement.	Verbal praise will be given after successful completion of each step. When Patty performs 50% of the steps in the task analysis (TA) independently, reinforcement will be given only after nonprompted correct responses and at completion of the entire task. When Patty completes 75% of the TA independently, reinforcement will be delivered on every other nonprompted correct response and at the completion of the entire task.
4. Specify time period within which the worker is to respond.	Patty will be given 10 seconds for self-initiation of a step of the TA.
5. Error correction procedure.	Errors will be interrupted using a system of least prompts (verbal, model, physical). Upon initiation of an incorrect response or no response within 10 seconds, the trainer will begin with the least intrusive prompt (verbal). If an incorrect response is initiated or there is no response within 10 seconds, a model prompt will be given. If Patty does not respond correctly in 10 seconds, a physical prompt is given.

pairs a controlling stimulus (prompt) with a second stimulus (task request and materials). Time delay can be implemented in two different ways: progressive time delay or constant time delay. To review: when implementing a progressive time-delay procedure, the trainer first selects a prompt that will consistently assist the worker to perform the task correctly. Initially the prompt is given simultaneously with the request to perform the task, this is referred to as 0-second delay (Snell & Gast, 1981). By initial pairing of the prompt with the request to perform a skill, the worker is not allowed to make errors (Snell, 1987). The trainer allows gradually increasing amounts of time (usually seconds) to elapse between giving the request to perform the task and providing the assistance or prompt to complete the skill correctly. For example, training for the initial set of trials is done at 0 seconds, the next set at 2 seconds, the next at 4 seconds, and so forth. The employment specialist provides the overall cue to complete the task and then delays the prompt to provide time for the worker to perform independently. The prompt is always delivered if the consumer begins to make an error or has not performed within the delay period.

Constant time delay also begins the training with a predetermined number of trials at 0-second delay. However, after the initial trials are conducted, a constant interval (e.g., 3 seconds) is selected for all remaining trials. Guidelines for training using a time-delay procedure are shown in Table 8.5. Also refer to Chapter 4 for additional information on the use of either time-delay strategy. Figure 8.2 is a completed program format for teaching an individual to purchase a snack at break time using progressive time delay.

Response Cues

Cueing is a method of prompting similar to model prompts and involves directing the employee's attention to appropriate materials without using physical contact. Cueing during job-site training normally means pairing one or more dimensions of color, shape, or

---

Table 8.5.   Guidelines for progressive time delay

1. Specify number of training trials to be conducted at 0-second delay.

2. Specify time-delay intervals (i.e., 2, 4, 6 or 1, 2, 3, 4) and number of training trials to be conducted at each interval.

3. Select a reinforcer and specify how it will be delivered.

4. Select *one* prompt for training that the employee consistently responds to correctly.

5. Design an error correction procedure; for example, specify that all errors will be interrupted immediately. If three errors occur consecutively, return to a pre-determined number of training trials at 0-second delay. When these are completed, return to the previous delay level.

6. Implement procedure:

   Have the employee move to the appropriate work area unless movement is part of the task analysis.

   Provide the overall cue to begin the task.

   Wait the specified time period based on the pre-determined time-delay intervals.

   If the worker performs independently, provide reinforcement and move to next step.

   If no response within the specified time, provide the prompt and reinforce the worker for step completion. Move to next step in the task.

   Interrupt all errors immediately and provide the selected prompt.

   Implement the error correction procedure if the worker makes 3 errors in a row on the same step of the task analysis.

NOTE: The guidelines for a constant time-delay procedure follow the same steps outlined above with one exception. After the initial trials at 0-seconds are completed, training during all other trials is done at the selected *constant delay*, for example, 3 seconds, until the worker meets skill acquisition.

Consumer: Chris
Job Site: Hotel
Position: Laundry attendant
Schedule: Tuesday–Saturday 11:30 A.M.–3:30 P.M.
Employment Specialist:
Program: Using a vending machine during break

Objective: Given a money card with a picture of an item to purchase and the amount it costs, Chris will match his coins to the card and purchase a snack with 100% accuracy according to the steps in the task analysis for three consecutive training sessions.

Data Collection Procedures: Provide the overall cue, "Chris, buy a snack." Wait 3 seconds for a response. If correct, record a (+) for all steps correctly completed. As soon as Chris makes an error score a (−) on that step of the task analysis and all remaining steps. Discontinue testing and implement training procedures.

Behavior Change Procedures:
1. Make arrangements with Chris's family for him to have change in his pockets on a daily basis.
2. Determine the snacks that Chris would like to purchase from the vending machine.
3. Make a money card for each of these items that will fit into Chris's wallet.
4. Develop a task analysis for the program including steps for using cue cards.
5. Provide a cue to signal break, that is, pair telling Chris that it is break time with break time for his coworker, Mary.
6. Say "Mary's taking her break, get your snack."
7. Use a progressive time day procedure with a model prompt for training in using the cards.
8. Train for two days during all breaks at 0-second delay.
9. That is, provide the cue and simultaneously provide the model prompt for the first step in the task analysis. As soon as a step is completed, provide verbal reinforcement and immediately model the next step in the task.
10. After 2 days at 0 seconds, follow by 2 days at 4 seconds.
11. After 6 days, training for all remaining trials will be done at 5-second delay until skill acquisition.

Error Correction: Interrupt any error with a physical prompt immediately. Do not reinforce Chris after error correction. If three errors occur in a row, drop back to the previous delay level for one session of training trials.

Intervention Data:

Score (+) for independent/unprompted responses
Score (m) for prompted correct responses
Score (−) for incorrect responses

Reinforcement Type and Schedule: Reinforce Chris with praise for all independent correct responses. Reinforce prompted correct responses with praise on the average of every three steps in the task analysis. The reinforcement of obtaining a snack occurs naturally at the end of the task. After skill acquisition, fade the use of praise by designing a strategy at that time.

Figure 8.2.   Instructional program for progressive time delay.

size—which are redundancy cues—with the correct choice (Snell, 1987). An example that was used in Chapter 7 is the employee who has to select his or her time card from a time card rack that holds the time cards of 60 employees. Attaching a sticker of a specific color to the employee's time card may be all that is needed for him or her to identify the correct card. An example of a permanent cue was used to assist an employee named Marie in remembering the correct sequence for hanging rubber curtain dividers inside a dishwasher. The employment specialist made a small color drawing of the correct order of curtains and taped it to the dishwasher. This picture cue allowed Marie to complete the step without trainer assistance. Eventually Marie no longer needed the picture, but the supervisor asked to keep the picture posted for the employees on the two other shifts who experienced difficulty with the same task.

Matching-to-sample is also a type of cueing that can be used easily during job-site instruction. When instructing using the match-to-sample method, the employment specialist cues the correct response by showing the learner a sample of the correct choice. For example, when the employee is required to stack clean dishes on a dish dolly, the employment specialist can place a sample piece of dinnerware into each appropriate compartment on the dolly. The employee is then able to match the dishes to be stacked with the sample of dinnerware already in each compartment. Other match-to-sample ideas that have been used on job sites include: 1) a picture of silverware placed next to slots on a cafeteria silverware holder, 2) a red mark on a scale indicating the appropriate weight for counting forms in lots of 50, and 3) a piece of tape on the wall marking the height for stacking 20 towels.

Response Chains

Nearly all vocational tasks can be classified as response chains, because in order for the worker to learn the next step of the task analysis, he or she must have attended to the previous step in the sequence (Chadsey-Rusch & Rusch, 1988; Mcloughlin et al., 1987; Snell, 1987). The steps of this chain (the task analysis) must be performed in sequence, but they can be taught in a forward or backward progression. Additionally, the entire sequence for a task can be taught during a training session.

Simultaneous training on all steps in the task analysis (teaching the total task) is the preferred strategy, since the worker can practice each step as it naturally occurs (Snell, 1987). With this method, response prompting techniques, such as the system of least prompts or time delay, can be applied easily. However, in some cases a forward chaining technique may be necessary.

Forward Chaining   When beginning instruction using the forward chaining method, the employment specialist instructs the employee to perform the first step of the task analysis. No other instruction takes place until the employee is able to perform this step of the task analysis independently. Once the employee performs step one independently, the employment specialist begins instruction on step two, but requires the employee to continue performing step one. As the employee learns to perform each new step independently, the chain of performance is lengthened until the employee can complete all steps in the task analysis independently (Bellamy et al., 1981; Mcloughlin et al., 1987; Snell, 1987).

Another method of forward chaining involves beginning by training the employee to complete all steps in the task analysis, proceeding from the first step to the last. The employment specialist gives a general cue for the employee to complete the entire task. If necessary, a prompt is provided for the worker to complete each step in the task analysis. Refer to the "Least Intrusive Prompts" section earlier in this chapter for more on instruction using the least prompt strategy for providing training in all steps of a task simultaneously. Figure 8.3 shows an instructional program using forward chaining to teach an employee named Michael the procedure for cleaning windows.

Backward Chaining   When using the backward chaining method of instruction, the employment specialist completes or assists the employee in completing all the steps in a task analysis and then instructs the employee to complete the last step in the chain. No other instruction takes place until the employee is able to independently perform this step. Once the worker is performing the last step independently, the employment specialist begins instruction on the next step, working backwards in the chain (Snell, 1987). The employee is required to independently perform the steps learned as instruction progresses from the last step to the first step in the task analysis. Please note that this procedure has not been used frequently in job-site training by RRTC staff. We have found that most job tasks lend themselves to instruction using a forward chaining procedure with simultaneous training in all steps in the sequence. Figure 8.4 shows an instructional program using time delay and backward chaining to teach an employee named Martha to press and stack napkins.

Deciding whether to teach all steps of a task simultaneously or to use a forward or backward chaining method should be determined after reviewing the results of the probe data. If the assessment data reflect correct performance consistently across the steps of the task, consider teaching all steps simultaneously. However, if the first few steps of the task are critical to the entire task (e.g., latching the sink drains to begin pot scrubbing) or if the data reflect very low performance, then a forward chaining method may be more appropriate.

Reinforcement Procedures for Job-Site Training

Before job placement, and during the orientation and assessment phase of job-site training, the employment specialist will spend time investigating the likes and dislikes of the new employee. This process was explained in Chapter 7 and involves interviewing the employee, the parent or guardian, and significant others who can provide a list of reinforcers for the employee. This list is used to select specific reinforcers to be included in the instructional program for training in a new job skill. It is hoped that only natural reinforcers, such as verbal praise or receiving a paycheck, will be necessary; however, other options may be needed during the initial phases of training. Regardless of the type of reinforcer chosen, the employment specialist must consider several factors, including the timing and the schedule of delivery. Table 8.6 shows guidelines to follow when using reinforcement at a job site (Barcus et al., 1987; Mank & Horner, 1988; Moon et al., 1986; Snell, 1987).

Timing   The timing of reinforcement delivery is critical when attempting to increase the probability of a behavior recurring. All reinforcement should be given quickly and immediately following the occurrence of the desired behavior. For example, the employment specialist for a worker named Marie immediately told her, "Good using two hands!" when she simultaneously picked up a glass in each hand. By immediately praising a specific skill, the employment specialist increased the likelihood of Marie repeating the desired behavior. If the employment specialist had waited until breaktime to tell Marie that she had done a nice job, an increase in the particular behavior praised would have been doubtful.

Sometimes it is not feasible to deliver a reward immediately. This is especially true if a tangible reward, such as a cup of coffee or a magazine, has been selected for use at the job site. The employment specialist would not want to provide a sip of coffee each

Consumer: Michael

Job site: Mall

Position: Janitor

Schedule: Monday–Friday, 7:00 A.M.–11:30 A.M.

Employment specialist:

Program: Training independent performance on cleaning upper window panes of the main entrances at the mall. Each window set must be cleaned one time per week. Michael currently cleans the lower panes at each entrance using a horizontal wiping pattern to complete these duties. Cleaning the upper panes will require the following task modifications:

1. Use of an extended step ladder to obtain the height needed to clean each upper pane.
2. Correct positioning of the step ladder in front of each window pane to be cleaned.
3. Fitting an extension pole on the handles of the squeegee and sponge to increase the area that can be covered by this equipment.
4. Use of a vertical wiping motion, moving from the top to the bottom of each window.

Skill training will be implemented in order to assist Michael in learning the new job task.

Consumer Characteristics: Michael demonstrates the ability to acquire new skills with verbal, gestural, and physical prompts. He responds to both verbal and tangible reinforcements by increasing the quality and quantity of his work.

Data Collection: Five separate, but identical task analyses will be used to monitor Michael's work progress at each of the five window sets. The use of five separate recording forms will allow the trainer to assess Michael's performance across different locations and time periods. Due to Michael's work schedule, probe and prompt data will be recorded once per week at each of the five window sets. Multiple opportunity probe data will be taken on the first single window pane cleaned each day. Correct performance will be defined as initiation of work within 3 seconds. A (+) will be used to designate correct performance of the step in the task analysis. Incorrect performance is designated by a (–). Prompt data will be recorded during cleaning of the second single window pane cleaned each day.

Baseline Performance: Michael independently completed 12 out of 41 steps (29%) of the task analysis.

Behavior Change Procedures:
1. A system of least intrusive prompts will be implemented to fade response prompts needed during initial training. A three-prompt hierarchy, including verbal, gestural, and physical prompts, will be used in conjunction with this system. Training will occur simultaneously on all steps of the task analysis (total task presentation). The criterion for skill acquisition is 100% performance on three consecutive probe trails.
2. Training will begin with the trainer within 3 feet of the base of the ladder. The trainer should be ready to mount the ladder at any time during the training period when physical assistance is needed for correct performance of a step in the task analysis. Movement from this distance is determined by the procedure outlined below. The trainer will initiate the training session with the cue, "Michael, clean the window."

Figure 8.3.   Instructional program using forward chaining.

(continued)

Figure 8.3.   (*continued*)

> If no response is given within 3 seconds or Michael begins to make an error, the
> trainer will introduce the first level of prompting (verbal) in the three-prompt hier-
> archy. If correct performance is not demonstrated at this level of prompting, the
> trainer will introduce the next more intrusive prompt of the hierarchy. At no time
> will the trainer allow Michael to make an error.
>
> 3. Verbal reinforcement will be delivered on each completed step of the task analysis
>   during the first 3 days of training at a particular window set. For example, if Michael
>   correctly wipes the window ledge with a physical prompt, the trainer will say,
>   "Good wiping the window ledge, Michael," at the completion of this task. Begin-
>   ning on the 4th day of training at a particular window set, verbal reinforcement will
>   be delivered on only those steps of the task analysis that have not been performed
>   correctly for three consecutive probe trials. This process will continue until rein-
>   forcement is required only at the conclusion of the entire task. When all steps of the
>   task analysis are completed independently for three consecutive trials, the trainer
>   will step back to a distance of 6 feet. When Michael independently performs at this
>   distance, the trainer will move back to a distance of 30 feet. When independent
>   performance is demonstrated at this distance, the trainer will fade from the work
>   site. Probe data will continue to be recorded on a weekly basis at each particular
>   window set.

time the individual exhibited a desired behavior. Instead, the use of exchangeable reinforcers would be necessary. These might include tokens, points on a card, checks on a
calendar, and so forth. The tokens, points, or checks would be exchanged later for an
item or activity that the employee had selected.

There are several advantages to using exchangeable reinforcers. First, like tangible rewards, they can be delivered immediately and can alert the individual that the preferred item will be available soon. A worker may receive a token for each independent
response made during pot scrubbing. If the worker earned 10 tokens, he or she would
then be able to exchange them for a preferred, more tangible reinforcer at a convenient time.

Another positive feature of using exchangeable tokens is that reinforcement can
be gradually faded as other, more naturally occurring events become reinforcing to the
employee. For example, the employment specialist should always provide verbal praise
for a job well done when reinforcing the worker with tokens. As the worker becomes
more independent, verbal praise should become a stronger or more powerful reinforcer
than the tangible item, which would be faded gradually. Tokens can also be easily faded by
requiring the worker to complete an increasing amount of work before receiving the tangible item. For example, initially 10 tokens would have to be earned before receiving the
cup of coffee. This number could be increased gradually until the employee was working
a full day before receiving the item.

Schedule of Delivery   Setting up a schedule of reinforcement to plan frequency
of delivery is another important component of the employee's instructional program. The
employment specialist must decide between two types of reinforcement schedules: a
continuous reinforcement schedule or an intermittent reinforcement schedule. During
initial instruction of a new skill, a continuous reinforcement schedule generally is used.
This means that the employee receives reinforcement for each step in the task that is
completed correctly. As the employee's independent performance increases, the amount
of reinforcement is gradually decreased to an intermittent schedule. Intermittent reinforcement involves the delivery of a reinforcer after a predetermined number of correct

Consumer: Martha

Job site: Ramada Renaissance Hotel

Position: Laundry attendant

Date of hire: 11/12

Schedule: Monday–Friday, 11:00 A.M.–1:15 P.M.

Employment specialist:

Program: Training independent performance of laundry attendant job tasks

Objective: Martha will independently press and stack the napkins at the Ramada Renaissance Hotel with 100% accuracy for 3 consecutive days.

Rationale: Martha needs to press and stack the napkins correctly at a rate of four in 50 seconds in order to perform the job of laundry attendant to company standards.

Consumer Characteristics: Martha has cerebral palsy, mental retardation, and a visual impairment. She has perceptual difficulties, scoliosis, poor fine motor skills, visual impairment corrected with glasses, an unsteady gait, seizures controlled with medication, and clear speech. Martha wants to work and requires frequent reinforcement to complete a task. Martha has been observed to make errors when a modeling prompt is used. She has been observed to respond to physical prompts but has difficulty because the trainer must move Martha's hands opposite her spasticity. Martha has been observed to follow a gestural prompt.

Data Collection: A task analysis will be used to measure Martha's work performance.

Baseline Procedures: Martha performed the tasks with 4% accuracy according to probe data collected on 11-6.

Behavior Change Procedure: Give Martha the instructional cue, "Press the napkins." Use a time-delay procedure with a gestural prompt for training in all steps in the task analysis. Use a time-delay level of 0 seconds on all steps in the task analysis for 1 week. Begin week 2 using a backward chaining procedure with a constant delay of 3 seconds for the last step in the task analysis ("Rub napkins"). Continue all other steps in the task analysis at a time-delay level of 0 seconds. If Martha does not complete the step correctly within 3 seconds, use a gestural prompt for training in the step. When Martha performs the last step with 100% accuracy on all trials for one complete day, increase the time delay level of the second to the last step in the task analysis ("Put napkins on table") to a constant delay of 3 seconds. Continue all other steps in the task analysis at a time delay level of 0 seconds. Maintain a 3-second constant delay level for the last two steps in the task analysis. Martha will meet the program criterion when she performs the second to the last step with 100% accuracy on all trials for 1 complete day. Use a backward-chaining procedure with a constant delay level of 3 seconds to teach the remaining steps in the task analysis. When the program criterion of 100% correct responses during a 3-second time delay is met, increase the time-delay level to 3 seconds for the preceding step in the task analysis. Maintain a time-delay level of 0 seconds on all steps in the task analysis and a constant delay of 3 seconds on all steps meeting program criterion. Prevent errors by using a gestural prompting procedure with a 0-second time delay.

Interrupt errors during the 3-second time-delay level by giving a gestural prompt if an incorrect response is initiated during the 3-second delay. Use a physical prompt if no response is initiated in 3 seconds or if an incorrect response is initiated, both following a gestural prompt.

Figure 8.4. Instructional program using backward chaining.

(continued)

Figure 8.4. *(continued)*

Data Collection:
1. During week 1, probe data will be collected at the beginning of each work day. Record a (+) for an independent correct response and a (−) for an incorrect or no response. Discontinue the probe at the first (−) and begin training.
2. Beginning week 2, record a (+) or (−) on the step in the task analysis for which the backward-chaining training procedure is being used. If the step is performed incorrectly on any trial, record a (−).

Reinforcement: Provide praise on a variable ratio schedule of every 2 correct responses during the 0-second time-delay level. Provide praise for every step performed independently during the 3-second time-delay period. Use specific verbal reinforcement for: 1) correctly completing steps in the task analysis, 2) working quickly, and 3) working quietly. A calendar will be used and marked off daily. Paydays will be indicated with a fast food restaurant symbol. On paydays, Martha and the employment specialist will cash her paycheck and go out to eat at a fast food restaurant.

Error Correction: If 3 errors occur in a row, go back to 0-second delay for 10 trials. Return to 3-second constant delay.

Generalization/Maintenance Procedures: To be developed after all steps in the task analysis have met program criterion of 100% correct responses at a 3-second constant time-delay level.

responses or a predetermined period of time. When reinforcement is delivered based on a predetermined period of time, an interval schedule of reinforcement is being used. If reinforcement occurs after a predetermined number of correct responses, a ratio schedule is being utilized.

There are two types of interval schedules that may be useful at a job site. The first is a fixed-interval (FI) schedule, which requires that the reinforcer be given to the employee after a fixed interval of time. For example, Chris's employment specialist realized that he was spending too much time window shopping in the mall and not enough time on the task of cleaning with a dry mop. The employment specialist implemented a reinforcement program using a fixed-interval schedule of 5 minutes (FI:5) by setting Chris's alarm watch to beep every 5 minutes. If Chris was on task and not staring at the store windows when the alarm sounded, he was reinforced with, "I like the way you're working," or "That's the way to go!", and so forth.

Any interval of time may be used when developing a program using a fixed interval schedule. However, the employment specialist should begin with an amount of time that allows the employee to be successful. The time allowed to elapse before reinforce-

Table 8.6.   Guidelines for using reinforcement at a job site

Reinforcement should be contingent upon the performance of specific job skills/duties.

Reinforcement should be delivered immediately following performance of the desired behavior.

The behavior being reinforced should be clearly specified.

Natural reinforcers, such as supervisor/coworker praise, should always be paired with tangible rewards such as movie tickets.

Age-appropriate reinforcers should be used.

As the worker successfully performs the desired job skill, the reinforcement schedule should be changed so that more job skills (steps of the task analysis) are required for each reinforcement.

ment is provided can be increased gradually. Chris's employment specialist determined that he was able to stay on task for 4–5 minutes. This fixed-interval schedule was increased when Chris received reinforcement for successful on-task behavior for 5 minutes. The program continued until Chris was able to remain on task until scheduled break times.

The second type of interval schedule is a variable interval (VI) schedule. It is similar to a FI schedule except that the time interval does not remain the same but is a predetermined average. For example, Chris's employment specialist may have reinforced him on an average of every 5 minutes. The timer or alarm would be set for 1–10 minutes so that over time an average of 5 minutes would be achieved. The employment specialist would still want to gradually increase the average so that Chris would eventually work on task without constant reinforcement.

If reinforcement is delivered contingent upon the number of responses, the employment specialist is using a ratio schedule of reinforcement. There are two types of ratio schedules: a fixed ratio (FR) and a variable ratio (VR) schedule. When using an FR schedule, the employee is reinforced after a predetermined fixed number of correct responses. For example, when Marie began her job of operating the dishwasher, she was reinforced with praise every time she completed a step correctly. Once she demonstrated competency on the job, her employment specialist began to gradually fade the reinforcement by selecting a fixed ratio schedule of 2 (FR:2). Under this program, Marie received praise for every two correct responses. This requirement was gradually increased to FR:3, FR:4, and so forth, until Marie received praise only after she completed the entire task correctly.

The other type of ratio schedule is a variable ratio schedule (VR). This is similar to the FR schedule except that the employee is reinforced after an average number of responses. If Marie's employment specialist had selected this schedule, Marie might have received reinforcement after 1, 2, or 3 correct responses, which over time would average out to 2 responses. As with an FR schedule, the average used in a VR schedule would gradually be increased until Marie received reinforcement only after completing the entire task.

Establishing the Paycheck as a Reinforcer Many individuals with severe handicaps have had little exposure to money or the idea that a paycheck represents money for work completed. This will present a problem to the employment specialist since the paycheck is a naturally occurring reinforcer that obviously has the potential for providing a strong motivation for work. There are many different ways to teach a person the meaning of a paycheck. Some individuals may quickly benefit from simply going with the employment specialist to immediately cash the check and use some of the money to buy a desired item. Another person may grasp the concept of a paycheck by marking off days on a calendar with the employment specialist indicating that payday will be approaching and that money will be used to buy an item. Still other individuals may understand the concept of a paycheck if a graph is made showing how many dollars were earned every day.

These ideas, however, may not work for the individual who does not realize that working results in earning money and that money can be used to buy things that she or he likes. Table 8.7 outlines a program developed for John, an individual who had difficulty with these concepts. In fact, John often refused to work or comply with the employment specialist's requests. A program was developed to help him understand the concept that working resulted in earning money and that money could be used at the job site to buy preferred items.

Table 8.7.   Establishing John's paycheck as a reinforcer

Phase 1:

The workday was divided into 5-minute intervals.

John could earn a check on a card for working during an entire 5-minute interval.

After he earned two checks for working, John immediately received a nickel.

The workday was divided into four segments/breaks during which John could spend whatever nickels that he had earned.

After 2 consecutive days of John not refusing to work, the program moved to Phase 2.

Phase 2:

The workday was divided into 10-minute intervals.

The other factors of the program remained the same.

After 2 consecutive days of John not refusing to work, the program moved to Phase 3.

Phase 3:

The workday continued to be divided into 10-minute intervals. Checks were earned on a card for working during an entire interval.

As soon as two checks were earned, John received a nickel.

However, John could only use his nickels to buy preferred items during two scheduled breaks. One occurred during the midpoint of the day and the other at the end of the day.

After 2 consecutive days of John not refusing to work, the program moved to Phase 4.

Phase 4:

The workday was divided into 15-minute intervals.

John no longer earned a nickel after every two checks were earned. Instead the checks were added up during the midpoint of the day and at the end of the day for spending.

After 2 consecutive days of John not refusing to work, the program moved to Phase 5.

Phase 5:

The workday was divided into 20-minute intervals.

At this point checks were added up at the end of the day, and John was able to spend his money on a preferred item.

After 2 consecutive days of John not refusing to work, the program moved to Phase 6, and so forth.

Note: The program was written to gradually increase the length of the intervals before John received a check on his card. The amount of the payment also gradually increased until payment at the end of the day was one dollar. Payment every day faded to payment every other day, and so forth, until payment occurred naturally on payday.

Fading Trainer Presence from the Immediate Work Area

The employment specialist must gradually fade his or her physical proximity to an employee as the employee begins to independently perform the steps of the task analysis for a job duty. Ultimately the employment specialist must remove his or her presence from the immediate work area in which the job duty is performed and eventually from the job site altogether. The removal of the trainer's physical presence from the immediate work area must be systematically planned and based on the performance of the employee.

Initially the employment specialist should be located beside the employee in a position to provide direct instruction. (Barcus et al., 1987; Moon et al., 1986). When the employee is independently performing approximately 80% of the steps in the task analysis for the job duty and the remaining 20% with a verbal prompt, the employment specialist should move 3–6 feet away from the employee. At this time, if it is necessary for the employment specialist to prompt the employee on a step, he or she should move up to the employee to give the prompt. Once the employee initiates the appropriate response, the employment specialist should move back to the designated distance. This distance should be maintained until the employee performs the task for at least three consecutive probe trials with no more than 20% of the task requiring verbal prompts.

At this point, the trainer's distance from the employee should be increased to 6–10 feet and maintained until the employee performs the task for three consecutive probe trials with no more than 10% of the task requiring verbal prompts. Again, if an instructional prompt is necessary, the employment specialist must move to the employee and give the prompt while beside her or him.

Next, the distance from the employee should be increased to across the room (10–20 feet) and maintained until the employee performs the task independently for three consecutive probe trials. At this point, the employment specialist should leave the immediate work area and continue to monitor the worker's performance of the job duty. As long as the employee's performance is maintained, the trainer should stay out of the immediate work area in which the duty is performed. The program in Figure 8.5 is an example of a systematic plan to fade the presence of the trainer from the immediate area in which a job duty is performed.

DATA COLLECTION, GRAPHING, AND ANALYSIS

Recording and graphing data is crucial to the success of an initial skill training program. Measurement procedures are a vital component of the systematic instructional plan in that they allow the employment specialist to monitor the progress of the employee, as well as determine whether the instructional format is successful or needs to be modified. Probe and prompt data are recorded during this phase of training. Both are based on the individualized task analysis of each major job duty and indicate whether the employee is beginning to work independently.

Probe data represent how well the employee performs a job duty independently, with no prompting or reinforcement from a trainer. Probe data should be collected a minimum of once each week. Typically, a job task is considered learned when the employee independently and correctly performs every step of an individualized job duty task analysis for a minimum of three consecutive probe trials.

Prompt data indicate the kinds of prompts that are provided for the employee during the performance of the job duty. It is recommended that the recording of prompt data be limited to only one or two tasks per day (Barcus et al., 1987; Moon et al., 1986; Wehman et al., 1988). It is more important for the employment specialist to collect data on a predetermined schedule and to analyze data freqently, than it is to collect data on a daily basis. We suggest collecting prompt data on at least one trial (a complete task analysis) on every job duty in which the worker is being instructed once each day (Barcus et al., 1987; Moon et al., 1986).

Data Collection Using the Least Intrusive Prompt System

The same task analysis recording sheet used for probe data collection is also utilized for recording prompt data (Moon et al., 1986). Recording is done in the left corner for each step of the task (see Figures 8.1 and 8.7). In this case, the employment specialist records a symbol representing either independent performance of a step (+) or use of a verbal (v), model (m), gestural (g), or physical prompt (p) (Wehman et al., 1988). It is also important to keep track of the number and type of prompts that are provided for the worker on a specific task over a period of time. This allows the employment specialist to determine when it is possible to start gradually moving away from the worker during training. Movement away from the employee helps reduce dependency on the employ-

Program: Fading during task acquisition

Worker: Paul

Job site: The Center

Instructor: Martha

Objective: Paul will complete all tasks with 100% accuracy with the employment specialist out of sight for 3 consecutive days.

Worker Characteristics: Paul is a hard worker who learns the unchanging portions of his tasks very quickly. He has some difficulty with changes in routine. He responds well to verbal praise and to smiles as reinforcement, but does not like being corrected. Any error correction should be phrased very tactfully. Paul can become sullen and abrasive if corrected, and the best response seems to be silence until a positive action can be reinforced, and then an economy of positive words should be used, for example, "That's it," or "You've got it." Paul enjoys working independently. He has excellent problem-solving skills and finds the most efficient way to accomplish a task. The order of the TA steps need not be strictly followed in order for him to complete the task correctly.

Data Collection: Task analyses of each task should be used to record progress in task independence as well as employment specialist distance. Data should be taken daily. No prompts should be given unless an error occurs.

Reinforcement: Verbal reinforcement will be used during training. Praise for independent work will be stressed as fading progresses.

Fading Procedure: During acquisition (performance of less than 100%), employment specialist should remain at 3–10 feet (closer than this seems to annoy Paul). Move to 3 feet for problem areas of the task as indicated by previous data, and back to 10 feet for steps Paul has completed correctly for several days. Give reinforcement for correctly completed steps that had been trouble spots and responses done correctly after prompting, and reinforce at task completion.

Phase 1:   When Paul completes the task independently with 100% accuracy for 3 consecutive days, fade to 10–20 feet. Reduce verbal praise so that it is given at task completion only. Smile instead of praising verbally during task, and look at his hands instead of making eye contact to reinforce attending to task rather than looking up. If an error is made, step in and tactfully correct, maintaining positive attitude. Praise correct response ("That's it." "You've got it."), and move back to a 10–20 foot distance.

Phase 2:   When Paul completes the task with 100% accuracy for 3 consecutive days independently with the instructor at 10–20 feet, fade to over 20 feet. Continue to smile during correct work, and add periods of looking away or doing something with hands when Paul is performing steps he has had no trouble with. If an error is made, follow procedure in Phase 1 and step back to over 20 feet. Verbally praise task completion and reinforce independent work.

Phase 3:   When Paul completes the task with 100% accuracy for 3 consecutive days independently with the trainer at over 20 feet, fade to out of sight (preferably to area of next task if it is performed out of sight of work area of first task). When Paul moves on to next task, approach and reinforce independent task completion and move on to next task. Inspect work completed when possible (during another task at Phase III or during Paul's break). If no error is apparent, continue Phase 2 the next day and inspect. If no error is apparent, continue Phase 3 the next day. If no errors are found for 3 consecutive days, inspection may be done on an intermittent basis.

Figure 8.5.   Fading trainer presence from the immediate work area.

ment specialist's physical proximity. Table 8.8 outlines steps that should be used when recording prompt data for the least prompt strategy (Barcus et al., 1987; Snell, 1987; Wehman et al., 1988).

Data Collection with a Time-Delay System

The task analysis sheet used for probe and prompt data collection should also be used for collecting training data for a time-delay program. The employment specialist should select symbols to represent independent performance of a step, correct performance of a step after a prompt is delivered, and incorrect responding. A ($+$) can be used for independent performance and a ($-$) for incorrect performance. The first letter of the prompt selected for training could be used to indicate that a prompt was required, for example, (P) for physical prompt. Incorrect responding during training may be an indication that the prompt selected for delay is not successful. In this instance, the employment specialist may need to select another prompt for training.

Graphing Data

Improvement in an employee's ability to perform job skills independently is easier to analyze if prompt and probe data are displayed graphically. Figure 8.6 is a sample of how a graph should be formatted. Begin by plotting the days of the week along the horizontal axis. Label the work days consecutively (Monday through Sunday) and include holidays and weekends. The vertical axis is used to plot prompt or probe information. For probe data the employment specialist may plot percentage or number of steps completed correctly. If prompt data are to be graphed, the employment specialist can indicate number or percentage of steps completed with a verbal, model, or physical prompt or independent responses. The vertical axis should be divided into intervals of the same size, such as increments of 5%–100%.

Interpreting Probe Data

Tracking the percentage of steps an employee performs independently, without prompts or reinforcement, allows the employment specialist to determine the rate at which the employee is acquiring the job skills. If the percentage of steps the employee completes

---

Table 8.8.   Recording prompt data using a least prompts strategy

1. Have the employee move to the appropriate work area unless movement is part of the task analysis.
2. Stand behind or beside the worker so that prompts can be provided quickly if necessary.
3. Give the worker a general cue to begin the task, such as "Operate the dishwasher."
4. Wait 3–5 seconds for self-initiation of Step 1 of the task analysis.
5. If correct, record ($+$) and proceed to Step 2.
6. If no response is given after a verbal prompt, provide a model or gestural prompt specific to Step 1, with same verbal prompt.
7. If correct, record (v) by step and proceed to Step 2.
8. If no response is given after a verbal prompt, provide a model or gestural prompt specific to Step 1, with same verbal prompt.
9. If correct response is given, record (m) by the step and proceed to Step 2.
10. If no response is given after a model prompt, provide a physical prompt to complete the step.
11. Record (p) by the step and proceed to Step 2.
12. Repeat this procedure for each step until the employee completes the entire task.
13. Always interrupt an error immediately with the next prompt in the least prompt system.

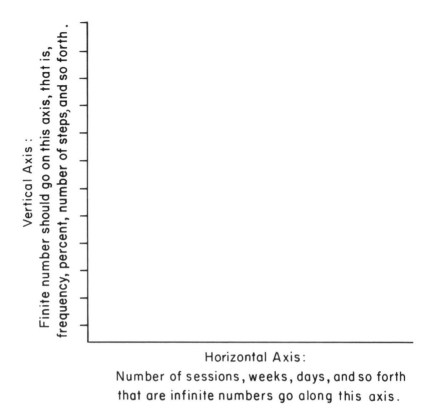

Figure 8.6. Organization of graph data.

independently and correctly increases steadily, continue the instructional program until all the skills in the task analysis are performed independently. If the probe data indicate no significant increase in independence over a 2-week period, the employment specialist should review the prompt data that have been collected between probes according to the procedures outlined in the instructional program. If the probe data indicate some improvement, such as a decrease in physical prompts and an increase in verbal prompts, the program is working and should be continued. However, if no decrease is noted in the level of prompt required, then a new procedure should be developed.

Interpreting Data: A Case Study Using Least Intrusive Prompts

The following program is offered as an example of job-site training. There are basic procedures to follow, but no two instructional programs are ever the same. For example, no two programs for operating a dishwasher would be identical, since different employees, environments, and equipment create differences in the programs.

Figure 8.7 is a task analysis recording sheet that shows data collected during the first week of instruction with Chris on the task of dry mopping. On February 2, the employment specialist began using the system of least intrusive prompts to instruct Chris in his dry mopping task. Using the same recording sheet that was used for probe data, the employment specialist recorded the type of instruction provided to Chris in the left corner of each box next to the task steps. The right corner of each box contains a notation of the trainer's physical proximity to Chris during the training session.

Figure 8.8 shows the probe data taken after 1 week of instruction to determine if

	Probe 1/31	Probe 2/1	Probe 2/2	Training 2/2	Training 2/3	Training 2/4	Training 2/7	Probe 2/8
Trainer: Elizabeth Long Employee: Chris Environment: First floor of mall Instructional Cues: Use your dry mop								
6.1 Remove dry mop from cart.	+/1	+/1	+/1	+/1	+/1	+/1	+/1	+/1
6.2 Place head of mop on floor.	+/1	+/1	+/1	+/1	+/1	+/1	+/1	+/1
6.3 Pick up dry cloth.	+/1	+/1	+/1	+/1	+/1	+/1	+/1	+/1
6.4 Place cloth in pocket of uniform.	+/1	+/1	+/1	+/1	+/1	+/1	+/1	+/1
6.5 Pick up damp cloth.	+/1	+/1	+/1	+/1	+/1	+/1	+/1	+/1
6.6 Hold cloth in hand around mop.	+/1	+/1	+/1	+/1	+/1	+/1	+/1	+/1
6.7 Push dry mop towards store.	+/1	+/1	+/1	+/1	+/1	+/1	+/1	+/1
6.8 Angle mop around customers.	−/1	−/1	−/1	p/1	p/1	m/1	m/1	−/1
6.9 Push mop down each entrance hall.	−/1	−/1	−/1	p/1	p/1	p/1	m/1	−/1
6.10 Push mop back to main traffic area.	−/1	−/1	−/1	p/1	p/1	m/1	m/1	−/1
6.11 Push mop towards store.	−/1	−/1	−/1	p/1	p/1	m/1	v/1	−/1
6.12 Stop at each sitting area.	−/1	−/1	−/1	p/1	p/1	p/1	p/1	−/1
6.13 Clean spills with damp cloth.	−/1	−/1	−/1	p/1	p/1	p/1	m/1	−/1
6.14 Wipe trash can lids with damp cloth.	−/1	−/1	−/1	p/1	p/1	p/1	p/1	−/1
6.15 Take cloth out of pocket.	−/1	−/1	−/1	p/1	p/1	m/1	m/1	−/1
6.16 Wipe seats with dry cloth.	−/1	−/1	−/1	m/1	m/1	m/1	m/1	−/1
6.17 Wipe tile with dry cloth.	−/1	−/1	−/1	p/1	m/1	m/1	m/1	−/1
6.18 Place cloth in pocket.	−/1	−/1	−/1	m/1	m/1	v/1	v/1	−/1
6.19 Push mop towards store.	−/1	−/1	−/1	p/1	p/1	p/1	p/1	−/1
6.20 Push mop across store entrance.	−/1	−/1	−/1	p/1	p/1	m/1	m/1	−/1
6.21 Position mop/self facing second store.	−/1	−/1	−/1	p/1	p/1	p/1	p/1	−/1
6.22 Repeat steps 6.8−6.10.	−/1	−/1	−/1	p/1	p/1	m/1	m/1	−/1
6.23 Push mop towards second store.	−/1	−/1	−/1	p/1	p/1	p/1	p/1	−/1
6.24 Repeat steps 6.12−6.16.	−/1	−/1	−/1	m/1	m/1	m/1	v/1	−/1
6.25 Push mop towards second store.	−/1	−/1	−/1	m/1	m/1	m/1	v/1	−/1
6.26 Push mop across entrance.	−/1	−/1	−/1	p/1	p/1	p/1	m/1	−/1
6.27 Push dry mop to supply cart.	−/1	−/1	−/1	m/1	m/1	m/1	v/1	−/1
6.28 Stay at supply cart.	−/1	−/1	−/1	p/1	p/1	p/1	p/1	−/1
6.29 Gently shake dry mop.	−/1	−/1	−/1	p/1	p/1	p/1	m/1	−/1
6.30 Clamp dry mop to cart.	−/1	−/1	−/1	p/1	p/1	m/1	m/1	−/1

(continued)

Figure 8.7. Task analysis data recording sheet.

Figure 8.7.   *(continued)*

Trainer: Elizabeth Long

Employee: Chris

Environment: First floor of mall

Instructional Cues: Use your dry mop

6.31	Place damp cloth on cart.	−/1	−/1	−/1	m/1	m/1	m/1	v/1	−/1
6.32	Sweep dirt into pile with broom.	−/1	−/1	−/1	m/1	m/1	m/1	m/1	−/1
6.33	Remove dust pan from cart.	−/1	−/1	−/1	m/1	m/1	v/1	v/1	−/1
6.34	Sweep dirt into dust pan.	−/1	−/1	−/1	p/1	p/1	m/1	m/1	−/1
6.35	Empty dust pan into trash bag.	−/1	−/1	−/1	m/1	m/1	v/1	v/1	−/1
Total steps correct		7	7	7	7	7	7	7	7
Percent correct		20%	20%	20%	20%	20%	20%	20%	20%

Instructional Code

+ = Correct   V = Verbal
− = Incorrect M = Model or gestural prompt
              P = Physical prompt

Distance Code

1 = within 3 feet
2 = 3–10 feet
3 = beyond 10 feet

Chris was learning his new dry mopping task. From a review of the probe data alone, it appeared that Chris was not making any progress, because his probe results were identical to the data prior to systematic instruction.

However, a close examination of the prompt data for that same period of time revealed that on the first day of instruction Chris needed physical assistance on 54% of his dry mopping task. At the end of that same week, Chris required physical assistance on only 17% of the job task. The results of the prompt data displayed in Figure 8.9 demonstrate clearly that trainer assistance was decreasing and Chris was learning to complete the dry mopping task.

The prompt data in the Figure 8.10 clearly show that Chris was learning his new job task of cleaning with a dry mop. At the end of the 3rd week of training, Chris no longer received any physical assistance and required only model prompts for 26% of the task. By the 5th week he was performing the majority of the job duty independently with only 11% verbal prompts. This information was helpful to Chris's employment specialist for determing how to fade physical proximity from Chris during instruction. Since he was performing well, the employment specialist moved back about 6 feet from Chris. As long as Chris maintained his performance at this level, or he did not require more than 20% of the task to be verbally prompted, the employment specialist remained at this distance. When independent performance increased, the trainer gradually moved across the room. After 100% independent performance for three consecutive probe trails was achieved, the employment specialist left the immediate work area.

The least prompts instructional strategy is frequently used by employment specialists. Table 8.9 lists guidelines that employment specialists at Virginia Commonwealth University's Rehabilitation Research and Training Center have found helpful when altering a least prompts instructional program.

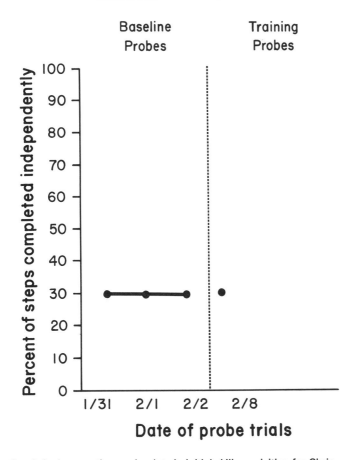

Figure 8.8.   Graph for interpreting probe data in initial skill acquisition for Chris.

JOB-SITE MODIFICATIONS

Modifications in the work setting and/or the use of adaptive devices can enable a worker to complete job duties successfully (Nisbet & Callahan, 1987; Wood, 1988). Wood (1988) suggests that modifications can be made: 1) to the equipment, 2) to the method or sequence of the task, or 3) to improve worker interaction in performance of the task. The necessity for and the type of job modification should be based on an analysis of the worker's progress through a review of the instructional data for the specific job duty. A plateau at a certain instructional level, such as the employee performing the steps of the task analysis (TA) only following gestural prompts, should alert the employment specialist to the possible need for: 1) a change in the task analysis, 2) a change in the instructional program, 3) a modification and/or adaptation to the work environment, or 4) a change in the worker's job responsibilities or work environment (Everson, Hollahan, Callahan, Franklin, & Brady, 1987).

Change in Instructional Program

Initially the employment specialist designs a systematic instructional program to teach a job duty and implements the training program. This plan includes: 1) a training schedule; 2) an individualized job duty task analysis specifying the sequential, teachable job skills

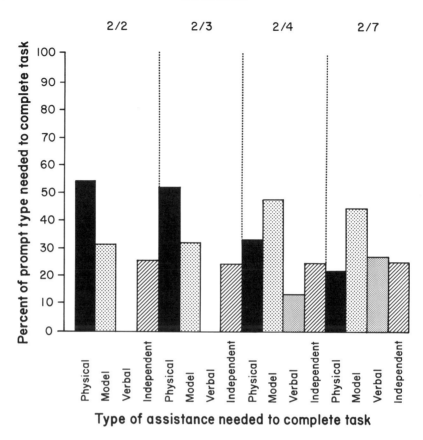

Figure 8.9. Graph of prompt data for first week of work.

involved in each major duty; 3) the specific instructional techniques, including prompting methods and reinforcement procedures; 4) the data collection procedures used for monitoring the employee's progress; and 5) procedures for fading instruction (Barcus et al., 1987; Mcloughlin et al., 1987; Snell, 1987).

In some instances the initial instructional plan does not result in the worker learning the job tasks. If this is the case, the employment specialist must revise the instructional plan based on the employee's progress (Gold, 1980). The data collected on the instructional program will allow the employment specialist to select a revised format that may result in the worker's acquisition of the necessary job skills. Table 8.10 shows a list of questions that employment specialists with Virginia Commonwealth University's Rehabilitation Research and Training Center ask when analyzing the effectiveness of a systematic instructional plan.

For example, for an employee named Michael, the trainer initially selected an instructional format of total task presentation using a least intrusive prompting system. After 1 week of instruction with Michael, it became evident that he was performing individual steps of the job task only upon receiving a model prompt. The employment specialist reviewed Michael's instructional data and decided to change the instructional format to a total task format using a time-delay procedure with a model prompt. After 2 weeks of instruction utilizing the revised format, Michael was performing all steps of the task independently.

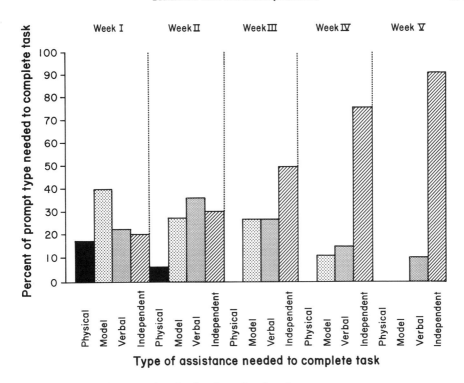

Figure 8.10. Graph of prompt data for first 5 weeks of work.

Adaptations to the Work Environment

If a worker can perform a job duty effectively and efficiently without specialized equipment or modification to the work environment, he or she should be expected to do so. However, in some instances use of adaptive devices such as a step stool, tilt table, or specialized chair, and/or modification to the work environment, such as rearrangement of the position of equipment, use of permanent visual or auditory cues, or changes to the sequence of the task, can enable a worker to complete a job task successfully. The employment specialist's job is to find ways to simplify task demands and identify modifica-

Table 8.9. Guidelines for altering a least prompts instructional program

Review the prompt data after three training sessions.

If the data show a steady decrease in the level of prompts, continue the program.

If no decrease is noted, continue the instructional program for three training sessions.

Review the data. If the level of prompts has begun to decrease, continue the program. If no decrease is apparent, change the level of reinforcement or the schedule of reinforcement.

After the level or schedule of reinforcement has been changed, review the program at the end of three training sessions. If the level of prompts has begun to decrease, continue the program.

If the level of prompts is not decreasing, break the steps of the job duty analysis into smaller steps. Implement the least intrusive prompting procedure with the new task analysis.

Review the new program at the end of three training sessions. If the level of prompts is decreasing, continue the program.

If the prompt data show no decreases, change or add response cue and/or response prompts.

Review at the end of three training sessions. If the level of prompts is decreasing, continue the program. If no changes are made, modify the job duty.

Table 8.10. Analyzing an instructional plan

Analyze the effectiveness of the training strategy

   Does the training strategy match the learning style of the individual?

   Is the person responding to the type of prompt(s) you have selected?

   Is he/she attending to the task?

   Are too many skills being taught at the same time?

Has the task analysis been individualized to match the individual's abilities?

   Has the task been broken down into small enough steps?

   Have the physical limitations of the consumer been taken into consideration, or was the task
   analysis written for someone without physical limitation?

   Can the task be taught in sections rather than in the entire chain?

   Does the task analysis eliminate the need to make quality judgments (e.g., four times around
   the sink results in a clean sink to employer standards)?

   Would external cues or adaptive equipment help the person learn the task if added to the task
   analysis?

Have all of the components of delivering reinforcement been considered?

   Is the reinforcement given immediately after the desired response?

   Has the amount of reinforcement been reduced too quickly?

   Does the reinforcement match the individual's current abilities (i.e., does the person need a
   material/food item paired with social praise?)?

   Does the individual have a behavior that is interfering with learning the task? Should a behavior
   program be developed in addition to the skill acquisition program?

---

tions or adaptive devices that meet the needs of the worker (Everson, et al., 1987; Wood, 1988). Sowers, Jenkins, & Powers (1988) suggest that the employment specialist must: 1) identify the aspects of the job duty where the worker is having difficulty, 2) identify a range of modifications and/or adaptive devices, 3) select the most appropriate modification and/or adaptation, and 4) implement its use on the job.

Some employment specialists may be skilled in identifying and designing modifications and/or adaptive devices, but, in many instances, the employment specialist may need the assistance of other professionals, such as an occupational therapist or a rehabilitation engineer (Wood, 1988). Whether the employment specialist or another professional identifies and designs a solution, the guidelines listed in Table 8.11 should be followed.

Change in the Worker's Responsibilities

In spite of efforts to change the instructional format, modify the work environment, and/or use adaptive devices, sometimes a worker still has difficulty with parts of a job duty. In this instance it will be necessary to determine if there is a coworker who could share the job duty. Another alternative is to identify a coworker's job duty that is of equal responsibility and duration to the task that is difficult for the employee. It may be possible to switch job duties with that individual as long as the supervisor and the coworker approve of the change. The employer, the worker, and the employment specialist should meet to discuss what, if any, alternatives are acceptable to everyone concerned. In some situations the employer may not be amenable to changes in the worker's responsibilities and may request that the employee resign from the position. However, frequently employers are willing to change their workers' responsibilities and will explain what alternatives they are willing to implement. The employer and the worker should agree on and specify the course of action and when the change is to be effective. A change in a worker's re-

Table 8.11.   Guidelines for adaptations to a work environment

Review the probe/prompt data to determine the specific problem area.

Determine alternatives and outline strategies for modifying the specific job task in question.

Review the alternatives/strategies with the employer.

Agree on the appropriate modification or adaptation.

Explain the changes to the employee.

Implement the modification and/or adaptation.

Provide systematic instruction.

Evaluate the employee's progress.

sponsibilities will require the development and implementation of an instructional plan for training the worker in performance of the new responsibilities.

INTERVENTION TIME DATA

Another type of data that should be collected throughout an individual's employment is the intervention time of the employment specialist. Intervention hours may fall into any number of categories, such as consumer training, travel/transportation, program development, employment advocacy, and so forth. Recording intervention time in these categories enables the employment specialist to identify areas of strength and need. For example, if the employment specialist notes that an inordinate amount of time is spent counseling the family, he or she may need to find additional sources of support and assistance for that family.

Analysis of intervention time during the initial stages of job-site training helps the trainer decide when to begin fading his or her presence from the job site. A review of intervention data on a regular basis may also reveal that an employment specialist is spending too much time in one specific area of job training and placement at the expense of another area where a problem may be occurring.

Following is a case study demonstrating the use of intervention time data. The employment specialist for a worker named Sue carried an intervention time recording sheet with her to the job site each day. Having this form accessible assisted her in keeping an accurate record of the time she spent working with Sue, both on and off the job site. Figure 8.11 shows an intervention time record kept by the employment specialist during Sue's 4th week of employment.

Analyzing the first 12 days of intervention data, along with the initial skill acquisition results, helped Sue's employment specialist plan a schedule for fading assistance. The employment specialist was concerned with her intervention time both on and off the job site. On February 8th, the employment specialist continued to stay at the job site for 8 hours; however, she began to reduce her active time with Sue to 7 hours. Three working days later the employment specialist had reduced her active time to 6.5 hours. During inactive periods, the employment specialist divided her time between getting to know Sue's coworkers and doing necessary paperwork. Again, using the results gathered from the intervention time and skill acquisition data, the employment specialist began to fade her travel training assistance on February 4. She also became concerned when the intervention data revealed that she had been meeting with Sue's family every night after work. In an effort to avoid any long-term problems, the employment specialist presented an every 3rd day meeting schedule to Sue's family. Eventually her parents became more

**VIRGINIA COMMONWEALTH UNIVERSITY
REHABILITATION RESEARCH AND TRAINING CENTER**

**CONSUMER SPECIFIC INTERVENTION TIME
RECORDING SHEET (REVISED 9/86)**

Consumer

Name: Sue

SSN: 210-44-9527

Recording period: February

Staff Member

Name: Vicki

ID Code: 06

Case manager, vocational rehabilitation: Mike Jones
Mental health, mental retardation: Sally Murphy

Date (month/date)	2/3	2/4	2/7	2/8	2/9	2/10	2/14
INTERVENTION TIME DIRECTLY RELATED TO JOB SKILLS TRAINING (hours, minutes)							
1. ACTIVE (time with consumer and time coordinating at job site)	8	8	8	7	7	6.5	6.5
2. INACTIVE (between periods of active intervention)	0	0	0	1	1	1.5	1.5
INTERVENTION TIME INDIRECTLY RELATED TO JOB SKILLS TRAINING (hours, minutes)							
1. TRAVEL/TRANSPORTING	2.5	1.5	1.5	1	.5		
2. CONSUMER TRAINING							
3. PROGRAM DEVELOPMENT (task analysis and behavioral intervention programs)							
4. DIRECT EMPLOYMENT ADVOCACY (work-site–related, includes consumer specific job development)							
5. INDIRECT EMPLOYMENT ADVOCACY (nonwork-site–related)	.5	.5	.5	.5	.5	.5	.5
6. SCREENING AND EVALUATION (screening consumer for service eligibility)							
TOTAL (daily)	11	10	10	9.5	9	8.5	8.5

Figure 8.11.　Intervention time results.

comfortable with the idea of Sue having a real job, and the employment specialist reduced her family contact to periodic telephone calls.

EMPLOYMENT EVALUATION

The employment specialist should send supervisor evaluation forms to the employee's supervisor on a regular schedule throughout the initial training/skill acquisition phase. Initially the form should be completed at least monthly. Information from each supervisor evaluation should be compiled by the employment specialist into a progress report and reviewed with the worker and his or her family or group home counselor. (Refer to Chapter 7, on orientation and assessment.) As the employee becomes stable in the position, quarterly reports may be sufficient and could be gradually reduced to one every 6 months. However, the employment specialist should solicit and be open to employer input throughout the course of employment.

SUMMARY

At this point in job-site training there are few legitimate reasons for termination of training and removal of the worker from the position. Possible reasons for termination of training are: 1) removal of the worker by family members, 2) the worker refusing to perform the particular job, 3) worker's health, or 4) the worker's involvement in action at the job site that warrants his or her resignation (e.g., stealing). Remember that the individual being placed into competitive employment through the use of supported employment strategies does not initially possess all of the work- and nonwork-related skills necessary to perform the job independently. It is the role of the employment specialist to provide training utilizing systematic instructional strategies described in this chapter.

REFERENCES

Barcus, M., Brooke, V., Inge, K., Moon, S., & Goodall, P. (1987). *An instructional guide for training on a job site: A supported employment resource.* Richmond, VA: Virginia Commonwealth University, Rehabilitation Research and Training Center.

Bellamy, G.T., Horner, R.H., & Inman, D.P. (1981). *Vocational habilitation of severely retarded adults* (2nd ed.). Baltimore, MD: University Park Press.

Buckley, J. (1988). *Employment training specialist: Job description, training and evaluation.* Eugene, OR: University of Oregon, Specialized Training Program.

Chadsey-Rusch, J., & Rusch, F.R. (1988). Ecology of the workplace. In R. Gaylord-Ross (Ed.), *Vocational education for persons with handicaps* (pp. 234–256). Mountain View, CA: Mayfield.

Everson, J., Hollahan, J., Callahan, M., Franklin, K., & Brady, P. (1987). *Getting the job done: A manual for the development of supported employment programs for people with physical and multiple disabilities.* Lancaster, PA: United Cerebral Palsy, Materials Center.

Gold, M. (1980). *Try another way training manual.* Champaign, IL: Research Press.

Kiernan, W.E., & Stark, J.A. (Eds.). (1986). *Pathways to employment for adults with developmental disabilities.* Baltimore: Paul H. Brookes Publishing Co.

Mank, D.M., & Horner, R.H. (1988). Instructional programming in vocational education. In R. Gaylord-Ross (Ed.), *Vocational education for persons with special needs* (142–173). Mountain View, CA: Mayfield.

Mcloughlin, C.S., Garner, J.B., & Callahan, M. (1987). *Getting employed, staying employed: Job development and training for persons with severe handicaps.* Baltimore: Paul H. Brookes Publishing Co.

Moon, S., Goodall, P., Barcus, M., & Brooke, V. (Eds.). (1986). *The supported work model of competitive employment for citizens with severe handicaps: A guide for job trainers.* Richmond, VA: Virginia Commonwealth University, Rehabilitation Research and Training Center.

Nisbet, J., & Callahan, M. (1987). Achieving success in integrated workplaces: Critical elements in assisting persons with severe disabilities. In S.J. Taylor, D. Biklen, & J. Knoll (Eds.), *Community integration for people with severe handicaps* (pp. 184–201). New York: Teachers College Press.

Rusch, F.R. (1986). *Competitive employment issues and strategies.* Baltimore: Paul H. Brookes Publishing Co.

Snell, M.E. (Ed.). (1987). *Systematic instruction of persons with severe handicaps.* Columbus, OH: Charles E. Merrill.

Snell, M.E., & Browder, D.M. (1986). Community-referenced instruction: Research and issues. *Journal of The Association for Persons with Severe Handicaps, 11*(1), 1–11.

Snell, M.E., & Gast, D.L. (1981). Applying delay procedure to the instruction of the severely handicapped. *Journal of The Association for the Severely Handicapped, 5*(4), 3–14.

Sowers, J., Jenkins, C., & Powers, L. (1988). Vocational education of persons with physical handicaps. In R. Gaylord-Ross (Ed.), *Vocational Education for Persons with Handicaps* (pp. 347–416). Mountain View, CA: Mayfield.

Touchette, P.E. (1971). Transfer of stimulus control: Measuring the moment of transfer. *Journal of the Experimental Analysis of Behavior, 15,* 347–354.

Wehman, P., & Moon, M.S. (Eds.). (1988). *Vocational rehabilitation and supported employment.* Baltimore: Paul H. Brookes Publishing Co.

Wehman, P., Moon, M.S., Everson, J.M., Wood, W., & Barcus, J.M. (1988). *Transition from school to work: New challenges for youth with severe disabilities.* Baltimore: Paul H. Brookes Publishing Co.

Wood, W. (1988). Supported employment for persons with physical disabilities. In P. Wehman & M.S. Moon (Eds.), *Vocational rehabilitation and supported employment* (pp. 341–364). Baltimore: Paul H. Brookes Publishing Co.

STABILIZATION OF WORK
PERFORMANCE

9

Once an employee has learned to perform all the skills necessary to execute a major job duty correctly and independently, the employment specialist must ensure that performance of the duty is maintained at company standards under normal working conditions (Moon, Goodall, Barcus, & Brooke, 1986). The employment specialist's focus at this phase of training is to increase the employee's production rate to standard on each major job duty, expand and maintain the employee's performance throughout the entire work environment, and systematically remove to the greatest degree possible his or her own presence from the job site (Barcus, Brooke, Inge, Moon, & Goodall, 1987). Supervision of the employee should be transferred to the employer and conducted under normal company standards (Mcloughlin, Garner, & Callahan, 1987).

Typically, the employment specialist moves into the stabilization phase of job-site training for a specific job duty when the employee has independently performed every step of the individualized job duty task analysis for that specific duty on three consecutive probe data trials (Barcus et al., 1987). At this point in the training the employment specialist is concerned with designing and implementing formalized instructional strategies to increase the employee's production rate to company standards (Barcus et al., 1987; Mcloughlin et al., 1987; Moon et al., 1986). At times, the employment specialist may be simultaneously providing initial skill training on a major duty, implementing strategies to increase production rate on other job duties, and fading from the work area on still more duties. In addition, the employment specialist will be collecting probe data on all other job duties being performed by the employee independently under the natural working conditions. Table 9.1 shows a real-life example of the various training phases in which one employment specialist was involved. As indicated, two skills are in the skill acquisition phase, while two others are in the stabilization phase.

This chapter describes strategies that can be used to assist the employee to function under the natural controls of the work environment including: 1) programming naturally occuring cues, contingencies, and reinforcers; 2) expanding worker performance across duties, supervisor's, job situations, and interpersonel interactions; 3) using co-worker mentors; and 4) fading the trainer presence from the work site.

159

Table 9.1. Examples of training phases

Job duty	Phase of job-site training	Employment specialist's training
Cleaning sinks in restrooms	Stabilization	Fade from immediate work area; continue to collect probe data on schedule.
Dry mopping mall floor	Skill acquisition	Provide systematic instruction at a distance of 6 feet.
Cleaning toilets	Stabilization	Implement a changing criteria program design to increase rate.
Cleaning windows at mall entrance	Skill acquisition	Implement systematic instruction program.

INCREASING PRODUCTION TO COMPANY STANDARDS

Once an employee has learned to perform a specific job duty correctly and independently, the employment specialist must ensure that performance of the duty is maintained at company standards under normal working conditions. This training is based on implementing the procedures outlined in Table 9.2 (Barcus et al., 1987; Mcloughlin et al., 1987).

Verifying Production Standards

The first step in increasing the employee's production rate is to verify a company standard with which to compare the employee's rate of production. This may be done by asking the supervisor if there is an established company production standard for each job duty that the worker is performing. If no standard has been established, the employment specialist must verify a rate based on the performance of other employees in the same position. This verification can be done during job-site observations before placement or during the orientation and assessment component of job-site training (Moon et al., 1986). Observe one or two employees for several days and take an average of their production rate.

If the production rate is defined by the length of time it should take to perform a job duty, complete the following steps:

1. Note the time when the employee begins the job duty.
2. Observe the employee performing the task.
3. Note the time when the employee completes the task.
4. Subtract the beginning time from the ending time to determine the amount of time it takes to complete the task.
5. Take an average production rate across several days to verify a company standard.

For example, a worker named Kathy was hired as a janitor at a local mall, and one of her major job duties was cleaning the restrooms. The employment specialist was in-

Table 9.2. Procedures for increasing production rate

1. Verify the job-site production standards for the job duty.
2. Determine the employee's current production rate.
3. Select instructional strategies to increase production rate.
4. Design program to increase production to standard.
5. Implement the program.
6. Evaluate the worker's productivity.
7. Modify the program as necessary.

formed that each restroom needed to be cleaned in 30 minutes. In the process of completing a job duty analysis for Kathy's position, the employment specialist had the opportunity to observe the supervisor cleaning a restroom on three occasions and a coworker twice. The supervisor cleaned the restroom in 27 minutes, 36 minutes, and 29 minutes, for an average rate of 30.7 minutes. The coworker took 28 minutes and 31 minutes, for an average of 29.5 minutes. Therefore, the employment specialist was able to verify that 30 minutes was standard for this job.

If the production standard is determined by counting the number of units completed during a given time period, complete the following steps to verify a company standard:

1. Identify two short time periods during the day to observe an employee performing the job duty.
2. Count and record the number of units completed (e.g., number of dishes washed) during the identified sample time period (e.g., 10 minutes).
3. Keep the time period constant across all observation periods.
4. Take an average of the employee's production rate to verify a company standard.

For example, an employee named Maggie worked at a local hospital laundry where she was required to fold laundry, which included towels, sheets, bed pads, and pajamas. The employment specialist asked what the production rate was for folding these items and was told that the pace was very fast, but no specific rate was given. In order to determine the hospital standard, the employment specialist observed workers within the laundry for four 10-minute periods throughout the day in an effort to identify the work rate for each item to be folded. In addition, the employment specialist completed the task herself to verify the production rate. Figure 9.1 shows the data for folding towels.

After review of the results with the supervisor, Worker A was identified as a 10-year veteran and the fastest worker at the work site. Therefore, the employer and the

Name: *Maggie*
Task: *Folding towels*   Month: *October*

	Date	Time started	Time ended	Total minutes worked	Units complete	Average
Worker A	10/5	9:30	9:40	10	25	23.7
	10/6	11:15	11:25	10	23	
	10/7	1:40	1:50	10	24	
	10/8	2:45	2:55	10	23	
Worker B	10/5	8:45	8:55	10	24	21.5
	10/6	10:30	10:40	10	21	
	10/7	1:15	1:25	10	20	
	10/8	2:30	2:40	10	21	
Employment specialist	10/5	9:00	9:10	10	22	21.5
	10/6	11:00	11:10	10	21	
	10/7	1:00	1:10	10	22	
	10/8	2:00	2:10	10	21	

Figure 9.1. Production rate for folding towels.

employment specialist agreed that folding 21.5 towels in 10-minutes was a more realistic standard for the job.

Determining the Employee's Current Production Rate

The second step in the process of increasing the employee's production rate to company standards is to determine the employee's current production rate. If the production standard is defined by the length of time it should take to perform the job duty (e.g., 15 minutes to break down and clean the dishwasher), the employment specialist should implement the procedures described in Table 9.3.

Job duties that must be completed within a prescribed period of time, such as cleaning the restroom or breaking down and cleaning the dishwasher, frequently must be done only one time during the employee's shift. In these cases, the employment specialist should record the production data over 3 consecutive days to determine whether the employee is performing at or near standard rates. In other instances, job duties, such as cleaning a hotel room within a 30-minute period, may occur repeatedly throughout the day. In these situations, the employment specialist should record production data, using the procedures stated in Table 9.3, two or three times per day for 2 days. An average company production standard can then be obtained.

For example, after working for 2 weeks, Chris required very little assistance in setting up his cart for work each day. Probe data were then taken on this skill, and the employment specialist determined that Chris was completely independent. While collecting probe data the employment specialist also determined whether Chris was completing the task according to the company's production standard of 18 minutes. In order to establish Chris's present production rate, the employment specialist recorded the times Chris started and completed the task. By subtracting starting time from ending time, the employment specialist was able to determine the total time it took Chris to set up his cart. The employment specialist then divided the company standard by Chris's total time and established his work rate.

Prior to assisting Chris in increasing his production rate, the employment specialist determined that he averaged 63% of the standard. (This was found by averaging Chris's production rates for 2/11, 2/14, and 2/15.) The employment specialist informed Chris of the need to work faster and provided reinforcement in the form of verbal praise and a daily production rate graph taped to Chris's cart. As seen in Figure 9.2, Chris met company standards within 1 week.

In situations where the production standard is the number of units completed during a given time period (e.g., scrubbing 30 pots in 10 minutes), the employment specialist should implement the procedures outlined in Table 9.4 to determine the employee's production rate.

The production data in Figure 9.3 show an example of determining employee pro-

Table 9.3.   Determining employee production rate defined by length of time

1. Note the time the employee begins the job duty.
2. Observe the employee performing the task.
3. Note the time the employee completes the task.
4. Subtract the beginning time from the ending time to determine the amount of time it takes to complete the task.
5. Divide the company standard by the time it takes to determine the amount of time it takes to complete the task.
6. Record on data sheet.

Name: *Chris*   Month: *February*

Task: *Setting up cart*   Standard: *18 minutes*

	Date	Time started	Time ended	Total minutes worked	Percent of standard
Production rate	2/11	3:02	3:28	26	69%
prior to	2/14	3:00	3:31	31	58%
instruction	2/15	3:01	3:30	29	62%
Production dur-ing instruction	2/16	3:00	3:25	25	72%
	2/17	3:02	3:23	20	90%
	2/18	3:02	3:23	21	86%
	2/21	3:01	3:19	18	100%
	2/22	3:02	3:20	18	100%
	2/23	3:01	3:19	18	100%

Figure 9.2. Production rate for Chris.

duction rate when the standard is a unit rate. As soon as the probe results indicated that an employee named Marie was independent in operating the dishwasher, the employment specialist collected data to determine Marie's production rate. This was established by taking data three times per day for 2 days. The employment specialist then realized that Marie was matching company production standards for all areas of dishwasher operation except for unracking the clean dishes.

Marie's employment specialist used the production recording form shown in Figure 9.3. The data were divided into two areas: work rate (percent of standard) prior to instruction and work rate (percent of standard) following instruction. Marie's employment specialist assisted her in increasing her production rate by giving immediate reinforcement for each rack of dishes completed within 1 minute and 10 seconds. At the end of seven sessions, the employment specialist recorded that Marie was unracking clean dishes at 100% of standard.

Strategies to Increase Production Rate

The employment specialist's next step, after determining the employee's current production rate, is to ensure that the employee performs the job to company standards under natural work conditions (Barcus et al., 1987). The best strategies for improving and maintaining production rates are those found naturally at the job site and typically used with all employees in the work environment. In Table 9.5 Mcloughlin et al. (1987) have identified a list of common strategies used by employers to increase the production rate of their employees.

Table 9.4. Determining employee production rate by the number of units completed

1. Identify two short time periods during the day to sample and record the employee's production rate.
2. Count and record the number of units completed (e.g., number of pots scrubbed) during the identified sample time period (e.g., 10 minutes).
3. Divide the number of units the employee completes by the company standard number to determine the production rate (percentage of standard).
4. Record rate on data sheet.
5. Collect and record rate at least two times during the day for 2 consecutive days.

Name: *Marie*   Month: *August*
Task: *Unrack clean dishes*   Standard: *6 racks (units) in 7 minutes*

	Date	Time started	Time ended	Total minutes worked	Units completed	Percent of standard
Production rate prior to instruction	8/ 3	9:45	9:51	7	3.5	50%
	8/ 3	1:40	1:47	7	3.75	63%
	8/ 3	2:47	2:54	7	3.5	50%
	8/ 4	9:30	9:37	7	3.75	63%
	8/ 4	1:31	1:38	7	3.75	63%
	8/ 4	2:50	2:57	7	3.5	50%
Production rate following instruction	8/ 5	9:42	9:49	7	3.75	63%
	8/ 5	1:43	1:50	7	4.5	75%
	8/ 5	2:28	2:36	7	4.75	79%
	8/ 6	9:42	9:47	7	5.5	92%
	8/ 6	2:29	2:36	7	5.75	96%
	8/ 9	9:50	9:57	7	5.5	92%
	8/ 9	1:51	1:58	7	6	100%
	8/10	2:30	2:37	7	6	100%
	8/11	9:41	9:48	7	6	100%

Figure 9.3. Production rate for Marie.

Frequently employees with severe mental retardation do not automatically function in response to these strategies. Several instructional techniques can be used to bring the employee under the controls of the natural work environment, including programming naturally occurring cues, programming naturally occurring contingencies, and programming naturally occurring reinforcers (Barcus et al., 1987). Regardless of which method or combination of methods an employment specialist chooses, she or he should use the following guidelines when appropriate to the employee's receptive language skills:

- Inform the employee of the company production standard.
- Inform the employee of her or his current production rate.
- Keep the employee informed of her or his progress.
- Model the appropriate production rate.

Programming Naturally Occurring Cues   A natural cue represents some feature of the work environment that indicates to the employee what should be done next. Examples include the placement or location of materials; the presence of a customer, coworker, or supervisor; a mechanical device such as an on/off indicator light on a dish-

Table 9.5.   Employer strategies for increasing production

Performance charts showing an employee's production rate
Bonus pay for work exceeding the production standard
Worker of the week or month commendation
Pay raises and/or promotions
Employees turn in daily production counts to the supervisor
Supervisor recommends solutions to the employee

washer; or verbal, gestural, or pictorial instructions. Additional examples of naturally occurring cues are provided in Table 9.6.

When a natural cue is presented or occurs, the employee can make either a correct response or an incorrect response. For example, when dish trays stack up at the end of the conveyor belt while the employee is operating the dishwasher, the employee could stop operating the dishwasher and clear the trays (the appropriate action) or he or she could continue to operate the dishwasher while trays continue to stack up on the conveyor belt (inappropriate action). If the employee consistently responds with the appropriate action of clearing the trays, no intervention is necessary. In the event that the employee does not maintain the appropriate response, the employment specialist should implement systematic instructional procedures. This is necessary in order for the trainer to eventually fade his or her presence from the work area. The example in Figure 9.4 shows how Michael was taught to respond to naturally occurring cues.

Programming Naturally Occurring Contingencies   Natural contingencies include natural corrections from persons in an employee's environment and the natural consequences of performing an action or job duty that can motivate an individual to continue the appropriate response or modify an inappropriate response. Examples of some naturally occurring contingencies are listed in Table 9.7.

If the natural contingencies maintain the employee's performance at the company standard, no intervention is needed. If the natural contingencies do not maintain the appropriate response or if allowing the natural contingencies to occur poses a threat to the employee's safety or the safety of others in the work environment, implementation of systematic instructional procedures is necessary.

For example, Marie's coworker would go to the employment specialist and complain that Marie was dripping too much water on the floor in the pot scrubbing area. Each time the employment specialist received a complaint he would ask Marie to mop the floor. This occurred for a week, after which the employment specialist asked Marie's coworkers to talk with Marie directly when they saw excess water on the floor in the pot scrubbing area. He also asked her coworkers to compliment Marie whenever the floor was dry. As soon as Marie started to get compliments and complaints from her new friends (coworkers), she started to mop the floor routinely while she was scrubbing pots. The coworkers who were once complaining about Marie's wet floor were now thanking her for keeping the floor dry.

Table 9.6.   Examples of naturally occurring cues

Types of naturally occurring cues	Corresponding examples of naturally occurring cues	Appropriate employee action
Placement of objects	Dirty dishes on empty restaurant table	Busing the table
Presence of customer/coworker	Presence of customer in cafeteria line	Ask, "May I help you?"
Supervisor	Supervisor in the work area	Being on task
Mechanical device	Indicator light on dishwasher	Refilling dishwasher with soap
Verbal instruction	Coworker request for assistance	Indicating willingness to help
Gestural instruction	Coworker points to clock on wall	Punching out for break
Pictorial instruction	Pictures for salad preparation in fast food restaurant	Completing duty as indicated in picture, then going on to complete next job duty

Employee: *Michael*   Job site: *Regency Square Mall*

Employment specialist: *John*   Date:

Objective: Within 10 seconds of seeing a medium size puddle of liquid on the mall floor, Michael will initiate emergency clean-up procedures with 100% accuracy for four consecutive sessions. (A medium size puddle is defined as any puddle of liquid measuring at least 5″ in diameter.)

Environment: First level of the mall.

Reinforcement: Michael will receive verbal praise each time he initiates the clean-up procedure within 10 seconds. Once he achieves 75% success, reinforcement will gradually be decreased to every other occurrence of the desired behavior.

Data Collection: Because spills occur on a sporadic basis, event recording will be taken for each possible occurrence of the behavior. The time will be recorded when the employment specialist feels Michael has seen the spill, and the time he begins to initiate clean-up procedures. A (+) will be recorded if Michael initiates the activity in the 10-second period and a (−) if he exceeds the time limit. These data will be converted into percentage of appropriate responses observed out of the total possible opportunities.

Intervention Program:
A.   When Michael observes a spill and subsequently exceeds the 10-second period, the employment specialist will tell Michael, "Clean up the water."
B.   As Michael achieves at or above 60% success, the employment specialist will use a indirect prompt (e.g., "Michael, what should you do now?") whenever he exceeds the 10-second period.

Program Evaluation: This program will be evaluated 6 days from the date of initiation. If Michael has not demonstrated success at this time, the program will be revised. If Michael has begun self-initiation, the program will continue as described above.

Figure 9.4.   Instructional program for responding to natural cues.

Programming Naturally Occurring Reinforcers.   Employees who work for reinforcers available in the work environment, such as paychecks, coworker and supervisor praise, positive written supervisor evaluations, pay raises, bonuses, and social interactions with coworkers are more likely to maintain their work performance. Initially, the naturally occurring reinforcers may not serve to maintain the employee's performance of his or her job duties. When this is the case, artificial reinforcers should be paired with the naturally occurring reinforcers. Once the job duty is being performed to standard, the non-natural reinforcers should be systematically withdrawn until the employee is performing the job duties for naturally occurring reinforcers only. Refer to Chapter 8, on initial training and skill acquisition, for procedures on using reinforcers during job-site training.

An employee named Jane needed programming for naturally occurring reinforcers. She was employed as a laundry attendant and required frequent reinforcement from the employment specialist to stay on task while pressing napkins and folding towels. The supervisor and coworkers rarely initiated positive reinforcement and interacted among themselves infrequently. The employment specialist observed that when a worker initiated contact with the supervisor, frequently the worker received verbal praise for completing his or her work. The employment specialist used a model prompt to train Jane to report to her supervisor every time she finished folding or pressing a cart full of laundry. The supervisor responded with praise for completing the work or with

Table 9.7. Example of naturally occurring contingencies

Types of naturally occurring contingencies	Action	Appropriate employee response	Inappropriate employee response
Natural corrections from coworkers and supervisors	Supervisor informs all employees to work faster.	Worker demonstrates on-task behavior and increases work rate.	New employee tells supervisor to get lost.
Consequences of performing an action	Chef requests assistance in carrying food through a door.	Worker holds door for chef.	New employee shuts door in chef's face.
Consequences of performing a job duty	New employee is thanked by a coworker for taking out trash.	Worker smiles at coworker.	New employee tells coworker that he hates this job.

verbal directions for the next task to be completed. The trainer faded to a verbal prompt as Jane learned to initiate the interaction with her supervisor. The checklist that was used to monitor Jane's independent response rate is located in Figure 9.5. The strategy used assisted her in receiving the reinforcement she required in an environment where minimal reinforcement was available. In addition, a natural cue for prompting the worker to perform the next task was naturally built into her job routine.

Attention to Task

During the stabilization phase of job-site training and all throughout the follow-along period, it is important to monitor an employee's on-task behavior. Knowing that an employee is attending to task allows the trainer to make decisions about how and when to fade from the job site. When a worker has problems staying on-task, this affects work rate as well as relationships with supervisors and coworkers.

A whole interval recording method can be used for assessing on-task behaviors during brief observation periods. With this method, the employment specialist defines what constitutes on-task behavior and off-task behavior. He or she then selects an interval of time to observe the employee unobtrusively. The interval is then divided into segments for observation. If the worker remains on task for the *whole* segment of time, the employment specialist scores ($+$) on the data recording form. If the worker is off task for any portion of the segment, ($-$) is scored. Intervals of data collection should be scattered across the day during all job duties. This will help the employment specialist determine whether the employee is consistently off task for a specific job duty or specific time

For example, an employee is observed performing a particular job task during a 30-minute interval. The employment specialist does not prompt or reinforce the worker in any way. Every minute the job trainer notes whether the employee is on task by recording ($+$), or off task by recording ($-$). At the end of the 30-minute observation period, the employment specialist calculates the percentage of time the employee is on task by dividing the number of ($+$) recorded by the total number of observations.

Figure 9.6 displays a data collection recording form for an employee named Mark for on-task behavior. The employment specialist wanted to obtain an accurate picture of Mark's independent work behavior during performance of his pot scrubbing job duty. The supervisor had suggested that he felt Mark was having difficulty with this task. Standing away from Mark's immediate work area, the employment specialist set aside a 30-minute

Date	Number of carts completed	Number and type of trainer prompts required	Number of independent responses
8/9	111	MMM	
8/9	111	MMV	
8/10	1111	MMVV	
8/11	111	MVV	
8/12	1111	VVVV	
8/13	111	VVV	
8/15	111	VV	1
8/16	1111	VV	111
8/17	111	V	11
8/18	111		111
8/19	1111	V	111
8/20	111		111
8/22	1111		1111
8/23	111		111

V = Verbal   G = Gestural   M = Model   P = Physical

Figure 9.5.   Checklist for monitoring Jane's response rate. (This program was developed and implemented by Wendy Parent, an employment specialist with the RRTC/VCU.)

period to observe Mark. Using the definitions of on-task behavior at the bottom of the recording form, the employment specialist observed Mark and recorded whether he was on task for each of the 1-minute time periods.

After sampling Mark's work regularity for 3 working days, the employment specialist was able to determine that Mark was 67% on task while scrubbing pots. The employment specialist then discussed the issue with one of Mark's coworkers who walked past the pot scrubbing area on a regular basis to set up her food preparation area. The coworker agreed to tell Mark that he was doing a good job scrubbing pots each day between 8:30 and 9:30. As reflected in the data, Mark showed a sharp increase in on-task behavior after the coworker started to reinforce Mark's work behavior.

Design and Implementation of a Program to Increase Production

At this point, the employment specialist should review the employee's production rate and on-task data. If the employee is still experiencing difficulty in performing the job task at company standards, the employment specialist should implement the process outlined in Table 9.8.

Several strategies can be used to improve a worker's production rate (Barcus et al., 1987; Mcloughlin et al., 1987; Moon et al., 1986; Wehman, Moon, Everson, Wood, & Barcus, 1988). The employment specialist can design and utilize a changing criterion reinforcement program in which the worker has to work progressively faster in order to receive reinforcement (Wehman et al., 1988). A self-management program, through which the employee monitors his or her own performance (Wehman et al., 1988; Wheeler, Bates, Marshall, & Miller, 1988), may be implemented. The employment specialist may have the worker talk about ways to improve her or his performance, and then meet with the worker before and after the task to discuss the worker's progress (Mcloughlin et al., 1987). In some instances the use of assistive devices such as a timer, alarm clock, or a mechanical pacing device may be used in conjunction with a self-monitoring or changing-criterion program design. If assistive devices are utilized, the employment specialist should systematically fade the use of them from the worksite

Trainee: *Mark*
Trainer: *Steve*

Job site: *Henrico Government Center*
Job duty: *Scrubbing pots*

Date	Observation period	Time started	Time ended	1-minute intervals (+ = on-task; − = off-task)	Percent time on-task	Job duty
Baseline						
8/9	30	8:30	9:00	+ + + + + − − − + + + + + − − − − + + +	53%	Scrub pots
8/10	30	9:00	9:30	+ + + + + − + − − − + − − − − + − − + +	57%	Scrub pots
8/11	30	8:30	9:00	+ − − + + + − + − − + + − − + + − + + −	53%	Scrub pots
8/12	30	8:30	9:00	+ + + + − + − − + + + + − + + + + + + +	77%	Scrub pots
Intervention						
8/12	30	8:30	9:00	+ + + + − − − + + + + + − + + + + + + +	83%	Scrub pots
8/15	30	9:00	9:30	+ + + + + + + + + − + + + + + + − + + +	93%	Scrub pots
8/15	30	8:30	9:00	+ + + + + + + + + + + + + + + + + + + +	100%	Scrub pots
8/16	30	8:30	9:00	+ + + + + + + + + + + + + + + + + + + +	100%	Scrub pots
8/16	30	9:00	9:30	+ + + + + − + + + + + + + + + + + + + +	97%	Scrub pots

Definitions
On-task: Hands in motion completing job task (i.e., wiping, sweeping, scraping, scrubbing, lifting, or stacking).
Off-task: Hands not in motion, walking away from work area, clapping hands or rubbing self.

Figure 9.6. Data collection record for on-task behavior.

Table 9.8.   Determining whether a formal program is necessary to increase production rate

Review probe data for the task. Make sure the employee is performing all steps of the task analysis (TA) as they were designed.

If the employee is not performing all steps, resume acquisition training until the employee performs the steps of the TA in order.

If all steps are being performed, review the TA. Make sure the task has been analyzed so that it is performed as efficiently as possible. (Reduce worker movement; make sure the TA facilitates the use of both hands if appropriate, and so forth.)

If the TA is revised, resume acquisition training until the employee performs all steps of the revised TA in order.

If the employment specialist is satisfied that the original TA is as efficient as possible, observe the worker to determine on/off task behavior.

If there is a high level of off-task behavior (more than 20%), the employment specialist should implement a training program.

If the employee is performing the TA as designed, and if the employment specialist is satisfied that the TA is efficient and on/off task data indicate the worker is on-task, design and implement a formal program to increase production rate.

(Mcloughlin et al., 1987; Wehman et al., 1988). Some of these program designs are described below.

Changing Criterion Design   Using the changing criterion program design the employment specialist systematically requires the employee to work progressively faster in order to receive reinforcement, until the worker can perform the task consistently at the company standard (Snell, 1987). First, the employee's production rate must be identified (baseline). In the beginning of the program, the worker is to meet a criterion that requires a minimal increase in his or her production. Gradually, as the worker meets the criterion and receives reinforcement, the criterion is increased so that it is closer and closer to the company standard. Table 9.9 describes guidelines that may be helpful to follow when using a changing criterion design. Figure 9.7 is a sample program used with an employee named Mary to increase her production rate.

Self-Management   Self-management refers to the ability of an employee to monitor his or her work performance through the use of external prompts or procedures such as self-instruction, labels, picture cues, checklists, pictorial job duty booklets, pretaped instructions, and/or tactile cues. Self-management procedures are commonly used at job sites to assist employees in, for example, following the daily job duty sequence, per-

Table 9.9.   Guidelines for using a changing-criterion program design

Establish a reinforcer.

Review production data to determine the worker's current production rate without reinforcement.

Establish an initial criterion for the worker to meet based on the worker's baseline performance.

Set an objective for changing the criterion.

Determine subsequent increase in the criterion level.

Begin the program.

Change the criterion as the worker meets the established objective based on his or her performance.

Evaluate the worker's performance.

If performance is unsuccessful, check to see if you have increased the criterion too quickly.

Check the reinforcer.

Change criterion and reinforcer if necessary.

Consumer: *Mary*
Job site: *Ramada Renaissance Hotel*
Employment specialist: *Sue*
Program: *Increasing work rate using a changing criterion design*

Objective: Mary will fold 21 towels correctly in 10 minutes over 90% of her workday for 3 consecutive days.

Rationale: Mary is currently performing her job with 95%–100% accuracy but is working at a rate below the employer's standards. She has met criterion on the behavior intervention program to increase on-task work behavior

Baseline data: Data collected on June 16, 1988, show that Mary is folding 15 towels in 10 minutes, which is 60% of the standard required of laundry attendants.

Data collection: A permanent product recording method will be used to count and record the number of towels folded correctly. The frequency and type of errors made will be recorded on the data sheet.

Reinforcers: A multi-element design was used to compare the effects of a timer, candy, and a picture checklist. The timer was found to be the most effective with 12, 26, and 23 towels folded respectively during 10-minute intervals. Candy will be purchased on an intermittent schedule at the end of the workday.

Changing Criterion Design Procedure:
1. Show Mary the timer and tell her that you are going to set it for 10 minutes. Explain that she needs to fold 12 towels before the bell goes off. The trainer will set the timer and leave the room.
2. When the timer goes off, the trainer will return and count the number of towels that are folded correctly. Mary and the trainer will plot the data point on the graph together. If she folds 12 towels or more, provide verbal praise. If she folds fewer than 12 towels, say: "You folded _____ towels. We need to work faster to fold 12 towels. Let's try it again.
3. When Mary meets the criterion of 12 towels and 2 consecutive trials, increase the criterion to 14 towels in 10 minutes. Follow the same procedures as above.
4. When Mary meets the criterion of 14 towels for 3 consecutive trials, increase the criterion to 16 towels. Follow the same procedures as above.
5. When Mary meets the criterion of 16 towels for 3 consecutive trials, increase the criterion to 18 towels in 10 minutes. Follow the same procedure as above.
6. When Mary meets the criterion of 18 towels for 4 consecutive trials, increase the criterion to 21 towels in 10 minutes. Follow the same procedure as above.
7. When Mary meets the criterion of 21 towels for 3 consecutive trials, a fading and maintenance schedule will be developed.
(If Mary exceeds the criterion set at any level (i.e., consistently folds 14 towels during the 10-towel critierion) the new criterion will be based on her actual performance.)

Figure 9.7.   Changing criterion program to increase production.

forming a specific job duty appropriately, operating mechanisms (e.g., turning on/off a piece of machinery), determining the appropriate supplies for restocking a supply cart, or breaking down or reassembling a piece of machinery. Table 9.10 provides examples of typical self-management procedures that have been used at job sites.

Some new employees with severe mental retardation will require formal self-management programs to guide them through the performance of their duties. A self-

Table 9.10.   Examples of self-management procedures

EXTERNAL PROMPT(S)	EXAMPLE
Self-recording	A worker charts her or his performance on a daily basis.
Self-instruction	A person in a janitorial position must clean several shower rooms in a truck stop. In each room, the employee verbally states the tasks to be completed (e.g., "Clean the sinks") and then performs the job. This is repeated for each job duty. The process is simply one of saying, then doing.
Labels	A pot scrubber discriminates pots that need to be soaked versus those to be scrubbed immediately by picking up a pot and verbally labeling each one as a "soaker" or a "scrubber." This process allows the employee to organize the work area independently.
Picture cues	A drawing that shows the appropriate sequence for replacing the divider curtains in a dishwasher can assist the employee.
Checklist	A list of the sequence of job duties can be developed using a single picture to represent each major duty. The employee can check off each duty upon completion.
Pictorial job duty booklet	A multiple page booklet can be made in which snap shots depict the job sequence for the employee.
Pretaped instruction	A prerecorded tape with verbal instructions can be used by the employee. The tape (in a portable cassette tape player) is turned on and the employee listens to the instruction, turns off the player, and completes the duty. Then the employee turns the tape on to receive the next instruction. This process is repeated until the job is completed.
Tactile cue	A piece of sand paper can be glued to the "OFF" button for a garbage disposal. The employee identifies the rough surface as the button to push when turning off the garbage disposal.

management program should not stigmatize the worker and must be approved by the supervisor. Whenever possible, an employee's self-management program should be gradually faded. Table 9.11 outlines guidelines for developing a self-management program.

Figure 9.8 is an example of a program for teaching Michael self-management in his work routine. Michael was able to perform his work tasks independently but did not get started on time. After determining that Michael was having difficulty initiating his work duties, the employment specialist selected a self-monitoring cue to assist Michael in getting to work upon arrival at the job site. She then designed a program to instruct Michael to use a picture cue flip book.

EXPANDING WORKER PERFORMANCE

The employment specialist must ensure that the employee is able to consistently and appropriately perform all aspects of his or her job. This requires the systematic expansion of the number of job duties that the employee performs and maintains at company standards until she or he is able to complete all job duties independently. In addition, supervision of the worker must be conducted by the supervisor(s) for the job site. The employment specialist may need to develop a systematic plan for transferring supervision to the appropriate company personnel.

All job sites have situations occurring that are not controlled by the employee, such as the fire alarm sounding, and require the development of a system to ensure that the employee responds appropriately. Before an employment specialist can consider removing his or her presence from the work site, the employee must be able to respond to a

Table 9.11.   Guidelines for developing a self-management program

Review probe data. If the employee is having specific difficulties in sequencing or discriminating, consider using self-management procedures.

Select a self-management strategy that is not stigmatizing to the new employee and is appropriate for the situation and the job site.

Get the supervisor's approval for the procedure before utilizing it.

Design and implement a systematic instructional program to assist the employee in learning to use the self-management procedure. Involve the supervisor in this process if appropriate.

Monitor the procedure and modify if necessary.

Fade the self-management procedure whenever possible.

variety of situations and function within the parameters of the social culture for the work site. Appropriate interpersonal interactions with coworkers, supervisors, and patrons of the company must occur regularly in order for the employee to become an integral member of the work force.

Expanding Performance Across Supervisors

The employee ultimately will have to perform all job duties under the natural system of supervision at the job site. In some instances the employee may have only one supervisor, but frequently there are several supervisors at a job site. In other situations, for example, there may be two managers who alternate between the day shift and the afternoon shift; or, the employee may be under the supervision of the cook while in the kitchen, the assistant cook at the cafeteria line, and the head custodian while collecting trash and putting it into the dumpster. When an employment specialist is faced with these or similar conditions, she or he should include the appropriate supervisor throughout the training process, particularly during the stabilization period. The employee should be instructed to direct any questions that are not related to training, such as asking for leave time or problems with equipment malfunction, to the appropriate company supervisor, (Mcloughlin et al., 1987) rather than depending on the employment specialist. The employment specialist's role is to provide instruction to the worker to perform the job, and all work-related issues should be handled by the company supervisor(s) from day 1 of employment. Guidelines for ensuring supervisor involvement are described in Table 9.12.

Expanding Performance Across Situations

Occurrences at the job site that cannot be controlled by the employee or the employment specialist include safety signals flashing or sounding (e.g., fire alarm), supplies in the work area running out (e.g., the dishwasher running out of detergent), and machinery breaking down. These situations may occur so infrequently as to make it difficult for the employment specialist to train the employee to respond to all possible situations. Therefore, the employment specialist must plan for the most likely of these situations by checking with supervisors to determine the procedures to follow when they do occur. The following general guidelines help in planning for these infrequent occurrences.

- Identify the possible situations.
- Meet with the supervisor to discuss company policy and outline procedures.
- Explain situations and procedures to the employee and coworkers (if appropriate).
- Elicit a coworker to assist the employee when necessary.

Consumer: *Michael*

Job site: *Azalea Mall*

Work time: *7:00 A.M.—11:00 A.M.*

Employment specialist: *Donna*

Objective: Upon arrival at Azalea Mall, Michael will independently use a picture cue and flip book to: 1) begin work withing 1 minute of arrival and 2) move from task to task for 3 consecutive days with 100% accuracy.

Rationale: Michael is currently delaying work approximately 10–20 minutes upon arrival. At present he waits until Donna arrives to initiate his job duties. He needs a self-monitoring cue to get started in the morning.

Student Characteristics: Michael has little difficulty following a task sequence. He is able to perform his work independently but experiences difficulty getting started on time.

Baseline Procedures:
1. Assess the length of time it takes for Michael to get started on his job duties for 3 consecutive days. Also assess the time it takes him to complete each of his assigned tasks (duration).
2. Probe for 1 day Michael's ability to use the picture flip book. Ask Michael to begin the task by saying, "Michael, it's time to work; use your picture book," (see Behavioral Change Procedures below). Wait 5 seconds for him to initiate the task. If he is performing correctly, score a (+). As soon as he makes an error or fails to initiate a step in the task analysis, discontinue the probe and score a (−) for all remaining steps.
3. Develop a graph for each type of data collection.

Training Data: 1) Continue to collect duration data daily; 2) probe Michael's use of the flip book every 3 days by completing procedure # 2 under Baseline Procedures.

Behavioral Change Procedures;
1. *Develop a flip book of pictures* for Michael's use. The first picture should show Michael setting up his cart. Each remaining picture should show his job duties:
   a. Job cart set up
   b. Cleaning the restrooms (Men's)
   c. Mopping the restroom floor
   d. Cleaning the restrooms (Women's)
   e. Mopping the restroom floor
   f. Setting up cart for cleaning the windows
   g. Cleaning windows of first store
   h. Cleaning windows of second store
   i. Cleaning windows of third store
   j. Cleaning windows of fourth store
   k. Cleaning windows of fifth store
   l. Sweeping the hallway
2. *Develop task analysis and attach to program.*
3. *Use a system of least prompts* for instructing on the use of the picture cue and book. The employment specialist should remain within sight of Michael until he reaches 100% correct performance using the picture book for 3 consecutive days. Meet Michael at the door to the Mall between fourth and fifth store. Before he enters the Mall provide the cue "Michael, it's time to work. Use your picture cue." Wait 5 seconds for an independent response. If correct, proceed to the next step in the task analysis. If incorrect or no response, provide a model/gesture cue. Wait 5 seconds for an independent response. If incorrect or no response, provide a physical prompt. Teach *all* steps in the task analysis in this way. If an error occurs at any time, stop Michael immediately and proceed to the next prompt in the sequence.
4. *Reinforcement strategy:* Coordinate with Michael's family on his bringing a thermos to work with his favorite beverage daily. Train Michael to do self-reinforcement after each job duty completed using his picture cue book.

Figure 9.8. Self-monitoring using a flip book.

Table 9.12. Ensuring supervisor involvement

The supervisor should communicate job-related information directly to the employee as with any other staff member.

The supervisor should be included throughout all phases of training.

The supervisor should communicate natural corrections to the employee as with any other staff member.

The supervisor should reinforce the employee for acceptable work performance as with any other staff member.

The supervisor should discuss work-related issues with the employee.

Table 9.13 provides an example of a situation where procedures were developed to expand a new employee's performance across situations that occur infrequently at a restaurant.

Expanding Performance Across Interpersonnel Interactions

The establishment of interpersonnel relationships with coworkers and supervisors is an important aspect of becoming an accepted member of the work force (Maynard, 1986; Taslimi, 1980). Henderson and Argyle (1985) reviewed studies of interactions on the job and found that 35%–90% of work time is spent interacting with others. Common types of interactions between workers are: helping with work, discussing work, discussing personal life, joking, teasing, asking for or giving advice, and demonstrating work tasks (Nisbet & Hagner, 1988).

Mcloughlin et al. (1987) recommend that the employment specialist consider the steps in Table 9.14 to assist the worker to develop relationships with other employees.

Interfering Behavior Employees who have severe mental retardation sometimes engage in mannerisms, such as finger flapping, or inappropriate talking, such as protesting against working or yelling at coworkers. These type of behaviors can bring on unwanted attention (Mcloughlin et al., 1987). An employment specialist dealing with this type of situation may need to develop a formal program to eliminate or reduce the occurrence of these or other types of interfering behaviors. Figure 9.9. shows a program that was developed to eliminate the interfering behavior exhibited by Michael, who would refuse to work. Figure 9.10 shows a graph of the data on this program.

Coworker Mentor or Advocate A common strategy used in business involves one worker acting as a mentor to assist another worker in the work place (Kram & Isabella, 1985). The employment specialist, in conjunction with the employer, should identify an experienced, competent coworker who has a thorough understanding of the overall operations at the job site and who generally gets along well with everyone, to be a

Table 9.13. Examples of infrequent job situations that must be addressed

Situation	Procedure	Person(s) responsible
Bomb threat or fire alarm	Leave building through nearest exit	Security guard and second floor janitor
Wet floor: mop not in supply closet	Request assistance from coworker	Second floor janitor
Dishwasher breaks down	Inform immediate supervisor	Chef
Water begins to back up through drain	Request assistance from coworker	Supervisor or coworker

Table 9.14.   Facilitating co-worker relationships

Learn coworkers' names.

Fade your presence at lunch and break times.

If the employee needs some information, have him or her ask coworkers or the supervisor.

Questions about the job during training should be directed to coworker or the supervisor.

Encourage the employee to interact with his or her coworkers at break, lunch, and after work.

Encourage the employee to become involved in company-sponsored activities: softball team, carpool, company party, and so forth.

Adapted from Mcloughlin, Garner, and Callahan (1987).

mentor or advocate. Often a coworker who initially shows a great deal of interest in the new worker and the training procedures being implemented is a good choice as coworker advocate. The guidelines in Table 9.15 should be helpful in working with coworkers on the job in this function.

The employment success of an employee with severe mental retardation is often determined by the support and understanding of coworkers at the job site. If the employee is perceived as reliable, cooperative, competent, and dependable, the potential for long-term employment in that job is increased. Identifying at least one coworker at the job site who can eventually serve as an unofficial trainer and facilitator for the employee will help facilitate the integration of the new employee into the work force. Table 9.16 lists examples of ways in which coworkers have served as facilitators.

FADING FROM THE JOB SITE

The process of fading the employment specialist's presence from the job site begins the first day of a worker's employment and takes several weeks to several months to accomplish (Barcus et al., 1987; Moon et al., 1986; Wehman et al., 1988). During this time the employment specialist will fade the instructional prompts used to teach the worker specific job tasks, systematically fade from the immediate work area, and gradually leave the job site for longer periods of time.

The information that assists an employment specialist in determining when to begin fading and whether to continue the process comes from analyzing the following data: on/off task, probe, prompting assistance, and production rate. These data are recorded on a regular basis during initial skill training and acquisition and provide a measure of the employee's job performance (Barcus et al., 1987). In addition to these data, the degree to which the employee performs her or his duties under the control of the naturally occurring cues, contingencies, and reinforcers, as well as under the supervision of the company manager, will influence the schedule and rate at which the employment specialist's presence can be faded. Therefore, the actual schedule of fading is influenced by the employee's performance, the characteristics of the job, the work environment, and the needs of the supervisor(s) and coworker(s) (Barcus et al., 1987; Moon et al., 1986).

Fading Instruction

The fading of instructional cues and prompts is an essential first step in the process of removing the trainer's presence from the job site. Fading of instruction begins the first day of training and involves the purposeful reduction of the level and intensity of instructional assistance that the worker requires to perform the job task independently. The

Consumer: *Michael*

Job Site: *Pizza parlor*

Program: *Eliminating work avoidance (i.e., sitting down on the job, going to the break area inappropriately, not engaging in work tasks for longer than 5 minutes)*

Objective: Michael will complete all of his job duties without exhibiting work avoidance behaviors with 100% accuracy for an entire week (Thursday–Sunday).

Rationale: Michael must learn to work without exhibiting work avoidance behavior in order to maintain employment at the pizza parlor.

Student Characteristics: Michael enjoys work but has not shown ability to deal with work frustration. He shows some interest in self-monitoring. Michael does not respond well to verbal interaction.

Baseline/Data Collection: Duration of work avoidance across an entire workday for 3 workdays will be collected for baseline. The same procedure will be used after program implementation.

Behavior Change Procedure:

1. Develop a picture book of job duties. A picture will represent each major job task . There will be a page for checking off tasks completed without work avoidance.
2. Make a reinforcement check sheet with a picture (drawing) of a pizza divided into eight sections. These sections will represent earning slices of pizza.
3. At the beginning of the day, show Michael the book and picture of the pizza. Explain that for each task completed he will earn a slice of pizza at the end of the day. Begin work. As soon as the first task is completed (without Michael avoiding work) tell him to check off the task in his picture book. Show him the reinforcement sheet and check off one slice. Say in a matter of fact voice "You have earned the first slice of pizza. That's good. Now earn the next slice." Move in this way through the morning tasks.

For the afternoon, Michael has the opportunity to earn three checks. He earns the first immediately upon getting back to work after his break. The remainder of the afternoon should be divided into two equal parts. One should approximate the midpoint of the afternoon. The final check should run up to just before the time to order the pizza. (This is 15 minutes prior to departure time.)

If Michael displays work avoidance behavior, beyond **5** minutes, give him **one** warning. Say, "Michael, you must work to earn your pizza." Remove yourself for **2** minutes. If he comes back to work within this time period, he may still earn the pizza. If not, he has lost it for the job duty period. Stand next to Michael and say "Go to work, now." Stand and wait. As soon as he goes to work say, "Good, you can begin earning pizza now." As long as Michael refuses to work, repeat your verbal command every 5 minutes. Tell him you will move away from him as soon as he begins to work.

At the end of the day the employment specialist needs to cut the pizza into eight sections. Remove any slice that Michael has not earned. Present Michael with the slices earned. Say, "This is how much pizza you earned today."

Maintenance and generalization procedures will be developed. Specifically a self-monitoring program will be developed when Michael reaches program criterion.

Figure 9.9. Program for eliminating interfering behavior: work avoidance.

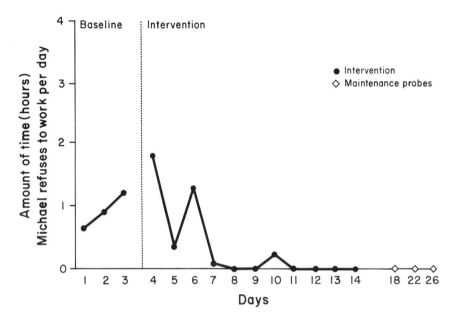

Figure 9.10.   Graph of data on program for eliminating work avoidance behavior.

employment specialist can consider the fading of instruction for a job task complete when the worker no longer depends on him or her to perform the job duty.

Fading from the Work Area

Once the employee is correctly performing a specific job duty for three consecutive data sessions, and is working at the company's production standard under the natural work conditions, the employment specialist should remain out of the immediate work area while that job duty is being performed. For example, the employment specialist may go to the break area to catch up on paper work while the employee sets up the salad bar. However, the employee may still require training assistance from the employment specialist on all other job duties. As each major job duty is performed independently by the employee, the employment specialist fades her or his presence from that specific work area. For example, when an employee named David began to take greater responsibility for each job duty, the employment specialist faded his presence from David's immediate work area. The employment specialist scheduled his time with David to assist him in meeting the production demands for pot scrubbing and operating the dishwasher. Table 9.17 reflects the employment specialist fading schedules for a 2-week period in August.

Fading from the Job Site

When the employee is working approximately 50% of his or her work day without the presence of the employment specialist in the immediate work area, the employment spe-

Table 9.15.   Guidelines for working with coworkers

Ask a coworker if she or he is willing to assist the new employee by acting as a coworker advocate.

Model appropriate interactions with the new employee; the coworker will follow your lead.

Encourage questions from the coworker.

Discuss ways in which the coworker advocate can be of assistance.

Table 9.16. Example of coworker involvement

Prevents the employee from always being assigned to the least prestigious jobs

Ensures that the employee is not being taken advantage of by coworkers

Assists the employee in appropriately handling confrontations with other coworkers

Makes sure the employee understands schedule changes and that the employee communicates this information to parents/guardians and employment specialist

Assists the employee in responding properly to situations such as safety signals (fire alarms), running out of supplies in the work area, and machinery break downs

cialist should begin removing his or her presence from the job site. The employee's first time alone for a portion of the day at the job site is a significant step. The employment specialist should clearly explain to the employer, coworkers, and the employee that she or he can be contacted and will return to the job site immediately should a problem arise. If the employee continues to do well based on data results and supervisor and coworker comments, then the employment specialist should gradually stay on site only during that part of the employee's work day in which his or her presence is necessary (e.g., during the lunch rush). When the employee is successfully completing all job duties under natural work conditions, the employment specialist should remain away from the job site for an entire day. Initially, the employment specialist should stop by the job site at the end of the workday and determine if all went well for the day. The guidelines in Table 9.18 are useful when the employment specialist fades from the job site (Barcus et al., 1987; Moon et al., 1986).

The following is a brief description of the fading process that Chris's employment specialist used to fade her presence from the job site. On February 7th, Chris and the employment specialist independently met with two coworkers and the shift supervisor to inform them that Chris would be alone at the job site for a portion of the workday. The employment specialist explained that Chris was already doing well by himself when she left the immediate work area. A schedule was given to the supervisor and Chris for the first week; a telephone number at which the employment specialist could be reached was

Table 9.17. Example of reducing the trainer's presence in the immediate work area

Approximate time job duty is completed	Job duty	Trainer time with Marie in immediate work area
8:00	Punch in	8:00– 8:55 = 55 minutes
8:00– 8:30	Set up dishroom	
8:30– 9:00	Clean dishroom	
9:00–10:25	Operate dishwasher	9:10–10:30 = 1 hour, 20 minutes
10:25–10:55	Clean equipment	
10:55–11:10	Break	
11:10–12:30	Scrub pots	11:10–12:00 = 50 minutes
12:30– 1:00	Lunch	
1:00– 3:00	Operate dishwasher	1:00– 1:10 = 10 minutes 2:00– 3:00 = 1 hour
3:00– 3:30	Collect, clean, and return ash trays	
3:30– 4:00	Break down dishroom	3:30– 4:00 = 30 minutes
4:00	Punch out	
	Total time	4 hours, 45 minutes

Table 9.18.   Guidelines for fading trainer presence from the job site

Discuss the fading schedule with the employer.

Agree on a day to begin fading trainer presence.

Inform the employee and coworkers (if appropriate) that you are leaving the work site.

Give the employer a telephone number where you can be reached.

Leave for no more than 1 or 2 hours the first time.

Continue to collect probe, on/off task, and production data on the established schedule.

Increase your time off the job site as the employee continues to show independence, until he or she can work for the entire day without assistance.

also provided. Everyone was assured that the employment specialist would return if any problems occurred. Each successive week, the employment specialist drew up a new schedule for fading her time from the job site and gave a copy to Chris, his coworker facilitator, and his supervisor. Many times during the fading process, Chris told his employment specialist that he did not need her anymore. These comments, along with daily evaluations, helped the employment specialist determine that Chris could do his job without a trainer present. Figure 9.11 shows the schedule for reducing the trainer's presence at the job site and corresponding objectives and methods of evaluation.

FOLLOW-ALONG

Job-site training involves direct systematic instruction in job duties and related nonvocational skills (Barcus et al., 1987; Moon et al., 1986). The employment specialist's role is to facilitate the worker's successful performance of job duties, to be available to support the worker, and to fade from the work site to the greatest degree possible (Mcloughlin et al., 1987). Once the employment specialist has implemented the procedures outlined in each of the three components of job-site training (orientation and assessment, initial skill training, and stabilization) and the worker independently completes her or his job duties under the controls of the natural work environment, the employment specialist moves into the follow-along phase of supported employment.

It is critical that the employment specialist devise a method for regular follow-along of the worker's progress after fading from the job site (Moon et al., 1986). Follow-along should be individualized, systematic, and focused on enhancing the quality of the worker's employment experience. It is a proactive process that relies upon the cooperation and involvement of key people who are important to the worker and her or his maintenance of employment. Table 9.19 lists persons who may be involved in the follow-along planning and support for a worker.

Follow-along planning involves: 1) reviewing the worker's current work experience, 2) planning follow-along activities, 3) establishing a follow-along schedule, and 4) implementing the follow-along plan (Rusch, 1986). The objectives of the follow-along process are to identify activities necessary to support the worker in maintaining a high quality work experience and to develop an agreement among the people and resources whose cooperation and participation will support the activities (O'Brien, 1987). It is a structured process designed to improve understanding of the worker's situation and create agreement on cooperative actions for supporting the worker. Table 9.20 outlines guidelines for proactive follow-along.

Date	Trainer schedule	Objectives	Method of evaluation
2/8	3:03–11:00	Determine if employee has independently: 1. Entered buiding 2. Punched time clock 3. Initiated cart set up	1. Coworker observation 2. Checking time card 3. Trainer observation

Sunday	Monday	Tuesday	Wednesday	Thursday	Friday	Saturday
		2/14 At job site	2/15	2/16	2/17	2/18
				3:03–11 P.M.		
		2/21	2/22	2/23	2/24	2/25

Date	Trainer schedule	Objectives	Method of evaluation
2/23	4:15–11:00	Determine if employee has independently: 1. Maintained above objective 2. Set up cart at correct production rate 3. Cleaned station #1 4. Dry mopped first floor of the mall 5. Initiated sweeping task	1. Coworker observation 2. Job duty analysis 3. Observe station #1 4. Observe floor, check with mall security 5. Trainer observation

Sunday	Monday	Tuesday	Wednesday	Thursday	Friday	Saturday
		2/21 At job site 3:03–11:00 P.M.	2/22	2/23 **Begin new schedule** At job site	2/24	2/25
				4:15–11:00 P.M.		

	4:45–11:00	Determine if employee has independently: 1. Maintained above objectives 2. Completed sweeping of first floor of the mall	1. Coworker observation, shift supervisor observation, trainer observation, job duty analysis 2. Trainer observation

Sunday	Monday	Tuesday	Wednesday	Thursday	Friday	Saturday
		2/28 **Begin new schedule** At job site	2/29	3/1	3/2	3/3
		4:45–11:00 P.M.				

3/1	6:30–11:00	Determine if employee has: 1. Maintained above objectives 2. Initiated collecting trash	1. Coworker observation, shift supervisor observation, job duty analysis 2. Trainer observation

Figure 9.11. Fading schedule for February and March. Note: The employment specialist conducted spot checks at 10:45 P.M. every other night until March 24. At that time Chris began receiving only two 10:45 P.M. checks per week.

(continued)

Figure 9.11. *(continued)*

Date	Trainer schedule		Objectives		Method of evaluation	
Sunday	**Monday**	**Tuesday**	**Wednesday**	**Thursday**	**Friday**	**Saturday**
		2/28 At job site 4:45–11:00 P.M.	2/29	3/1 **Begin new schedule** at job site ──────────→ 6:30–11:00 P.M.	3/2	3/3
		3/6	3/7	3/8	3/9	3/10 ──────────→
3/10	6:45–11:00		Determine if employee has: 1. Maintained above objectives 2. Collected trash		1. Coworker observation, shift supervisor observation, job duty analysis 2. Trainer observation	
		3/6 At job site 6:30–11:00 P.M.	3/7	3/8	3/9	3/10 **Begin new schedule** At job site 6:45–11:00 P.M.
		3/13	3/14	3/15	3/16	3/17 ──────────→
3/15	10:45		Determine if employee has: 1. Maintained above objectives		1. Coworker observation, shift supervisor observation, trainer observation, job duty analysis	
		3/13 At job site 6:45–11:00 P.M.	3/14	3/15 **Begin new schedule** At job site 10:45–11:00 P.M.	3/16 **Begin new schedule** No trainer present at job site	3/17 At job site 10:45–11:00 P.M.
		3/20 No trainer present at job site	3/21 At job site 10:45–11:00	3/22 No trainer present at job site	3/23 At job site 10:45–11:00	3/24 No trainer present at job site

Table 9.19.   Persons involved in follow-along planning

Worker

Coworker mentor/advocate

Supervisor(s)

Family member(s)

Neighbor(s) / friend(s)

Coworkers

Human service personnel (e.g., group home manager, rehabilitation counselor, employment specialist, rehabilitation engineer)

Designing a Proactive Follow-Along Plan

A frequently cited reason for establishing follow-along services has been to identify problems in need of remediation in order to prevent the worker from losing his or her job (Kreutzer & Morton, 1988; Rusch, 1986; Wehman and Kregel, 1985). The aim of proactive follow-along is to maintain and enhance the dignity and position of the worker as a valued member of the work force rather than just determining causes of deficiencies in the worker's performance.

The quality of a worker's employment experience should be reviewed routinely. There are several outcomes an employment specialist should consider when planning and implementing a proactive follow-along plan. Table 9.21 briefly describes these outcomes.

Review of a worker's job performance begins the first day she or he begins a job. Daily analysis and feedback from the instructional data; observations; and interactions with the worker, supervisor(s), coworker(s), and family member(s) keep the employment specialist informed of the worker's performance and acceptance within the work place and is a measure of job satisfaction. Methods of reviewing the worker's status and determining follow-along activities include: 1) supervisor(s) evaluations, 2) worker self-evaluations, 3) family member evaluations, 4) coworker mentor input, 5) on-site visits, 6) off-site visits, and 7) telephone contact (Hill, Cleveland, Pendleton, & Wehman, 1982; Moon et al., 1986; Rusch, 1986; Wehman & Kregel, 1985). Table 9.22 gives a brief description of each of these methods.

It is imperative that the employment specialist establish a regular ongoing schedule for review of the worker's employment after fading from the work site. A follow-along schedule should be established to include preset dates and times when each follow-along activity will be conducted. Legal and accountability responsibilities required by funding sources (Mcloughlin et al., 1987) will have a direct impact on the schedule. For example, current vocational rehabilitation regulations stipulate that follow-along activities must oc-

Table 9.20.   Guidelines for proactive follow-along

Identify the worker's satisfaction with her or his work.

Identify the supervisor(s) satisfaction with the worker.

Identify the coworker mentors satisfaction with the worker.

Identify the family member(s) satisfaction with the worker's experience.

Plan follow-along activities.

Establish a follow-along schedule.

Implement the plan.

Review the worker's employment experience.

184 MOON ET AL.

Table 9.21. Worker outcomes

Choice	Does the worker have automony in everyday work-related matters and in larger work matters concerning where and what type of work she or he will perform?
Competence	Is the worker performing meaningful work with whatever level or type of assistance that is required?
Respect	Is the worker holding a valued place among the network of coworkers and valued roles in the work place?
Community participation	Is the worker having the experience of being a part of a network of personal relationships?
Community presence	Is the worker involved in the community environment that defines work life?

Adapted from O'Brien (1987); Shafer (1987).

cur at the work site a minimum of two times per month (Federal Register, 1987). Follow-along services should be designed to provide the necessary supports to the worker for as long as they are necessary and will last for an indefinite length of time.

Table 9.22. Nature of follow-along

Supervisor evaluations	Solicit employer satisfaction with the worker's productivity and integration into the work-site culture. What is the potential for career advancement?
Worker self-evaluations	Solicit worker satisfaction with her or his current position. Is the work challenging, meaningful, and of interest to the worker? Has he or she received a pay raise? What are his or her career aspirations?
Family evaluations	Identify the satisfaction of family members with the worker's performance. Look for changes in family culture that may potentially affect the worker's performance.
Coworker mentor input	Identify the coworker mentor's perception of the worker's integration into the work force. Does the worker enjoy regular access to and intergration with coworkers?
On-site visits	Visits to the job site maintain personal contact and enable first hand observation of the worker's performance and integration into the work force culture.
Off-site visits	Visits with worker and family members off-site maintain personal contact.
Telephone	On-site or off-site visits are not always feasible and/or necessary. Some people are more candid about their perceptions over the telephone.

Adapted from materials developed by Barcus (1985); Shafer (1987).

REFERENCES

Barcus, M. (1985). *Materials developed for a four day internship.* Virginia Commonwealth University: Rehabilitation Research and Training Center. Richmond, VA.

Barcus, M., Brooke, V., Inge, K., Moon, S., & Goodall, P. (1987). *An instructional guide for training on a job site: A supported employment resource.* Richmond: Virginia Commonwealth University, Rehabilitation Research and Training Center.

Federal Register, May 27, 1987.

Henderson, M., & Argyle, M. (1985). Social support by four categories of work colleague: Relationships between activities, stress, and satisfaction. *Journal of Occupational Behavior, 6,* 229–239.

Hill, M., Cleveland, P., Pendleton, P., & Wehman, P. (1982). Strategies in the follow-up of moderately and severely handicapped competitively employed workers. In P. Wehman & M. Hill

(Eds.), *Vocational training and placement of severely disabled persons* (Vol. 3, pp. 160–171). Richmond, VA: Virginia Commonwealth University, Project Employability.

Kram, K., & Isabella, L. (1985). Mentoring alternatives: The role of peer relationships in career development. *Academy of Management Journal, 28,* 110–132.

Kreutzer, J.S., & Morton, M.V. (1988). Traumatic brain injury: Supported employment and compensatory strategies for enhancing vocational outcomes. In P. Wehman and M.S. Moon (Eds.). *Vocational rehabilitation and supported employment* (pp. 291–312). Baltimore: Paul H. Brookes Publishing Co.

Maynard, M. (1986). Measuring work and support network satisfaction. *Journal of Employment Counseling, 23,* 9–18.

Mcloughlin, C.S., Garner, J.B., & Callahan, M. (1987). *Getting employed, staying employed: Job development and training for persons with severe handicaps.* Baltimore: Paul H. Brookes Publishing Co.

Moon, S., Goodall, P., Barcus, M., & Brooke, V. (Eds.). (1986). *The supported work model of competitive employment for citizens with severe handicaps: A guide for job trainers.* Richmond, VA: Virginia Commonwealth University, Rehabilitation Research and Training Center.

Nisbet, J., & Hagner, D. (1988). Natural supports in the workplace: A reexamination of supported employment. *Journal of The Association for Persons with Severe Handicaps, 13*(4), 260–267.

O'Brien, J. (1987). A guide to life-style planning: Using The *Activities Catalog* to integrate services and natural support systems. In B. Wilcox & G.T. Bellamy. *A comprehensive guide to the Activities Catalog: An alternative curriculum for youth and adults with severe disabilities* (pp. 175–189). Baltimore: Paul H. Brookes Publishing Co.

Rusch, F.R. (Ed.). (1986). *Competitive employment issues and strategies.* Baltimore: Paul H. Brookes Publishing Co.

Shafer, M. (1987). *Presentation on follow along.* Paper presented for a 4-day internship at Virginia Commonwealth University: Rehabilitation Research and Training Center, Richmond, VA.

Snell, M.E., (1987). *Systematic instruction of persons with severe handicaps* (3rd ed.). Columbus, OH: Charles E. Merril.

Taslimi, M. (1980). A study on the role of informal relationships among service employees of a work organization. *Dissertation Abstracts International, 41A,* 1235.

Wehman, P., & Kregel, J. (1985). A supported work approach to competitive employment of individuals with moderate and severe handicaps. *Journal of The Association for Persons with Severe Handicaps, 10*(1), 3–11.

Wehman, P., Moon, M.S., Everson, J.M., Wood, W., & Barcus, J.M. (1988). *Transition from school to work: New challenges for youth with severe disabilities.* Baltimore: Paul H. Brookes Publishing Co.

Wheeler, J.J., Bates, P., Marshall, K.J., & Miller, S.R. (1988). Teaching appropriate social behaviors to a young man with moderate mental retardation in a supported competitive employment setting. *Education and Training in Mental Retardation, 23*(2), 105–116.

ADVOCACY AND SUPPORTED EMPLOYMENT

10

Mutual respect, honesty, and consideration are all words that have been used to characterize the client-advocate relationship. An advocate is an individual who seeks change by supporting, speaking out, or acting on behalf of another individual or group of individuals (Anderson, Chitwood, & Hayden, 1982; Sullen, 1979; Wehman, Renzaglia, & Bates, 1985). Although the entire notion of advocacy is a relatively old phenomenon in the field of developmental disabilities, it was not until the civil rights struggle in the 1960s and the consumer-participation movements of the 1970s that persons with disabilities, family members, and some professionals began to seek to change the discrimination practices against persons with developmental and other disabilities (Asch, 1985).

People with mental retardation and their family members have long been accustomed to speaking out on their own behalf against more traditional service delivery options in order to promote increased understanding, independence, and positive legislation for all individuals with developmental disabilities (Scheerenberger, 1987). One prominent example of the advocacy work done by persons with disabilities and their parents was the 1971 landmark case, *Pennsylvania Association for Retarded Citizens (PARC) v. the Commonwealth of Pennsylvania.* For the first time the courts upheld the right to a free and appropriate education for school age children with mental retardation. This action led to the 1975 passage of Public Law 94-142, the Education for All Handicapped Children Act. This law mandated school programs to serve all children regardless of their disability and made parents equal partners in the educational process. A later advocacy example is a text that is designed to guide self advocates and their family members through a decision-making process to obtain and to evaluate the important changes that they seek (Turnbull, Turnbull, Bronicki, Summers, & Roeder-Gordon, 1989).

If advocacy is a critical component in the delivery of human services, then it should serve a major function in high quality supported employment services. From the initial business contact during job development to the periodic contacts during follow-along, supported employment program managers and employment specialists act as advocates on behalf of all persons with severe disabilities and, specifically, the individuals they serve. Modeling is a key component of any helper or advocate relationship and as such requires supported employment service providers to act sensitively when representing persons with disabilities. For example, many of the behaviors in our repertoires,

187

both appropriate and inappropriate, have been modeled from coworkers, friends, or from the media. Similarly, our behaviors are being observed as we travel throughout the community presenting our supported employment service and representing persons with severe disabilities.

This chapter takes a close look at advocacy and explores its role in providing high quality community supported employment services. A supported employment service provider's general attitudes and knowledge are discussed. As well, specific advocacy guidelines to help ensure greater employment success and community acceptance for persons with severe mental retardation are presented.

THE NATURE OF ADVOCACY

Next to self advocacy, which involves persons with disabilities acting on their own behalf, citizen advocacy is perhaps the truest or purest form of advocacy. This approach calls for the use of "unpaid volunteers who act as free agents and who do not serve at the pleasure of any agency" (Wolfensberger & Zauha, 1973, p. 12). This important safeguard is built into the citizen advocacy operation to ensure that the needs and desires of the individual are being met, as opposed to the desires of a particular agency. Due to the potential conflict of interest issues that may arise between service providers and the clients they serve, supported employment specialists and program managers can never be "pure" advocates when compared to the volunteers associated with the citizen advocacy program. Yet, in order to implement supported employment services effectively, managers and employment specialists need to spend a large portion of their total working time advocating for persons with severe disabilities (Brooke, Sale, & Moon, in press; Kregel & Sale, 1988). For this reason the entire nature of advocacy deserves a closer examination.

There exists a certain set of values that frequently have been associated with high quality supported employment services (Bellamy, Rhodes, Mank, & Albin, 1988; Inge, Barcus, & Everson, 1988). Underlying these values is the *belief* that all persons, regardless of their disability, have the right to employment opportunities (Will, 1984). Commitment to this one belief is what drives quality supported employment programs. Service providers working in supported employment programs need to determine if they too subscribe to this basic belief.

Persons with severe mental retardation have a right to expect that supported employment personnel will work to ensure that their interests are articulated. The active nature of advocacy requires an employment specialist to acknowledge and, on some occasions, to confront the competing value systems of the individuals, the agency, and the business involved. For example, a supported employment agency, which needs to make a certain number of job placements within a given period of time, may tell its employment specialist to fade from the new employee's job site before the employee is truly ready for this step. In this instance the employment specialist may have to advocate for the employee with severe mental retardation and confront the agency values by explaining why it is not in the best interest of the new employee or the agency to fade too quickly from the job site.

Another example of competing values could arise between an employment specialist and an employer who focuses too heavily on the personal details of a potential employee's disability and relies on arbitrary medical standards to discourage the employment specialist from gaining additional information about a prospective job. The employment specialist in this case could communicate the interests of the individual with severe mental retardation by shifting the focus of the interview away from personal details and medical biases and on to the specific details of the job, the necessary qualifications, and the service that is provided through supported employment.

ADVOCACY PRACTICES IN SUPPORTED EMPLOYMENT PROGRAMS

Awareness of one's own personal values and realization that one's values can relate directly to how unconditional or nonjudgemental we are when interacting with various groups of people is a basic personal requisite of an effective helper or advocate (Gazda, Asbury, Blazer, Childers, & Walters, 1984). Therefore, it is of critical importance for supported employment advocates to remain aware of their own values as they communicate and work with persons with severe mental retardation, family members, employers, coworkers, community service providers, and the general public, all of whom will have their own unique and diverse value systems. One of the best ways to begin to analyze our own values is to critically review our outcomes and everyday practices. Judging the disparity between the values we hold and our practices will assist us as supported employment personnel in our advocate role. If a supported employment program manager reported that she subscribed to the value that persons with severe mental retardation have the right to employment where they can be successful and earn a fair wage, but she only served persons with mild and moderate mental retardation, then that manager would need to reflect on her personal values in light of her program outcomes.

Table 10.1 shows a list of essential advocacy practices through which persons with severe mental retardation and other severe disabilities would experience high quality supported employment outcomes. Most of the practices listed in Table 10.1 are directly initiated by the supported employment service provider advocating on behalf of persons with severe mental retardation.

High quality practices by supported employment advocates require employment specialists and program managers to work actively with new employees with severe mental retardation to meet their desired community employment-related goals. Meeting these

Table 10.1.   Essential practices of supported employment advocates

Persons with severe mental retardation and other severe disabilities have the right to employment opportunities where they . . .

Benefit from best practices

Receive ongoing support

Are accepted by coworkers

Receive the same employment benefits as coworkers

Have an opportunity to receive a fair wage

Have the same protection that is provided to all workers under federal labor laws

Choose their own trainers

Have opportunity for job advancement

Can reject job opportunities

Can change jobs

Can make decisions

Have dignity

Receive training in public transportation skills

Receive training on work-related skills

Are informed of community services

goals requires effective advocates who are knowledgeable of local community services, well trained in systematic instruction, and comfortable meeting and talking with members of the business community (Kregel & Sale, 1988; Sale, Wood, Barcus, & Moon, 1989).

OBTAINING EMPLOYMENT

When attempting to secure employment for persons with severe mental retardation, the employment specialist must be able to effectively represent his or her program while communicating with both family members and business people. Advocating for persons with severe mental retardation with two groups of people and their distinctly different interests necessitates following separate sets of guidelines.

Families who have watched a family member with severe mental retardation go through a traditional special education program in all probability never have had an opportunity to observe the student's vocational or social competence. Therefore, it is very understandable that family members might approach supported employment with a great deal of skepticism. It is the job of the supported employment service provider to explain how an individual with limited strength, endurance, and social and community skills will be able to work with the aid of an employment specialist and natural community supports.

In the same regard, business people may initially appear reluctant to become involved with a supported employment program because of past experiences with other types of employment services or because of some stereotypical notions that they may have about persons with severe or multiple disabilities. It is up to the employment advocate to convey the vocational competence of persons with severe mental retardation and the unique service to be found in a supported employment program.

Table 10.2 shows a list of guidelines that have been developed to assist the supported employment advocate in his or her communication with family members and employers. While Table 10.2 does not present an exhaustive listing, it gives enough information to help guide the supported employment service provider as he or she seeks support in obtaining employment for persons with severe mental retardation.

Table 10.2. Advocacy guidelines for approaching parents and employers to obtain competitive employment for persons with severe mental retardation

With parents	With employer
Be sensitive and empathetic.	Discuss the capabilities of the individual with severe mental retardation.
Employ active listening skills and identify underlying feelings.	Employ active listening skills and identify underlying feelings.
Discuss benefits of competitive employment.	List business advantages for hiring persons with severe disabilities.
Describe the role of the supported employment specialist and/or job coach and the training process.	Review the unique role of the supported employment specialist and/or job coach.
Remember parents know their children best.	Remind the employer that job completion is guaranteed from day 1.
Give information on how government benefits will be affected by employment.	Solicit questions and feedback.
Assist in working out transportation.	Use testimony from satisfied employers and companies.
Eliminate all professional jargon.	Be informed of national data on the safety record of persons with disabilities.
Give telephone numbers of other parents involved in supported employment.	Eliminate all professional jargon.
Give parents enough information to decide if competitive employment is appropriate at this time.	

The following two case study examples demonstrate how an employment specialist applied the advocacy guidelines in obtaining employment for Marie, a 21-year-old woman diagnosed as having severe mental retardation. The first case study portrays the employment specialist meeting with Marie and her family to discuss the possibility of Marie getting a job through a supported employment program. The second case study describes an employment specialist meeting with an employer to present the service available through the supported employment program.

Advocacy Case Study #1: Obtaining Employment—Approaching the Family

During the initial family meeting at Marie's home both parents immediately expressed their concern with regard to Marie's low stamina and her inability to work independently. The employment specialist acknowledged that those characteristics were not uncommon in the individuals with whom she typically worked, and she explained how her role as a job coach addressed those and a number of other training concerns. As the employment specialist went on to explain in detail some of the important facets of supported employment, Marie's mother and father would periodically interject statements about how Marie could never possibly work. The employment specialist realized that she might be putting Marie's parents on the defensive so she acknowledged the family's feelings of "fear" and "responsibility." This act of genuine warmth and empathy led to a very open discussion about the family's specific concerns about riding a city bus and meeting strangers. This meeting did not immediately lead to employment for Marie. The family chose to talk with several other parents who had sons or daughters in supported employment programs before making a decision. Four months later Marie's mother called the employment specialist to thank her for arranging the appointments with the other parents and requested supported employment services for Marie.

Advocacy Case Study #2: Obtaining Employment—Approaching the Employer

The employment specialist contacted the manager at a local hotel in response to an advertisement for attendants to work in the hotel laundry. The employment specialist knew that the hotel offered an excellent benefit package and that a laundry attendant position might be an excellent employment opportunity for a person with severe mental retardation. Dressed professionally, the employment specialist initiated her first meeting with the manager by describing the many benefits of a supported employment service. During this meeting the employer asked the employment specialist to specifically describe what she meant by "disabled" and then went on to request the IQ score of the individual he was considering for the hotel's laundry attendant position. While the employment specialist felt slightly irritated by the employer's request for an IQ score, she did not let herself respond with anger. Instead, the employment specialist acknowledged that, of course, all workers are individuals with their own unique set of strengths and weaknesses and that she personally found IQ scores to be meaningless. She then went on to describe some general behavioral characteristics of persons with severe mental retardation, using functional work-related examples. This explanation seemed to satisfy the employer, as indicated by her willingness to spend an additional 30 minutes with the employment specialist describing the job and answering questions about work-related responsibilities of the laundry attendant position.

In these case study examples the employment specialist could have experienced very different outcomes if, for example, she had patronized Marie's family by giving them a lecture on the dignity of risk or if she had told the employer that IQ scores are confidential information and therefore none of her business. Both of these responses would have broken off communication and would not have allowed the supported employment specialist to accomplish her goal of obtaining employment for Marie.

MAINTAINING EMPLOYMENT

Once an individual has agreed to competitive employment and an employer has agreed to hire the supported employment employee, then the advocacy role becomes more structured and complex. The ultimate success and acceptance of an employee at a job site is determined during job-site training. During this phase of supported employment, the employment specialist must: 1) stay in close contact with parents and families, 2) create an environment where the employers and coworkers feel comfortable interacting with the new employee, 3) confront incorrect or stereotypical attitudes or perceptions about persons with severe mental retardation, and 4) develop natural supports such as the use of coworkers as job-site advocates. Table 10.3 presents some advocacy guidelines that are commonly utilized to assist persons with severe mental retardation in maintaining competitve employment. These guidelines should be helpful to a supported employment service provider in his or her advocacy role.

The next two case study examples demonstrate how a supported employment specialist utilized the guidelines for maintaining employment as he advocated for Chris, a supported employment employee with severe mental retardation. Case study #3 reviews the interactions between the employment specialist and Chris's family when they expressed their desire for Chris to quit his job. Case study #4 describes how the employment specialist responded when Chris's coworkers started to ask specific questions about his job and about Chris.

Advocacy Case Study #3: Maintaining Employment—Family Concerns

Chris had been employed for 1 week in the food court area of a local mall. On Friday afternoon when Chris had completed his first week of work and returned home, his father called the employment specialist to tell him that Chris was quitting his job and would not be returning to the mall on Monday. The employment specialist was angry and upset but was able to arrange a meeting with Chris and his family for the following afternoon. During this meeting Chris's father explained how tired Chris had been since he started work and stated that the job was just too much for his son. While listening to Chris's parents explain why they wanted Chris to quit work, it quickly became apparent to the employment specialist that he had not spent enough time talking with Chris's family to keep them informed about what was occurring at Chris's job. Due to Chris's limited ability to communicate, his family did not have enough information about the job site, coworkers, or, most importantly, Chris's progress. Once the employment specialist acknowledged his failure to communicate and reviewed how well he thought Chris was doing, the family agreed to allow Chris to return to work on Monday. Before the employment specialist left Chris's home, he set up a regular schedule of appointments to meet with Chris's mother and father. Within a couple of months Chris's family and the employment specialist were only meeting formally twice a month, with the promise to call each other if anything came up.

Advocacy Case Study #4: Maintaining Employment—Coworker Concerns

The coworkers at Chris's job were very inquisitive and wanted to ascertain specific information about Chris and the employment specialist's role at the mall. Rather than feeling defensive or annoyed with the many questions, the employment specialist and Chris

Table 10.3. Advocacy guidelines for addressing parent and employee/coworker concerns to maintain competitive employment for persons with severe mental retardation

With parents	With employer/coworkers
Explain the job benefit package.	Allow time to talk to the employer informally before or after work hours.
Transport the worker during initial days of training.	Solicit the employer's feedback on worker's job performance.
Meet often with the family.	
Discuss positive job performance.	Ask for input on sequence of job duties.
Give the name, address, and telephone number of the employer to the parent/guardian or group home staff.	Verify production data.
	Have the employer check job duty analysis.
	Give the employer a copy of job duty analysis for the company's file.
Discuss the rules of the job site.	Learn unwritten rules of the job site.
Tell parents the names of coworkers who have established friendships with their son or daughter.	Identify person or persons who may become advocates at the job site.
Keep the parent/guardian informed of work progress.	Learn names of the coworkers in immediate work area.
	Talk informally with coworkers.
Give written feedback on employer's perceptions of training.	Explain behavior characteristics of the new employee (e.g., "While Chris can't read the newspaper, he can identify signs like exit, telephone, or emergency").
Identify skills that could be practiced at home.	
Solicit parent/guardian feedback.	Identify employee's personal strengths for employer and coworkers.
Explain the fading process.	Model appropriate interactions for coworkers and employer.
Request any changes to personal information (e.g., address, telephone number, living situation).	Request regular written evaluations on employee progress.
Continue periodic telephone conversations.	Involve coworker/employer in training progress.
	Socialize with coworkers at break.
Give office telephone number.	Discuss job modifications with employer, if needed.
	Recognize employers/coworkers who promote the employment of persons with disabilities (e.g., a special certificate, civic presentations).
	Maintain regular follow-up to ensure that natural supports are not affected by coworker turnover.

made time to meet individually with each of the coworkers who had expressed an interest. These informal talks led to identification of job-site advocates and/or friends who continued to support Chris long after the employment specialist faded from the job site.

In both of these case study examples the employment specialist demonstrated a keen awareness of his own strengths and weaknesses, which ultimately led to facilitating communication rather than cutting it off. The fact that the new employee was present for the problem-solving in each of the above situations demonstrates how the advocate relationship can be a collaborative process.

REDUCING CONFLICT OF INTEREST ISSUES

Advocacy plays a critical role in the provision of high quality supported employment services. Yet, as discussed earlier in this chapter, a supported employment direct service provider may be faced with potential conflict of interest situations as he or she advocates for an individual with severe disabilities and at the same time responds to the demands of an agency and/or company.

One of the best ways to reduce conflict of interest concerns is to use a voucher system, by which a person with severe mental retardation could contract with a trained supported employment professional for specific employment services. With this strategy the employment specialist would be responding directly to the request of the new employee with severe disabilities as opposed to an agency. Presently we are not aware of any program using this system.

Organizing a governing board is another strategy that deserves the consideration of a supported employment organization. The board would be made up of persons with disabilities, family members, business people, and the general public, all of whom would have the power to affect service delivery practices. Transferring this type of power to an impartial group of people would go a long way in ensuring fair and consistent practices. Additionally, if the board were designed to meet on a regular basis to review *all* the business from the preceding period, board members would become very familar with the day-to-day operation of the program and would then be in a better position to do problem-solving and to offer unique insights.

SUMMARY

Presently, effective advocates cannot be described by any particular behavioral characteristics. However, there are some broad, basic beliefs to which supported employment personnel must be committed prior to delivering services. These beliefs form the foundation on which the advocate relationship is built. Supported employment program managers and employment specialists must agree that individuals with severe mental retardation have the same rights to employment and community participation as other individuals. Second, the supported employment service provider must recognize his or her role as a community model and as such be informed and act sensitively when representing persons with disabilities. Third, and perhaps most important, supported employment personnel must be committed to remaining aware of their own values to help increase their effectiveness as advocates.

There should be little or no discrepancy between the values we subscribe to and the outcomes we achieve. Following the guidelines and strategies described in this chapter will not guarantee effective advocacy practices but will assist in the development of a well organized, high quality supported employment program.

REFERENCES

Anderson, W., Chitwood, S., & Hayden, D. (1982). *Negotiating the special education maze.* Englewood Cliffs, New Jersey: Prentice-Hall.

Asch, A. (1985). Understanding and working with disability rights groups. In H. McCarty (Ed.), *Complete guide to employing persons with disabilities* (pp. 170–212). Albertson NY: Research and Training Institute National Center on Employment of the Handicapped at Human Resource Center.

Bellamy, G.T., Rhodes, L.E., Mank, D.M., & Albin, J.M. (1988). *Supported employment: A community implementation guide.* Baltimore: Paul H. Brookes Publishing Co.

Brooke, V., Sale, P., & Moon, S. (in press). An analysis of job duties performed by supported employment program managers. *Rehabilitation Counseling Bulletin.*

Gazda, G., Asbury, F., Blazer, F., Childers, W., & Walters, R. (1984). *Human relations development.* Boston: Allyn & Bacon.

Inge, K.J., Barcus, J.M., & Everson, J.M. (1988). Developing inservice training programs for supported employment personnel. In P. Wehman & M.S. Moon (Eds.), *Vocational rehabilitation and supported employment* (145–162). Baltimore: Paul H. Brookes Publishing Co.

Kregel, J., & Sale, P. (1988). Preservice preparation of supported employment professionals. In P. Wehman & M.S. Moon (Eds.), *Vocational rehabilitation and supported employment* (pp. 129–144). Baltimore: Paul H. Brookes Publishing Co.

Sale, P., Wood, W., Barcus, J.M., & Moon, M.S. (1989). The role of the employment specialist. In W.E. Kiernan & R.L. Schalock (Eds.), *Economics, industry, and disability: A look ahead* (pp. 187–206). Baltimore: Paul H. Brookes Publishing Co.

Scheerenberger, R.C. (1987). *A history of mental retardation: A quarter century of promise.* Baltimore: Paul H. Brookes Publishing Co.

Sullen, D. (1979). *Mental retardation: Nature, needs, and advocacy.* Boston: Allyn & Bacon.

Turnbull, H.R., Turnbull, A.P., Bronicki, G.J., Summers, J.A., & Roeder-Gordon, C. (1989). *Disability and the family: A guide to decisions for adulthood.* Baltimore: Paul H. Brookes Publishing Co.

Wehman, P., Renzaglia, A., & Bates, P. (1985). *Functional living skills for moderately and severely handicapped individuals.* Austin: Pro-Ed.

Will, M.C. (1984). *Supported employment for adults with severe disabilities: An OSERS program initiative.* Washington, DC: United States Department of Education.

Wolfensberger, W., & Zauha, H. (1973). *Citizen advocacy and protective services for the impaired and handicapped.* Toronto: National Institute on Mental Retardation.

INDEX